Fashion

Inspired by a rapidly changing fashion landscape, *Fashion: New Feminist Essays* offers historical and contemporary studies that reveal the relationships between fashion and gender, sexuality, race, and age.

Fashion is a rich terrain for feminist scholars in the twenty-first century. Explicit engagements with feminist and queer politics, critical interventions by industry outsiders across digital platforms, diversifying images of stylish bodies, and ongoing discussions of the ethics and sustainability of fashion production: all of these point to an urgent need to reappraise the relationship of fashion to feminism and other justice-seeking movements. The essays in this collection take up fashion as a feminist critical tool that uniquely holds together the lived and represented body with larger cultural structures. Contributors unearth surprising new lines of connection between gender, sexuality, race, age, and religion in their relationship to capitalism, both historically and in the present.

Bringing together established and emerging scholars and perspectives from gender studies, history, sociology, philosophy, and literary studies, *Fashion: New Feminist Essays* traces the far-reaching impact of this most feminized of forms, underscoring the significance of fashion studies for understanding the politics of culture. This book was originally published as a special issue of the *Australian Feminist Studies* journal.

Ilya Parkins is Associate Professor of Gender and Women's Studies at the University of British Columbia, Okanagan Campus, Canada. She specializes in feminist theory, mass culture, fashion, and femininities.

Maryanne Dever is co-editor of *Australian Feminist Studies* and has published widely on feminist literary and cultural studies. Her previous Routledge edited collections include *Archives and New Modes of Feminist Research* (2018). She works in the Faculty of Arts and Social Sciences at the University of Technology Sydney, Australia.

Fashion
New Feminist Essays

Edited by
Ilya Parkins and Maryanne Dever

LONDON AND NEW YORK

First published 2020
by Routledge
2 Park Square, Milton Park, Abingdon, Oxon, OX14 4RN

and by Routledge
52 Vanderbilt Avenue, New York, NY 10017

Routledge is an imprint of the Taylor & Francis Group, an informa business

© 2020 Taylor & Francis

All rights reserved. No part of this book may be reprinted or reproduced or utilised in any form or by any electronic, mechanical, or other means, now known or hereafter invented, including photocopying and recording, or in any information storage or retrieval system, without permission in writing from the publishers.

Trademark notice: Product or corporate names may be trademarks or registered trademarks, and are used only for identification and explanation without intent to infringe.

British Library Cataloguing-in-Publication Data
A catalogue record for this book is available from the British Library

ISBN-13: 978-0-367-43688-9

Typeset in Myriad Pro
by Apex CoVantage, LLC

Publisher's Note
The publisher accepts responsibility for any inconsistencies that may have arisen during the conversion of this book from journal articles to book chapters, namely the inclusion of journal terminology.

Disclaimer
Every effort has been made to contact copyright holders for their permission to reprint material in this book. The publishers would be grateful to hear from any copyright holder who is not here acknowledged and will undertake to rectify any errors or omissions in future editions of this book.

Contents

Citation Information vii
Notes on Contributors ix

Introduction: Fashion and Feminist Politics of the Present 1
Ilya Parkins

1 Sisters in a Fashion: Martha Ansara and Elaine Welteroth 7
  Kath Kenny

2 'I Want to Wear It': Fashioning Black Feminism in *Mahogany* (1975) 22
  Kimberly Lamm

3 Interview with Reina Lewis 41
  Ilya Parkins

4 Digital Fashion Engagement Through Affect, Personal Investments and Remix 55
  Rosa Crepax

5 Cindy Sherman in a New Millennium: Fashion, Feminism, Art and Ageing 75
  Pamela Church Gibson

6 Fashionable 'Formation': Reclaiming the Sartorial Politics of Josephine Baker 92
  Jennifer Sweeney-Risko

7 Just Use What You Have: Ethical Fashion Discourse and the Feminisation of Responsibility 109
  Kathleen Horton

8 Performative Rhetorics in Invisibility: Phoebe Philo's Undone Authorship 124
  Erin O'Connor

Index 143

Citation Information

The chapters in this book were originally published in *Australian Feminist Studies*, volume 33, issue 98 (December 2018). When citing this material, please use the original page numbering for each article, as follows:

Introduction

Introduction: Fashion and the Feminist Politics of the Present
Ilya Parkins
Australian Feminist Studies, volume 33, issue 98 (December 2018) pp. 423–427

Chapter 1

Sisters in a Fashion: Martha Ansara and Elaine Welteroth
Kath Kenny
Australian Feminist Studies, volume 33, issue 98 (December 2018) pp. 548–562

Chapter 2

'I Want to Wear It': Fashioning Black Feminism in Mahogany *(1975)*
Kimberly Lamm
Australian Feminist Studies, volume 33, issue 98 (December 2018) pp. 428–446

Chapter 3

Interview with Reina Lewis
Ilya Parkins
Australian Feminist Studies, volume 33, issue 98 (December 2018) pp. 447–460

Chapter 4

Digital Fashion Engagement Through Affect, Personal Investments and Remix
Rosa Crepax
Australian Feminist Studies, volume 33, issue 98 (December 2018) pp. 461–480

Chapter 5

Cindy Sherman in a New Millennium: Fashion, Feminism, Art and Ageing
Pamela Church Gibson
Australian Feminist Studies, volume 33, issue 98 (December 2018) pp. 481–497

Chapter 6

Fashionable 'Formation': Reclaiming the Sartorial Politics of Josephine Baker
Jennifer Sweeney-Risko
Australian Feminist Studies, volume 33, issue 98 (December 2018) pp. 498–514

Chapter 7

Just Use What You Have: Ethical Fashion Discourse and the Feminisation of Responsibility
Kathleen Horton
Australian Feminist Studies, volume 33, issue 98 (December 2018) pp. 515–529

Chapter 8

Performative Rhetorics in Invisibility: Phoebe Philo's Undone Authorship
Erin O'Connor
Australian Feminist Studies, volume 33, issue 98 (December 2018) pp. 530–547

For any permission-related enquiries please visit:
http://www.tandfonline.com/page/help/permissions

Notes on Contributors

Pamela Church Gibson is Reader in Historical and Cultural Studies at the London College of Fashion, UK. She has published extensively on film and fashion, gender, history, and heritage.

Rosa Crepax is Associate Lecturer at Goldsmiths, University of London, UK, in the Department of Sociology, where she also completed her PhD in 2017.

Kathleen Horton teaches fashion theory and communication in the School of Design at Queensland University of Technology, Australia. Her teaching and research centers on the aesthetic, political, and social aspects of fashion practices.

Kath Kenny has been a doctoral candidate and Australian Postgraduate Award recipient at the Department of Media, Music, Communication and Cultural Studies, Macquarie University, Australia.

Kimberly Lamm is Associate Professor of Gender, Sexuality, and Feminist Studies at Duke University, USA.

Erin O'Connor is a PhD candidate in the Moody College of Communication with a focus on Rhetoric and Language at the University of Texas at Austin, USA.

Ilya Parkins is Associate Professor of Gender and Women's Studies at the University of British Columbia, Okanagan Campus, Canada.

Jennifer Sweeney-Risko received a PhD in English Literature from Binghamton University, USA, in 2016. Her research interests include fashion, material culture, modernism, and writing pedagogy.

Introduction: Fashion and Feminist Politics of the Present

Ilya Parkins

ABSTRACT
This introduction features an analysis of the current state of the relationship between the fashion system and feminist scholarship. Important points of convergence are identified, including the link between the socalled democratisation of fashion and the recent resurgence of feminism in mass culture, fashion's introduction of complex models of identity, embodiment and materiality, its foregrounding of class, and its ability to shed light on the relationship between feminism and neoliberal capitalism. Altogether, fashion emerges as an ideal diagnostic tool for the feminist politics of the present.

If there were ever a moment for feminist studies to take on fashion, this would be it. Over the last couple of years, the industry has framed itself as a diversity vanguardist—with an especially visible promotion of transgender and non-binary, and fat or 'plus-size', models. Pointed invocations of feminism appear regularly at couture houses like Chanel and Dior, trickling down to affordable mass like ASOS and sitting uneasily with the wider cultures of conspicuous luxury consumption and white slenderness that frame them. It is surely tempting to dwell in this stratum of the fashion system but feminist scholars will find it more fruitful to look beyond the industry's own self-fashioning and the attendant risk of becoming mired in stale debates about fashion's feminist credentials. At its best, feminist fashion scholarship demonstrates that fashion is a powerful methodological tool that allows us to home in on urgent questions in ways that are always in some sense materialist, always gendered, always alert to temporal and affective complexity, and always attuned to the operation of capitalism and its consequences.

Indeed, it is precisely because of its relationship with capitalism that fashion becomes so helpful to think with. Moments of apparent convergence between the concerns that animate feminism and those that—provisionally—preoccupy the fashion industry raise important questions about the relationship to capitalism of a feminism that has been globally resurgent over the last half-decade. As Laura Favaro and Rosalind Gill (2018) note in an analysis of mediations of feminism in women's fashion and beauty magazines in the UK and Spain, 'the stripping back and hollowing out of this movement for radical social transformation within the spaces of commercial magazines, and the ease with which it can then be connected to the economic imperatives of capitalism and the political logics of neoliberalism is troubling … ' (62). Certainly, analyses of fashion in the cultural studies tradition, with their emphasis on the expression of personal identity, have sometimes unwittingly colluded with the choice-driven logic that imagines consumerism as a playground for personal communication, hiving it off from the systems—including capitalist patriarchy—in which it is embedded. The ability to do this depends on a conscious splitting of individual subjectivity from the grand and spectacular sweep of the fashion industry, so that individual choices can appear to have sprung from the glamorous ether of self-expression rather than a locatable world-historical mood. The new fashion scholarship avoids this tendency to bifurcation, tracing as it does the mutual imbrication of fashion production and mediation, and individuals' expressive 'choices'. In large part, this turn is prefigured by the turn to the digital. Digital media—which encompasses, in the realm of fashion, everything from style blogging, to YouTube 'haulers', online shopping, and new online fashion magazines—ostensibly ushered in another era of 'democratisation' for fashion, following that of the late nineteenth and early twentieth centuries (whose democratic reach is itself contested). Rather, it seems that the digitisation of fashion cultures and representations helps to highlight the relationships between individual desires and practices, and the fashion and style superstructure, whose relationship to democratisation is at best contested. The result is a clear picture—reflected in this volume in particular by Kath Horton's and Rosa Crepax's essays—of the inextricability of gendered subjects from capitalism. They remind us of the structural constraints that condition fashion choices, while taking seriously the forms of expression that are thereby enabled, which we also see in Jennifer Sweeney-Risko's treatment of Beyoncé and Erin O'Connor's analysis of Phoebe Philo.

If the relationship between the self and structures of capital becomes glaringly apparent in contemporary fashion mediation, so too does the bleed between the physical and virtual spaces of fashion. The commingling of bricks-and-mortar retail with online community-building—as in the US feminist store Wildfang, discussed in my interview in this issue with Reina Lewis—the spaces occupied at live couture shows by fashion bloggers, and the online circulation of various forms of 'streetstyle' photography: all of these highlight bodies moving across spheres. If feminism's most potent contributions to fashion studies have been to underscore the importance of the material body and to stress the material dimensions of culture, then today's fashion structures challenge us to further refine our very ideas about the material. What happens to the body as it moves online? What happens to the promise of the material garment—much-vaunted in feminist theory—as it is rendered in pixels, on a screen? The notable thing about fashion is that it travels. To say that the garment, for instance, dematerialises as it moves onscreen, does not do justice to the complex ways that clothing—or a dressed body—transforms as it travels between virtual and physical space. With its liberal trafficking across such boundaries, today fashion defies entrenched feminist understandings of materiality, prompting us to rethink this category that has been so central to gender scholarship because of its alignment with the feminine and its consequent dismissal. Fashion today does not afford us the safety of dwelling in some pure materiality or of being given over to a utopic terrain of dematerialised, floating signifiers. Rather it highlights the relationship of body and worlds as these migrate, offering an intriguing model of itinerant, unstable matter that nonetheless maintains a strong connection to lived conditions of embodiment and sociality.

Fashion, with this same material dimension, also connects helpfully to mood, another category that troubles orthodoxies that feminists have been both interested in challenging and implicitly invested in upholding. Mood, as Jennifer D. Carlson and Kathleen C. Stewart (2014) write, is 'both a distribution across a field of subjects, objects, orientations, agencies, boundaries and institutionalized kernels of force or ideology and a fine point of affective sense that takes root in subjects to become the small and strangely shared lines of a life' (115). That is, moods knit together individual and collective: they are subjectively experienced and expressed, but it is their social circulation that defines them. Fashion functions like this, too—it is, famously, an expression of individuality and a technology that links the individual to the collective, blurring the line between the two because the form discursively insists upon their interdependence. Like mood, though, fashion is a social modality that does not subordinate individual to social, while it refuses to disentangle the two. In this sense, it approximates the workings of moods as a relative of affect, but guards against the tendency to individualise that theories of affect can lead us to, despite our best intentions. And, too, fashion is of course about the capturing and material translation of moods, seen as it is to express a generally ephemeral *zeitgeist*. The form thus creates a useful equilibrium between the empirical and the intangible, asserting the importance of the barely perceptible, much less nameable, in social worlds. For feminists, this materially inflected abstract realm of mood that fashion translates so well can help mitigate the lasting effects of schisms between theoretical and empirical work—splits which, though their heyday is past, continue to inform feminist scholarship. In its harnessing of mood, fashion offers a model— or, even, a series of models — for feminist scholarship interesting in accounting for the world creatively, generatively.

It allows us to do such work in particular with categories of identity. Of all the themes in this issue, class is the most notable for its expansiveness, its reach across all of the essays collected here. Of course, fashion has historically been a class marker *par excellence*, functioning as a highly visible form of cultural capital, and heavily invested—at the upper reaches of the industry—in maintaining status distinctions. The so-called democratisation of fashion that occurred in the late nineteenth century with the advent of new techniques for mass production occasioned immense class anxiety in the middle and upper middle classes. The explicit acknowledgement of class that threads through the essays collected here is striking, however, from the point of view of a (feminist) history of engagements with the category. While class is understood as a central category here—and not merely namechecked—it is not boldly or singularly marked out in any of the pieces. Rather, the salience of class is taken for granted, and the category is one among several strands of identity, in a model in which identity categories are not privileged but are not altogether absent, either. The writing collected here, in fact, seems to take as its starting point a diffracted model of identity. Perhaps because of fashion's mobile and itinerant nature, its ephemeral quality, analyses of it tend to adopt a similarly diffuse approach. Writing about fashion today has moved well beyond the approach dominant in the 1990s, in which a kind of utopian potential for the dissolution of identity seemed to reign, in keeping with the broader moment of postmodern cultural criticism. Fashion studies has recommitted to identity, on some level, as these pieces illustrate with their discussions of intricate connections between class, race, age, and femininity. But the example of class, which threads through the works but does not stand out as definitive, seems to indicate a model of identity as materially locatable and linked to oppression, yet capacious and flexible, again short-circuiting unproductive antinomies that have sometimes befallen feminist theory.

In this sense, fashion studies holds the potential to recall us to categories that have been receding; alongside class, of course, sits femininity. While the fashion world is currently embracing gender fluidity, it is notable that our issue can be read as an extended meditation on femininity. Indeed, fashion's longstanding feminisation and trivialisation offers feminists an important vantage point from which to engage with femininity, one that begins from fashion and beauty's 'double bind', described thus by Ellen Rosenman: 'women are required to invest themselves deeply in their appearance and then derided for this obsession' (2011, 89). Feminist fashion studies—including virtually all the essays contained in this issue—is typically engaged, whether explicitly or not, with the forms of cultural fallout from this longstanding double bind. It thus offers a potent tool for assessing the persistence of tropes of the feminine over time, into an era in which the stakes appear to have dramatically changed. Fashion's place in a discursive economy of beauty makes plain the ways that this domain is used to promote misogyny, less in the way it styles or pictures feminine bodies and more in the way that it functions to discipline feminine people for their socially constituted investments in appearance. As all of our authors show, fashion promotes and indeed requires a significant outlay of 'aesthetic labour' (Elias, Gill, and Scharff 2017), connecting it to an increasing attention to forms of labour in social inquiry—and adding nuance to the discussions of class that are also so pervasive among these authors, by suggesting that class and capital are forged as much in the closet and dressing room as in national and international institutions and structures.

This 'double bind' of beauty and fashion, which trades on the deep psychic investments of feminine subjects, can in fact be related to broader structural questions in the fashion industry. Consider the recent work of Giulia Mensitieri, whose book *'Le Plus Beau Métier du Monde': Dans Les Coulisses de l'Industrie de la Mode* traces how the luxury fashion industry relies on exploitation of its workers, who are psychically invested in the 'dream' that fashion represents and put up with unpaid labour for the access it affords to beauty, glamour, and luxury. Mensitieri argues that 'capitalism needs this dream: it is fuel for fashion not only in terms of consumption, but in terms of work' (Mensitieri and Lacroix 2018, my translation). Her work exposes 'the coexistence of utmost luxury and precarity' (Mensitieri and Lacroix 2018). Fashion thus points us toward some of the gendered and affective dimensions of precarity, that term that is so crucial for understanding the politics of the present.

The politics of the present: fashion can take us straight there. With its embedded relation to global capitalism, its ability to penetrate the psychic lives of consumers and wearers, and its expressive power, the fashion system is an ideal diagnostic tool for the contemporary moment. What is more, its unique time signature—relentlessly attuned to present moods, yet always turned to the past—provides an inbuilt mechanism with which to scrutinise the history of the present, and thus to denaturalise it. Responding in turn to various aspects of the contemporary present—or, in the case of essays by Kimberly Lamm and Jennifer Sweeney-Risko, to past presents—the essays collected here model feminist interventions in the politics of the present: always attuned to the subjective and the structural, the economic and the expressive, and the concretions and diffractions of identity.

Disclosure statement

No potential conflict of interest was reported by the author.

References

Carlson, Jennifer D., and Kathleen C. Stewart. 2014. "The Legibilities of Mood Work." *New Formations* 82: 114–133.
Elias, Ana Sofia, Rosalind Gill, and Christina Scharff. 2017. *Aesthetic Labour: Rethinking Beauty Politics in Neoliberalism*. London: Palgrave Macmillan.
Favaro, Laura, and Rosalind Gill. 2018. "Feminism Rebranded: Women's Magazines Online and 'the Return of the F-Word.'." *Digitos* 4: 37–65.
Mensitieri, Giulia, and Marion Raynaud Lacroix. 2018. "Tyrannie, burn-out et précarité: faut-il en finir avec le rêve de la mode?" *I-D*, March 13. https://i-d.vice.com/fr/article/bj59j5/tyrannie-burn-out-et-precarite-faut-il-en-finir-avec-le-reve-de-la-mode.
Rosenman, Ellen Bayuk. 2011. "Fear of Fashion; or, How the Coquette Got Her Bad Name." In *Cultures of Femininity in Modern Fashion*, edited by Ilya Parkins, and Elizabeth M. Sheehan, 89–102. Durham: University of New Hampshire Press.

Sisters in a Fashion: Martha Ansara and Elaine Welteroth

Kath Kenny

ABSTRACT
This article discusses Martha Ansara and Elaine Welteroth, two US born feminists who came to Australia during two key moments in feminist history, as a way of thinking about the relationship between feminists and fashion. Ansara arrived in Sydney in 1969 carrying women's liberation literature in her suitcase; she became an important generative figure in the Australia's women's liberation movement, particularly as an independent filmmaker and proponent of consciousness raising. Welteroth arrived in 2017 to speak at the Sydney Writers' Festival during a period of international resurgence of feminist activism. She brought with her images of women of colour she had featured in *Teen Vogue* and she invoked second wave consciousness raising, albeit in a remodelled, corporate-led form when she talked about the title's plans to bring young girls around kitchen tables to 'solve' political problems. The article uses comments both women have made in relation to fashion and beauty, close readings of their works, and a discussion of their respective feminist milieus to suggest a trajectory of feminism's relationship to the fashion industry that appears to have changed from a position of opposition to one of open embrace. It also complicates this reading by pointing to the resonances between these women of different feminist eras.

Introduction

In May 2017 the US-based editor of the Condé Nast title *Teen Vogue*, 30-year-old Elaine Welteroth, flew to Sydney to speak at various Sydney Writers' Festival events. She arrived in the middle of what appeared to be an international resurgence of feminist activism. Just a few months earlier an estimated five million people had taken part in Women's Marches in 673 cities across the world.[1] By the year's end the Merriam-Webster dictionary would declare 'feminism' its Word of the Year. In a festival event hosted by the editor-in-chief of *Slate* magazine Julia Turner, Welteroth (2017) outlined what she sees as the productive relationships between fashion, feminism and politics. She presented images of African-American and other diverse models she has featured in *Teen Vogue*, and she spoke about the title's much-praised American presidential election coverage (*The Atlantic's* Sophie Gilbert (2016) had congratulated the magazine's activism and nuanced coverage of politics, for example, and *The Guardian's* Hannah Jane Parkinson (2016) commended its politically savvy, fighting spirit). Arriving in Sydney on this wave of acclamation, Welteroth argued fashion and beauty could function as gateways to sisterhood and political awareness. As her conversation with Turner concluded, Welteroth (2017) appeared to invoke second wave feminism's consciousness raising, describing *Teen Vogue's* plans to bring young women together 'around kitchen tables' to tackle the world's problems.

As Welteroth spoke I was reminded of the way feminism continues to enter 'into every nook and cranny of social life' even as the more radical aims of the women's liberation movement for total social transformation have not been achieved under contemporary capitalism (Fraser 2009, 108). And I was also reminded of another US born feminist who came to Sydney carrying feminist literature in her suitcase at another key moment in feminist history. Martha Ansara was a 26-year-old single mother and aspiring filmmaker when she touched down in Sydney on a flight from California in October 1969, just in time to help fan the first sparks of women's liberation into a national fire (Ansara 2013). Although detective novels were her preferred reading material, as Ansara told the Coming Out Show (Australian Women's Broadcasting Cooperative 1977), she also carried pamphlets her sister-in-law had given her from the burgeoning US women's liberation movement. Within a few weeks of her arrival, Ansara was visiting Bob Gould's Third World bookshop where she met other women who had recently travelled to the States (Magarey 2014, 25). Together they made their own pamphlet advertising Sydney's first public women's liberation meeting, handing it out at an anti-Vietnam war rally in Sydney on 14 December (Ansara 2013, 84; Magarey 2014, 26).[2] Ansara stayed on in Sydney, where she introduced the concept of consciousness raising to early feminist groups and became involved in a self-consciously feminist publication as a member of the women's liberation collective behind *MeJane*. She also made films about women's lives and about *images* of women: she was a driving force behind *Film for Discussion* (Sydney Women's Film Group 1974), an early women's liberation film which opens with a montage of models and Hollywood stars.

This article looks closely at these two women as a way of thinking about the complicated and developing relationships between feminism and the fashion and beauty industries. Although Welteroth was in Australia briefly and Ansara stayed, a comparison of their respective contributions acknowledges a movement that, while always locally specific, has also been characterised by international flows of key figures and texts.[3] In the following pages I consider: comments Ansara has made in articles and interviews (including an interview I conducted with her in 2017); a close reading of Ansara's short film, *Film for Discussion;* Welteroth's Sydney Writers' Festival talk; a 2016 *Guardian* profile of Welteroth; and selected articles Welteroth has published in *Teen Vogue*. I also briefly discuss key actions and texts relating to beauty and fashion that shaped the early women's liberation movement. Unless otherwise stated I am using the term 'fashion' here to refer to the fashion industry and the term 'beauty' in a simple sense. However, as I will discuss throughout, I acknowledge there has always been an interplay between feminism, feminist fashions and the fashion industry, as Petra Mosmann recently argued (2016).

Discussing key texts and activist moments is one important way of understanding a cultural context; but by also considering specific individuals, their words and their work, a more complicated picture can emerge. Using this wide angle and zoom lens approach I am also guided by what Catharine Lumby (2011, 97) describes as cultural studies research that pays attention to the particular and attempts to 'grapple with contradiction and ambiguity' as well as 'context, location, and history'. Clare Hemmings (2011, 4–6) similarly warns feminist scholars to avoid narratives of feminist history that elide complexity and specificity, and which may owe more (for example) to the contemporary feminist scholar's need to either lament feminism's (supposedly) lost radical past or, alternatively, to unreflexively locate themselves as part of a more sophisticated feminist present. In the following pages, therefore, I want to consider these two women's approaches to beauty and fashion (two closely related terms, as I discuss below) for their complexities and ambiguities, as well as for differences and their resonances.

On one reading it is possible to sketch a simple and evolving relationship between feminism, beauty and fashion—one where feminism and feminists move from opposition to the fashion and beauty industries in the 70s, to a contemporary position, articulated by Welteroth in 2017, which argues these industries are not only compatible with feminism, they can be *a portal* to feminism and political awareness. And in discussing these two figures I *do* find evidence for such a narrative arc. But I argue there are also commonalities and resonances between these two women's approaches to fashion. And I suggest it may not be possible (nor even reasonable) to demand feminist figures approach questions of fashion and beauty in ways that map neatly onto one feminist era. Nor can we reasonably demand any one feminist present a unified or coherent stance towards a subject such as fashion.

Second wave feminism as oppositional to the fashion and beauty industry

As Susan Magarey recently persuasively argued (2018), second wave feminism, in many ways, initially defined itself in opposition to the fashion and beauty industries. In *The Feminine Mystique*[4] Betty Friedan (drawing on her experience as a contributor to women's magazines, as well as interviews with magazine editors and advertisers) famously argued that women's magazines were central to creating the feminine mystique, an infantilising image of women as housewives, tasked with beautifying themselves, their families and their homes. Listing the contents of 1960s edition of *McCall's* magazine, Friedan (1963/2013, 25–26) suggests articles about losing weight, 'glamourous' maternity clothes, home-sewing and making 'Bewitching' folding screens formed a metanarrative about beauty, the fashion industry and domesticity. For Friedan, the typical women's magazine (working in concert with key advertisers) sold women an image and ideology of fashion as a route to beauty and beauty as the key to finding a mate; once married, reproduction and homemaking was to be carried out with a homemaker's cultivated eye for fashionable beauty. Friedan wrote that this image left women strangely 'childlike' and 'passive' in a 'world of bedroom and kitchen, sex, babies, and home': women's magazines are 'crammed full of food, clothing, cosmetics, furniture, and the physical bodies of young women … do no work except housework and work to keep their bodies beautiful to get and keep a man' (1963/2013, 26–27). In 1975 Anne Summers wrote that the principal 'raison d'être' of popular magazines was 'the codification and constant updating of femininity. By consulting these magazines women can gain a pretty good idea of how to behave and dress' (1975, 239). Summers criticised women's magazines for focussing on the domestic while ignoring issues such as abortion, equal pay, child care, equality at work (1975, 438).[5]

As Magarey points out (2018, 32–4) second-wave feminist activism, particularly in its early phase, often paralleled this textual critique of beauty and fashion and antipathy to women's magazines. Women's liberationists' first national action in the United States was a protest against the 1968 Miss America pageant in Atlantic City; organisers invited women from all walks of life (including students, black women, women in the peace movement and anti-abortion activists) to protest 'an image that oppresses women' (Morgan 1970, 584–585). A media release (written by Robin Morgan) announced a boycott of commercial brands supporting the pageant and promising a 'huge Freedom Trash Can' to throw 'woman-garbage' into: 'bras, girdles, curlers, false eyelashes, wigs' and 'issues of *Cosmopolitan, Ladies' Home Journal, Family Circle*'. Organisers also cited the pageant's implicit racism as one of ten reasons for a boycott: 'Since its inception in 1921, the Pageant has not had one Black finalist [nor] a Puerto Rican, Alaskan, Hawaiian, or Mexican-American winner. Nor has there ever been a true Miss America – an American Indian' (Morgan 1970, 585).

Magarey (2018, 33–4) notes that the Australian women's liberation movement followed the US activists' lead with a 1970 protest against Adelaide University's 'Miss Fresher' beauty contest. Marilyn Lake (1999, 225–226) similarly writes that while the early 1970s was a time of great 'diversity and creativity of political action', opposition to beauty contests was common, with protests against the Miss Teenage Quest and beauty contests in universities and high schools. An early issue of *MeJane* reported the Labor Club entering a cow wearing a 'charming black and white coat' in the ANU's Miss University Competition ('Miss Daisy Bovine Robbed of Title', *MeJane*, no. 3, July 1971). While the early women's liberation movement also quickly took up issues such as access to contraception, abortion, divorce, equal pay and violence against women, 'a concern about beauty as oppressive continued, too, like a bass note in a song' Magarey suggests (2018, 40).

In a recent discussion of Germaine Greer's complicated relationship to fashion, viewed through the prism of a home-made paisley coat Greer wore on the cover of *Vogue* and *Life* magazines in 1971, Petra Mosmann (2016, 85–87) also cites the Miss America protest and critiques of fashion and the fashion industry made by feminists such as Kate Millett and Greer. She notes that Greer advocated for women to reject the norms of the fashion industry and urged women to think of beauty and fashion as sites of creativity and pleasure they could remake on their own terms. But Mosmann complicates the story of Greer's (and by extension second wave feminism's) adversarial relationship to the fashion industry with a close examination of Greer's own counter cultural fashion—the fox fur Greer said she wore 'for fun and satire', the paisley coat she had sewn herself—and the *Vogue* and *Life* photo shoots of the tall, strikingly attired and frequently laughing Greer; these were inextricably linked to the way in which Greer (unlike Millett) could position herself within, and was positioned by, the media as the 'fashionable, attractive and funny' feminist (2016, 84–85). Further, Mosmann argues the counter culture styles worn by Greer and other feminists were 'selectively commodified' (89) by the fashion industry, further complicating the notion of a simple opposition between feminism and the mainstream fashion industry in the 1970s.[6] Using both Magarey's and Mosmann's articles as stepping off points, I want to now consider how the figures of Martha Ansara and Elaine Welteroth similarly complicate easy narratives that position feminists as either *for* or *against*, *inside* or *outside*, fashion. I also want to suggest that both figures' approach to fashion can (productively) contain contradictions and ambivalences, and that there as many similarities between these two feminists' approaches to fashion as there are differences.

Martha Ansara's flexible fashion

In the late 1960s Ansara, a film-loving young mother of Syrian-Lebanese descent, had dropped out of the University of Chicago after becoming pregnant with her first child and was living with her husband in Boston (Ansara 2013, 83). Although women's liberationists in Boston boarded busses in 1968 to protest the Miss American pageant in Atlantic City, she wasn't among them. Her first experience of the women's liberation movement came, instead, when her sister-in-law took her to a women's liberation conference. She wasn't impressed, as she told me in a recent interview: 'They weren't talking about regular life. They were talking about the Russian revolution and I just thought, ugh! I didn't see the relevance really' (Kenny 2017). Ansara did join the anti-war movement though, and when she fell in love with an Australian filmmaker and left her husband, the couple joined the California-based anti-war film group Newsreel (Ansara 2013, 83–84). And as Ansara told me, any feminist consciousness of a link between the objectification of women and their oppression was still to come.

> We invited some women to come [to Newsreel]. We had a big billboard poster of a woman in a bikini that went along one side of the wall and they tried to point out something about sexism in relation to this and I just thought, huh? (Kenny 2017)[7]

At that stage Ansara was more intrigued by the possibilities of a woman being *behind* the camera, as she relates in this anecdote about catching sight of the French documentary-maker Agnes Varda across a crowded rally in 1967: 'She was directing her own film crew. Quietly, I spent that month's supporting mother's pension on a Super 8 camera' (Ansara 1987, 180). The pamphlet Ansara made with women she met at Gould's bookshop advertising Sydney's first public women's liberation meeting ('Only the Chains have changed') didn't tackle questions of fashion or beauty either. Helen Jarvis, who helped distribute the leaflet, has said the leaflet intended to make the links between women's liberation and the war in Vietnam: just as there is 'class' and 'national' oppression, there is also sexual oppression' (Cheng 1995). The leaflet linked women's oppression to their position in the domestic sphere and their unequal access to paid work:

> As women we learn that our proper aim in life is to be a good wife and mother above everything else. A woman who rejects this confining definition to seek satisfaction outside the home meets with constant frustration. Most jobs available to her are unskilled and unrewarding. She is told she is not capable of anything better. When a woman has the same job as a man she invariably gets less pay and less hope of advancement … She is forced into a woman's role, regardless of her interests and abilities. To be a woman is to be oppressed. (Australian Women's Broadcasting Cooperative 1977)

For Ansara then, her feminism initially didn't emerge from opposition to the fashion and magazine industries and commercial images of beauty. Rather it emerged from her involvement in the anti-Vietnam war left, along with a nascent but persistent sense that women must participate in creative and political work. In my 2017 interview Ansara repeated an anecdote she has told elsewhere (Magarey 2014, 27) that serves to set her apart from women's liberationists whose interest lay in policing a 'correct' position in relation to clothes, make-up and the presentation of the body:

> I remember in May, 1970, there was a conference in Melbourne ... and there were women from the Communist Party including Mavis Robertson ... [Some other delegates] were ranting against lipstick and this and that, and I remember Mavis saying, 'Soon they'll be doing underarm checks to see if we shave or not'. She was always very wicked. (Kenny 2017)

In a 1993 interview with oral historian Wendy Lowenstein, Ansara says she gravitated to communist women in the movement, and she again suggests questions around clothing and fashion were largely irrelevant to women's liberation: 'The [Communist Party women] wore business clothes [they] weren't bohemian'. Ansara realised she felt more politically aligned with the communist women, despite their more traditionally feminine presentation:

> I thought hang on, wait a minute, and I suddenly realised I actually felt more at home with the knitters and the lipstick wearers ... The other thing about the knitters and the lipstick wearers was that when they said they would do something, not only did they do it, but they did it they did it well. Bit by bit I just drifted over that way [to the Communist Party]. (Lowenstein 1993)

Other activists remarked on conflicts between women's liberationists over questions of clothes and make-up. Anne Summers (1973, 6), writing in *MeJane*, said she was abused for wearing makeup at a Women's Liberation conference. 'One woman abused several of us for wearing makeup (some of us felt we needed to present a front to all those women we were meeting for the first time)'. Ansara suggested to me (Kenny 2017) that some women's liberationists' concern with the right kind of appearance (a fashion that was oppositional to a commercial and traditionally feminine fashion, but a fashion nonetheless)[8] was an affectation. 'I remember all this bloody overall business. Why would you wear overalls? You're not a person working on a building site' (Kenny 2017). Ansara then remarked that her early disinterest in clothing as either a mark of one's politics, or as a source of oppression, may have been related to her status as a mother (a position which perhaps gave her a sense of other sources of oppression):

> There's a picture of the Feminist Film Workers.[9] We're all in a little line and I noticed I had a skirt on and that was commented on. But you see, the other interesting thing is, I had a child and most of those young women were a bit younger than me and they didn't have children yet. (Kenny 2017)

The skirt-as-fashion-and-political-object appears again in Ansara's own recollection of those years. In an anecdote about visiting Film Australia in 1970 to apply for a grant, Ansara pragmatically and matter-of-factly describes wearing a non-feminist miniskirt to achieve a feminist aim on behalf of her filmmaking collective:

> [I] went up to Film Australia in Lindfield to meet producer Dick Mason, an assessor for the Experimental Film Fund, then administered by the Australian Film Institute. I was twenty-seven years old, wearing makeup and a miniskirt, which I thought might help. In any case, we got a grant of $1050. (Ansara 2013, 84)

Film for Discussion's fashion issue

Ansara and the newly-formed Sydney Women's Film Group used the money to produce *Film for Discussion*, a 24-minute black and white film about a day in the life of an office worker 'Jeni' (Jeni Thornley), as she begins questioning the roles laid down for women at work, at home and as consumers. Ansara (Kenny 2017) says she came up with the idea for the film on a train on her way to the conference where she was appalled that some women abused others for wearing lipstick. And Ansara sourced the money while wearing makeup and a miniskirt. Yet despite this background (and despite Ansara's feminism emerging initially from her involvement with the anti-war left, and her previous comments about the irrelevancy of clothing to one's feminist politics) the film she made can be read as a blistering critique of the fashion and beauty industries. The following reading of the film is not meant as a 'gotcha' moment to unmask Ansara's inconsistency (in any case, the film has always been referred to as a group-devised process, see for example Smith 1975, 48–49). Rather I want to suggest it is possible, and arguably often productive, for individual feminists to hold evolving, ambiguous, or even contradictory, stances towards a topic such as fashion and beauty.

Film for Discussion begins with a montage of images of women linking the worlds of work and the home with the world of consumption, fashion and celebrities: footage of Hollywood figures such as Marilyn Monroe is intercut with images of women in typing pools, operating cash registers, in clothes factories, performing in a strip show, trying on wedding dresses, and as models advertising bras and laundry detergents. Both the content and quick edit form of the film's opening suggest both femininity's constructed nature and the narrow range of roles socially prescribed for women. Occasionally interrupting these images are glimpses of women protesting, chanting and singing: women moving forward and using their voices as if they are the active subjects of their history.

As the film's narrative begins, we see Thornley's character, directed by a male boss standing over her (shown only as a torso), carrying out mundane office tasks while talking with a coworker about the coworker's upcoming wedding, her plans for a honeymoon, house and children (Friedan's feminine mystique). At lunchtime Jeni accompanies the bride-to-be to a department store. In scenes intercut with her friend trying on wedding dresses, Jeni tries on hats but appears barely more animated than the store dummies. The wedding dresses and hats function as a synecdoche for the already-written marriage script these women are heading towards. In an article published a few short years after its release, Kate Legge (1980, 33) wrote that inert figures such as dummies, which appear frequently in this scene, served as 'visual similes' in many feminist films of this period 'to satirise and symbolise the prescribed stereotypes of a sexist society'. Here, commercial fashion stands in for women's more general lack of social and creative agency.

Jeni next talks to 'Deirdre', an office temp and women's liberationist. Inspired by Deirdre's ideas, Jeni later argues on a drive home with her boyfriend about women's position in the workplace, asking why she should do extra work for him (he is also a colleague). Next a family dinner scene offers a glimpse of Jeni's future if she too marries: Jeni's parents argue, her boorish father complains about the dinner not being on the table and directs his conversation to Jeni's boyfriend. Washing the dishes, Jeni shares her worries with her mother, who suggests 'maybe you will be able to change him [her boyfriend]'. Jeni retreats to her bedroom and, in a three minute dialogue-free scene, sits at her dresser slowly removing makeup. It's as if she is trying to eliminate all the artifice and construction to see who she is (or who she might be).

Ansara played a key role in bringing consciousness raising methods to the Sydney women's liberation movement (Wills 1981, 46), and *Film for Discussion* was made using consciousness raising processes. In an interview made shortly after the film's release, Ansara said the film was made in a way 'typical of the women's movement: people had different jobs, but the content was determined together' (Smith 1975, 48–49). When completed, Ansara and her co-creators worked hard distributing the film to consciousness raising and community groups around the country, where it was used as a 'conversation' starter (Ansara 1977, 104). Ansara is rightly frequently credited as a driving force for the film: she was not only the cinematographer, she led the actors through workshops, Thornley told me (Kenny 2018). So although Ansara's feminism emerged from her involvement in the anti-war left, and despite her comments suggesting questions of clothes and fashion are, at best, secondary to larger political concerns, she *did* end up making a film which cogently links fashion and beauty (particularly in the form of the wedding dress, but also through images of women as models and movie stars) to an oppressive triad of domesticity, work and consumerism: spheres in which women were expected to serve men and appear beautiful.

Elaine Welteroth's fashionable feminism

As I have discussed, Ansara's politics emerged at a moment when many key actions and texts of the women's liberation movement opposed the fashion and beauty industries. By the time Elaine Welteroth arrived in Sydney in 2017, however, it was possible for many feminists to view the fashion and beauty industries as not only *not antithetical* to feminism, but to regard these industries as *embracing* feminism. This shift is in line with what Joanne Hollows and Rachel Moseley write is both the incorporation of feminist ideas in popular culture in recent decades, as well as the associated questioning of the notion that there is an 'inside' and an 'outside' to feminism, one where *authentic* feminism must stand outside popular culture (2006, 1–2). This development was perhaps most dramatically (and literally) demonstrated in 2006 when a *BUST* magazine fashion spread showed models emulating the fashions of Elizabeth Cady Stanton, Gloria Steinem, Bella Abzug, Camille Paglia, Angela Davis and Kathleen Hanna. It is important to note though that this process has not been unproblematic: as Elizabeth Groeneveld (2009) has argued, the *BUST* issue and its cover line—'be a feminist or just dress like one'—set up a caricatured, individualised and depoliticised version of feminist history.

While fashion magazines appear to have increasingly embraced feminism (however problematically), feminist scholars have also been rethinking assumptions that women's magazines and feminism were always necessarily in opposition to each other. As I mentioned earlier, Mosmann (2016) reminds us that Germaine Greer appeared in model-like poses in *Vogue* and *Life* magazine profiles in 1971. She also notes the way Miss America protesters used fashion in 'creative' ways, and the 'dynamic relationships' between feminists and the fashion industry (2016, 87); rather than being *outside* the fashion industry, counter cultural feminists were creating fashion trends, even if unintentionally. Megan Le Masurier (2007), in a sympathetic reading of the pages of the Australian women's magazine *Cleo* in the 1970s, likewise questions the notion that women's magazines were always inherently antifeminist: she finds many articles and letters in *Cleo* articulating concerns that also engaged women's liberationists. Welteroth herself (2017) has cited predecessors to *Teen Vogue* in feminist-influenced magazines such as *Marie Claire*, *Sassy* and *Ms. Magazine*. It is in this briefly sketched context that few commentators would suggest anything incongruous about Welteroth's arrival in Sydney in 2017, hailed as a feminist fashion magazine editor who has described her young readers as both 'woke' to sexism and racism and hungry for 'beauty tips' (Warrington 2017).

In Sydney Welteroth told her audience that a magazine such as *Teen Vogue* did not have to be *either* for feminism *or* for the fashion and beauty industries: it could cover *both* hard-hitting political and social issues *and* beauty, fashion and fame. Welteroth also signalled a new accord, even a productive alliance, between fashion and feminism, claiming *Teen Vogue's* pairing of 'fashion and beauty' with 'radical information' is 'special and unprecedented' (Welteroth is not clear exactly how *Teen Vogue* represents a radical break from predecessor magazines. I read her comment as something of an embroidery in the context of a writers' festival with a significant public relations function). As if echoing (while also reversing) the second wave slogan 'the personal is political',[10] Welteroth said *Teen Vogue* takes news stories that 'maybe needed a little bit more context for a younger audience, needed maybe a personal narrative to make [them] seem relevant to them'. For Welteroth, fashion and feminism can not only *coexist*, but the fashion and beauty industry can be *portals* to sisterhood and political awareness:

> I can't tell you how many times I've been in the bathroom with another woman ... we feel we have nothing in common, but we talk about a great lipstick shade or great hair ... and it's just this doorway for connection and for understanding and for dialogue. (Welteroth 2017)

Fashion, beauty and politics do appear to have made a compact in *Teen Vogue;* often, the magazine also makes fashion and beauty political. In the months prior to Welteroth's talk, Lauren Duca's (2016) Trump-is-gaslighting-America column was *Teen Vogue's* most read story, followed by a story about how to apply glitter nail polish (Warrington 2017). In a *Guardian* profile shortly after she was appointed editor, Welteroth told Ruby Warrington (2017) her ambition for *Teen Vogue* is 'to highlight underrepresented voices and role models, and to create a magazine that didn't exist for me growing up'. Warrington notes Welteroth's term at *Teen Vogue* has been characterised by articles replete with political content and covers that have 'consistently featured women of colour' (as beauty editor in 2015 Welteroth helped produce the magazine's first issue to feature three black models on the cover, an issue that became the year's bestseller).[11] Welteroth herself (2016) wrote a feature about the cultural histories behind the hairstyles of seven women of colour, including a Native American woman, a Puerto Rican and a Jamaican and Haitian heritage woman.[12] However, *Teen Vogue's* articles are not a simple 'anything-goes' celebration of fashion. On April 14, 2017 Welteroth published what became the title's most-read story (Welteroth 2017), an article by Jessica Andrews about cultural appropriation at the Coachella music festival. Andrews argued western concert goers who wear Indian bindis and native American feathered headdresses are disrespecting those items' cultural and spiritual significance. Earlier Welteroth put the actress Amandla Stenberg on *Teen Vogue's* cover in February 2016 after Stenberg made a popular YouTube video about the way white artists and high fashion appropriate African American hair and music styles while staying silent on racism and police brutality. Stenberg 'basically schooled the world on what cultural appropriation is', Welteroth said, describing Stenberg as 'a voice for her generation' (Warrington 2017).

In championing women of diverse cultural backgrounds and a more inclusive definition of beauty and fashion, Welteroth's feminism can be read as answering the Miss America protestors' critique of the beauty and fashion industry's racism. And *Teen Vogue's* editorial approach, which has included a video collaboration with MuslimGirl.com (Al-Khatahtbeh 2016) featuring girls talking about the hijab, dating and Trump, can also be seen as a culturally aware improvement on *BUST*'s 'fashionable feminist issue' which, in an accompanying editorial, positioned burka-wearing women as the 'other' to liberal, hip, empowered, fashionable western feminists (Groeneveld 2009, 181). In embracing stories about swimsuit brands and nail polish in a popular magazine format, however, Welteroth and *Teen Vogue* are also repudiating the 1968 protestors' symbolic trash can rejection of women's magazines and the feminine fashion and accoutrements advertised within them.

Any attempt to sketch too-clear generational differences, or to attach Welteroth and Ansara too neatly to specific feminist waves, however, must also be confounded or complicated by the resonances between them. Welteroth's liberal embrace of fashion is arguably in sympathy with Ansara's own early accommodation of makeup and miniskirts in her political organising and strategic fundraising. And we can also hear, in Welteroth's comments about women bonding over beauty and fashion products in the bathroom, an echo of Summers' 1973 *MeJane* reference to wearing makeup to a conference as a way of building relationships with women new to the movement. *Teen Vogue*'s interrogation of who gets to wear what fashions can arguably also be read as having some affinities with second wave feminists for whom wearing overalls and not wearing makeup was a form of embodied activism. For Welteroth and *Teen Vogue*, though, 'correct' fashion does not mean forsaking feminine attire or makeup, like the feminists Ansara clashed with in 1970. Rather, it is concerned with cultural and racial sensitivity. Fashion still matters for feminists, though: for Welteroth the kinds of clothes you wear, the way you present yourself and your identity, are crucially important: 'Being yourself is a form of activism', Welteroth (2017) told her Sydney audience. Welteroth has described her own feminist consciousness as an 'intersectional feminism'—and her magazine accordingly gives weight to interconnected concerns of sexuality, race and gender (Warrington 2017). But to suggest that this approach is a *completely* new break from the early women's liberation movement would, I argue, be to forget the 1968 Miss America protestors were (for example) also keenly alert to the pageant's racism and ageism, and to the links between an imperialist war and the pageant winner's troop-visiting tour of Vietnam. Ansara, speaking under the commonly-used women's liberation pseudonym Vera Figner, was likewise keenly aware that the women's liberation movement must acknowledge the very different priorities of many Aboriginal women, and critique its often white and middle class assumptions (see Smith 1975, 52).

Welteroth's focus on issues around the body and appearance *can* be seen as evidence of Fixmer and Wood's (2005, 236) argument that, in contrast to second wave feminism's focus on central, juridical power, in its more recent manifestations feminism has often focussed on 'physical, bodily action that aims to provoke change by exercising and resisting power in everyday life'.[13] While I believe there is some compelling truth to this argument, it is important to recall second wave feminism's critique of fashion and concern with bodily forms of oppression. We also need to recognise that Welteroth (2017) concluded her Sydney talk with a reference to *Teen Vogue*'s plans to bring young girls around the kitchen table to 'solve' political problems in the world today, suggesting a clear interest in all forms of political power, micro and macro, while simultaneously invoking the consciousness raising practices of women's liberationists. Like Ansara's *Film for Discussion*, Welteroth envisages *Teen Vogue* as a consciousness raising text to provoke discussion and action. Though significantly, while Ansara and the Sydney Women's Film Group positioned themselves as against commercial films,[14] Welteroth's feminism not only embraces the commercial format, but replaces a grassroots-directed consciousness raising model with a top down, corporate-led consciousness raising. Welteroth suggests makeup and fashion can start 'important conversations' between women, and that *Teen Vogue* can help young girls to connect their own 'personal' lives with bigger 'political' issues (Welteroth 2017). This, in many ways, is a reversal of second-wave consciousness raising which, according to Susan Brownmiller (1999, 21), first emerged in a New York apartment in 1967 when a group of women, mostly veterans of the left already engaged with political organising, met to talk about their 'oppression as women' *in their own lives* (my italics).

Conclusion

Ansara, despite her ambivalence about questions of fashion, eventually developed a position in *Film for Discussion* that presented fashion, and the world of women as objects, models and dummies, as things which tied women to an oppressive system of work, consumerism and domesticity. Magarey (2018) suggests that now, however, women's increased participation in the labour market, 'combined with some—*some*—recalibration of the distribution of labour within households has made a bit of a difference to the need to cultivate beauty … to catch a husband'(40). This de-coupling of fashionable beauty as a route to a husband and financial security could perhaps explain, at least in part, a more relaxed attitude to fashion and fashion magazines we see in some contemporary expressions of feminism. But any narrative that positions women's magazines and the beauty industry as something second wave feminists were *against* and contemporary feminism are *for* fails when we consider (for example) Germaine Greer's 1971 appearances in *Vogue* and *Life*, or Ansara's embrace of the miniskirt. Or when we look at *Teen Vogue's* disapproving approach to cultural appropriation in the fashions of a popular music festival.

While we need to be careful to avoid too-simple historical narratives, I think it is nevertheless fair to say that for many second wave feminists who rejected the feminine mystique of women's magazines and who protested beauty pageants, the idea that fashion magazines and the beauty industry could be *uncomplicatedly* reconciled with feminism might have been unthinkable. Could they, for example, have imagined the editor of a fashion magazine leading a Women's March, as Welteroth did in January 2017? It is *hard* to imagine. For Welteroth, however, there is no contradiction; she regards *Teen Vogue* as being at the vanguard of contemporary feminism, recalling people at marches in different cities sending her pictures of 'banners talking about *Teen Vogue*' (Warrington 2017). Her favourite was a banner saying '*Teen Vogue* Will Save Us All!'. She tells Warrington: 'I honestly think our readers are gonna save the world'.

As Welteroth's comments show, feminists are still concerned with fashion, both as a source of oppression and liberation, and as something that can bring women together and divide women. Martha Ansara too saw fashion as a double-edged sword, where a fashion like the miniskirt could be used in aid of funding a feminist film that then critiqued the fashion industry. Ansara's politics were formed in the anti-war left, and only later did she develop a feminist critique of fashion. Welteroth talks about being a 14-year-old who was interested in fashion but didn't see herself represented in glossy magazines (Warrington 2017); her term at *Teen Vogue* began with championing models of colour, and only later did she 'pivot' *Teen Vogue* to bigger political questions such as 'politics and reproductive rights' (Welteroth 2017). Although just a brief discussion of two feminists from two different eras, this article sketches a broad shift in approaches to fashion and beauty, while also acknowledging many resonances across generations. It suggests it is not possible, nor perhaps reasonable, to look for a consistent or unified approach to fashion in either individual feminists or feminist generations. It is possible, and it might even be productive, for feminism and feminists to take evolving or even seemingly contradictory approaches to fashion.

Notes

1. The five million estimate comes from the US-based organisers of the Women's March (see www.womensmarch.com).
2. Martha Ansara dates the rally as 15 December.
3. The trend of feminists coming to Australia from the US had precedents as early as 1892, when Jessie Ackerman toured Australia (Lake 1999, 25). And the flow has never been one way: in the period Ansara first moved to Australia, Australian feminist Germaine Greer was based in the UK and touring the world, including the United States, publicising *The Female Eunuch*.
4. Brownmiller credits Friedan's key role in inspiring a mass form of consciousness raising: 'A revolution was brewing, but it took a visionary to notice … although Friedan had defined the problem in terms of bored, depressed, middle-class suburban housewives who downed too many pills … I saw myself on every page' (1999, 3).
5. Earlier, Simone de Beauvoir (1949/1972, 692) linked women's status as objects to, in no small part, the construction of femininity, 'artificially shaped by custom and fashion'.
6. Annemarie Strassel (2013, 38) locates an even earlier interplay between feminism and fashion in the bloomers advocated in the mid 1800s by Elizabeth Cady Stanton, Susan B. Anthony and Amelia Bloomer.
7. Ansara related the same anecdote to Felicity Collins (1995, 14) in an interview Collins conducted for her PhD research.
8. Petra Mosmann (2016, 83) makes a related point that the paisley coat Germaine Greer wore on the covers of 1971 issues of *Vogue* and *Life* magazines was part of a 'counter culture protest', but nevertheless still part of 'creating a fashion trend', one quickly taken up by the fashion industry and 'commodified' (2016, 88–89).
9. This picture is reproduced in Jennifer Stott's (1987, 119) overview of the feminist filmmakers, including Ansara, who were associated with the Sydney Filmmakers Cooperative.
10. Gloria Steinem has said to assign credit to anyone for coining the phrase 'the personal is political' would be as absurd as assigning credit to someone for inventing the phrase 'World War 11' (Burch 2012, 139), however its first use in a publication is commonly cited as the headline of an article by activist and writer Carol Hanisch in *Notes from the Second Year* (Shulamith Firestone and Anne Koedt 1970).
11. Recent *Teen Vogue* covers have featured Zoë Kravitz (March 2016), actress and singer Willow Smith (May 2016) gymnasts Simone Biles and Gabby Douglas (August 2016) and actress Yara Shahidi (December 2016).
12. Here Welteroth is, in Mimi Thi Nguyen's words, 'permit[ing] us to see what we have not been allowed to see' (quoted in Minh-Ha T. Pham 2011, 17).
13. They are careful to say scholars should not make too firm distinctions between second and third wave feminism: many second wave feminists can sound very third wave at times—for example, Germaine Greer tasting menstrual blood, and Susie Orbach writing *Fat is a Feminist Issue* (Fixmer and Wood 2005, 249).
14. In a flyer written to accompany *Film for Discussion* at consciousness raising sessions ("Winners/Losers", undated) the Sydney Women's Film Group says their work encourages active viewers, and was made in opposition to 'a profit-orientated society [where film] contests are used to promote and sell commodities to consumers'.

Acknowledgements

A paper presented by Susan Magarey at the How the Personal Became Political Symposium, held at the ANU Gender Institute, 6–7 March 2017, and later published as 'Beauty Becomes Political: Beginnings of the Women's Liberation Movement in Australia' in Australian Feminist Studies, was a formative influence for this article, and I am indebted to Susan for her work. I am also grateful to the blind reviewers of this article, and to my supervisor Dr Margie Borschke, for their invaluable comments and suggestions.

Disclosure statement

No potential conflict of interest was reported by the author.

Funding

This research is supported by an Australian Government Research Training Program (RTP) Scholarship.

Ethics

Interviews conducted by the author with Martha Ansara and Jeni Thornley were approved under Macquarie University's Human Research Ethics procedures.

ORCID

Kath Kenny http://orcid.org/0000-0002-2028-0666

References

Al-Khatahtbeh, Amani. 2016. "Watch Muslim Girls Get REAL About Love, Faith, and Donald Trump." *Teen Vogue*, May 9. https://www.teenvogue.com/story/muslim-girl-videos-islamophobia-america.
Ansara, Martha. 1977. "Interview with Martha Ansara." *Lip, Australian Feminist Arts Journal* 2 and 3: 104–105.
Ansara, Martha. 1987. "Martha Ansara." In *Don't Shoot Darling: Women's Independent Filmmaking in Australia*, edited by Annette Blonski, Barbara Creed, and Freda Freiburg, 180–181. Richmond: Greenhouse Publications.
Ansara, Martha. 2013. "Clapperboard." In *Things That Liberate*, edited by Margaret Henderson, and Alison Bartlett, 81–88. Newcastle-upon-Tyne: Cambridge Scholars Publishing.
Australian Women's Broadcasting Cooperative. 1977. *Mother I Can See a Light*. Coming Out Show. First broadcast on ABC Radio 2 (2FC) on Saturday 7 May, 1977.
Brownmiller, Susan. 1999. *In our Time: Memoir of a Revolution*. New York, New York: The Dial Press.
Burch, Kerry. 2012. *Democratic Transformations: Eight Conflicts in the Negotiation of American Identity*. London: Continuum.

Cheng, Eva. 1995. "Vietnam and the women's liberation movement." *Green Left Weekly*, April 26.
Collins, Felicity. 1995. "Ties that bind: the psyche of feminist filmmaking, Sydney 1969–1989." PhD diss., University of Technology Sydney.
De Beauvoir. 1949/1972. *The Second Sex*. Harmondsworth: Penguin Books.
Duca, Lauren. 2016. "Donald Trump Is Gaslighting America." *Teen Vogue*, December 10. https://www.teenvogue.com/story/donald-trump-is-gaslighting-america.
Fixmer, Natalie, and Julia T Wood. 2005. "The Personal is Still Political: Embodied Politics in Third Wave Feminism." *Women's Studies in Communication* 28 (2): 235–257.
Fraser, Nancy. 2009. "Feminism, Capitalism and the Cunning of History." *New Left Review* 56: 97–117.
Friedan, Betty. 1963/2013. *The Feminine Mystique, with an Introduction by Gail Collins and Afterword by Anna Quindlen*. New York: W.W. Norton and Company.
Gilbert, Sophie. 2016. "Teen Vogue's Political Coverage Isn't Surprising." The Atlantic, December 12.
Groeneveld, Elizabeth. 2009. "'Be a Feminist or Just Dress Like One': BUST, Fashion and Feminism as Lifestyle." *Journal of Gender Studies* 18 (2): 179–190.
Hanisch, Carol. 1970. "The Personal is Political." In *Notes From the Second Year: Women's Liberation, Major Writings of the Radical Feminists*, edited by Shulamith Firestone, and Anne Koedt, 76–78. New York: New York Radical Women.
Hemmings, Clare. 2011. *Why Stories Matter*. Durham: Duke University Press.
Hollows, Joanne, and Rachel Moseley. 2006. "Popularity Contests: The Meanings of Popular Feminisms." In *Feminism in Popular Culture*, edited by Jane Hollows, and Rachel Mosely, 1–22. Oxford: Berg.
Kenny, Kath. 2017. Interview with Martha Ansara, August 30. Transcript held by the author.
Kenny, Kath. 2018. Interview with Jeni Thornley, March 8. Transcript held by the author.
Lake, Marilyn. 1999. *Getting Equal: The History of Australian Feminism*. St Leonards: Allen and Unwin.
Legge, Kate. 1980. "The Problems of Pluralism: Women's Films and Feminist Films." *Lip 1980, Australian Feminist Arts Journal*, 131–133.
Le Masurier, Megan. 2007. "My Other, My Self." *Australian Feminist Studies* 22 (53): 191–211.
Lowenstein, Wendy. 1993. Martha Ansara interviewed by Wendy Lowenstein for the Communists and the Left in the arts and community oral history project. 3 digital audio tapes at the National Library of Australia.
Lumby, Catharine. 2011. "Past the Post in Feminist Media Studies." *Feminist Media Studies* 11 (1): 95–100.
Magarey, Susan. 2014. *Dangerous Ideas*. Adelaide: University of Adelaide Press.
Magarey, Susan. 2018. "Beauty Becomes Political: Beginnings of the Women's Liberation Movement in Australia." *Australian Feminist Studies* 33 (87): 31–44.
Morgan, Robin. 1970. *Sisterhood is Powerful*. New York: Vintage Books.
Mosmann, Petra. 2016. "A Feminist Fashion Icon: Germaine Greer's Paisley Coat." *Australian Feminist Studies* 31 (87): 78–94.
Parkinson, Hannah Jane. 2016. "Who will take on Donald Trump? Teen Vogue." *The Guardian*, December 12.
Pham, Minh-Ha T. 2011. "Blog Ambition: Fashion, Feelings, and the Political Economy of the Digital Raced Body." *Camera Obscura* 26 (1): 1–37.
Smith, Margaret. 1975. "A Personal View of the Women's Movement: Vera Figner, A Sydney Sister Interviewed by Margaret Smith." In *The Way Out*, edited by Margaret Smith, and David Crossley, 47–53. Melbourne: Lansdowne Press.
Stott, Jennifer. 1987. "Independent Feminist Filmmaking and the Sydney Filmmakers Co-Operative." In *Don't Shoot Darling: Women's Independent Filmmaking in Australia*, edited by Annette Blonski, Barbara Creed, and Freda Freiburg, 118–126. Richmond: Greenhouse Publications.
Strassel, Annemarie. 2013. "Designing Women: Feminist Methodologies in American Fashion." *Women's Studies Quarterly* 41 (1-2): 35–59.
Summers, Anne. 1973. "Where's the Women's Movement Moving To?" *MeJane* 10: 6–8.
Summers, Anne. 1975. *Damned Whores and God's Police*. Melbourne: Penguin.

Sydney Women's Film Group. "Winners/Losers: I lost it at the movies ... .it turned out to be my dignity." Undated flyer printed and authorised by 'Vera Figner, 25 Alberta St., Sydney'. Western Sydney University Library, Penrith Archives 305.420994 F1.

Sydney Women's Film Group. 1974. *Film for Discussion*. Hurlstone Park: Ballad Films.

Warrington, Ruby. 2017. "Inside Teen Vogue: 'Our readers consider themselves activists'." *The Guardian*, February 25.

Welteroth, Elaine. 2016. "7 Girls Show What Beauty Looks Like When It's Not Appropriated." *Teen Vogue*, April 21.

Welteroth, Elaine. 2017. "Elaine Welteroth: On Editing Teen Vogue." An in-conversation Sydney Writers' Festival session hosted by Julia Turner, Sydney, May 26.

Wills, Sue. 1981. "The Politics of Sexual Liberation". PhD diss., University of Sydney.

'I Want to Wear It': Fashioning Black Feminism in *Mahogany* (1975)

Kimberly Lamm

ABSTRACT
In this article I focus on the portrayal of fashionable clothing in the 1975 film *Mahogany* and connect it to the history of African American women engaging with sartorial self-representation as a means to assert their visibility in American culture. My aim is to analyse *Mahogany*'s emphasis on brightly-coloured highly-ornamented clothing, which has a long history of signifying bad taste and became part of accusations of racial and sexual inferiority. I want to show how *Mahogany*'s representation of fashion undermines the historically entrenched bias against colourful, highly adorned clothing while also revealing how this bias has played a subtle but significant role in the racism and sexism black women have encountered, further (but not finally) impeding them from the forms of recognition the category of femininity offers. *Mahogany* represents those impediments and repeats the sexual and racial commodification underlying them, but also resists them (albeit quite subtly) through the film's loving display of fashion and its attention to the work of designing and making clothes. *Mahogany* tells a story of bright sartorial resistance that can be understood as an articulation of black feminist desires for women of colour to be able to compose the images through which their bodies are perceived.

In the 1975 film *Mahogany,* the character Tracy Chambers – played by Diana Ross – aspires to be a fashion designer. Tracy lives on Chicago's South Side, works in the display department at Marshall Fields, and takes design classes at night. Animated by Tracy's talent and ambition, *Mahogany* makes fashionable clothing a prominent visual theme and scenes that focus on the creation and display of clothing highlight both the visual composition of the film and the creation of Ross as a celebrity image (Figure 1).

Ross designed all the costumes she wears in *Mahogany*. Her role as designer is stated prominently in the film credits – 'Costumes Designed by Diana Ross' – which gives the costume designer unprecedented prominence. In her biography *Secrets of a Sparrow*, Ross writes that *Mahogany* was her 'debut in the fashion business' and built upon what she learned in high school about 'fabrics, sewing, millinery, knitting, and crocheting' (Ross 1993, 175). She explains that she created the designs from a careful reading of the script and noting the places where she thought 'Tracy needed special clothes' and then writing down 'exactly what she needed to wear' (Ross 1993, 175). In his biography,

Figure 1. Diana Ross in a gown from *Mahogany*. Photo by Steve Schapiro/Corbis via Getty Images.

director Berry Gordy writes that Ross stayed up all night during the production of *Mahogany* to see her designs to completion and felt that Ross' devotion to the clothing compromised her on-screen performance (Gordy 1994, 341). Whether this assessment is true or not, the role of Ross as costume designer complicates the readily available story that Gordy, as head of Motown, transformed Ross into a harmonious image of black femininity that white audiences would be comfortable consuming, making her not only the star of the Supremes, but a perfect vehicle for what Mark Anthony Neal identifies as Gordy's corporate ambitions (Neal 1999, 89). The desire to become a fashion designer, which Ross and her character Tracy share, exceeds the demands to serve and please others and imprints the cinematic image with black women's agency.

The fact that Ross made her own costumes for *Mahogany* connects the film to the history of early cinema in which actresses had to provide their own on-screen attire. In 'Costume and Narrative: How Dress Tells the Woman's Story,' Jane Gaines charts the emergence of the costume designer in film history and analyses role that figure played in the tension between the film's narrative and its costumes, which, according to Gaines, indexes women's work and tells the woman's story. Gaines explains that actresses working in silent film had to either purchase or design their own costumes until they became stars (Gaines 1990, 182). The actresses Gaines refers to are white, and one could say that by entering this history of women designing and sewing their own costumes to place themselves within the cinematic frame, Ross makes *Mahogany* a meditation on challenging the implicit whiteness of femininity on screen, which reflects upon the difference fashioning her own iconicity entails.

Nicole Fleetwood's analysis of Ross in *On Racial Icons: Blackness and the Public Imagination* substantiates this reading. Fleetwood argues that, 'becoming a celebrity icon is a labor-intensive choice that involves sculpting one's features, developing public recognition, and turning oneself into a vehicle of desirability and adoration. In essence the celebrity icon is manufactured and groomed' (Fleetwood 2015, 55). Black female stars inherit pressures that make this labour particularly intensive. They have to contend with the fact that, as Fleetwood points out, their celebrity 'tends to be read within a representational space of negation' (Fleetwood 2015, 71). That is, the black icon is understood primarily in relationship to the restrictions US racism has placed on black life: not only 'the limited access blacks have had historically and presently to arenas of power, wealth, and possibility', but the subjection of black bodies to the commodification of slavery (Fleetwood 2015, 71). The images of Tracy designing clothing that appear early in the film – she is portrayed in her apartment studio shaping fabric draped on mannequins into dresses – can be read as meditations on the dense work of becoming a black female icon and claiming a place for black women within American culture's picture of femininity.

A 'fashion film', *Mahogany* contributes to a rich history in which fashion and film mirror each other and contribute to the visual ubiquity of consumer capitalism (Munich 2011, 260). In 'The Carole Lombard in Macy's Window', published just four years after *Mahogany* premiered, Charles Eckert argues that from the beginning of cinema, 'all of the elements of a new advertising form were implicit' (Eckert [1978] 1990, 103). With limitless potential for displaying products in idealising light, early films 'functioned as living display windows for all that they contained' (Eckert [1978] 1990, 103). As Eckert's research reveals, the beginnings of the Hollywood film industry inspired the development of the fashion and cosmetic industries, and together they produced the image of a young white woman as their star and primary consumer (Eckert [1978] 1990, 109–110). *Mahogany* intervenes in the racial premise of this history and addresses black women as consumers with dreams of making themselves into stars.

While *Mahogany* asks viewers to celebrate its intervention into the whiteness of American visual culture, scholars of the film have rightly pointed its political limitations. They argue that the film is not only a commercial for the star power of Diana Ross, but illustrates the capitalist appropriation of the anti-racist arguments that made an impact in the 1960s and 1970s and therefore offers restricted ideas how black men and women can appear. In her historically nuanced analysis, Miriam Thaggert reads *Mahogany* as an illustration of anxieties about 'career-oriented black women', which reflect the stubborn legacies of the Moynihan report on the post Civil Rights era (Thaggert 2012, 716). Thaggert highlights the anxious dismissals of what she calls Tracy's 'visual acumen' – her 'efficiency in *creating* images' – that run through *Mahogany* (Thaggert 2012, 720, 716). Highlighting how the film 'pathologiz[es]' Tracy's 'professional goals', Thaggert demonstrates how *Mahogany* reigns in a black woman's ambitions by reducing her to the work of submitting to and symbolising unthreatening iterations of black heterosexuality (Thaggert 2012, 716).

Thaggert's analysis of *Mahogany* builds on earlier readings by Robyn Wiegman, Jane Gaines, and Richard Dyer. These scholars draw attention to what Wiegman identifies as the film's 'reliance on narrative structures that foreground the bourgeois ideal as symbol of racial egalitarianism' (Wiegman 1991, 312). Wiegman also situates the film in relationship to American feminism, and reads *Mahogany* as an example of a feminism that gives 'equal access to corporate and commodity worlds' (Wiegman 1991, 308). By following how Tracy serves as a conduit for masculine rivalries, Wiegman argues that Tracy's self-commodification through fashionable display gives her access to a diluted form of feminist progress that replicates white and middle class ideals of femininity (Wiegman 1991, 308). In her well known analysis of *Mahogany*, which reads the film to demonstrate the limitations of feminist film theory's engagement with psychoanalysis, Gaines argues that in addition to making Ross a '"white"' model, the film 'hawks the philosophy of black enterprise and social aspiration' (Gaines 1988, 20). As though he was creating a template for *Mahogany*'s many negative reviews, Dyer focuses on the fact that Gordy made the film to appeal to both black and white audiences. He reads the film as a paean to consumption so full of clichés that any real political argument is diluted. 'As a vehicle for Diana Ross', Dyer writes, 'it chucks in something for everyone in her audience. The white audience is given a story of "success" and how "success doesn't bring happiness" that both celebrates the American way of life and keeps people (blacks) in their place' (Dyer 1986, 131).

These readings are convincing, but I approach *Mahogany* from a different angle. I read the film's focus on Tracy's fashionable clothing as more than a capitulation to white capitalist dominance, but a fashioning of black feminism that connects to the history of African American women's work with clothing. Focused on a black woman who takes pleasure designing brightly coloured, highly ornamented clothing, *Mahogany* alludes to the role clothing played in black women's resistance to slavery's punitive restrictions and defies a cultural history in which the construction of aesthetic taste and criticisms of fashion are intertwined with the production of racial and sexual difference, insidiously contributing to the limitations placed on black women. When read this way, *Mahogany* illustrates Gaines' argument that women's film costumes 'tell the woman's story' – the subjective landscape of the female character/star, which had to be seen and felt but could not stand out – but also highlights the impulse to make Tracy's ambition to be a fashion designer the primary narrative of the film (Gaines 1990, 180). I set this impulse against what is unquestionably considered *Mahogany*'s most prominent narrative – the contest between a black man and a white man for access to Tracy – and show how it *almost* erases the story of her ambitions to become a fashion designer, but not quite. By maintaining a consistent focus on Tracy's designs, *Mahogany* challenges this historically entrenched bias against colourful, highly adorned clothing while also revealing how this bias has played a subtle but significant role in the racism and sexism black women have encountered, further (but not finally) impeding them from the forms of recognition the category femininity offers. The film's loving display of Tracy's flamboyant designs resists these limitations and aligns with iterations of black feminist assertion that came alive in films and magazines addressed to African American audiences in the 1970s. Though quelled by a conclusion that reasserts the conservative assumption that the black woman's purpose is to serve her husband in his fight for racial justice, by fashioning a black feminism that actively embraces and defies stereotypes about black women in loud flashy clothes, *Mahogany* tells a story of bright sartorial resistance that can be understood as an articulation of black feminist desires for the story of a black woman who can imaginatively arrange her own image and have a say about how she is seen.

Defying taste

The intertwined themes of race, gender, and visual display are announced quite explicitly in the two scenes that open *Mahogany*. The first depicts a fashion show that takes place in an opera house in Rome. The second scene takes place in a classroom in Chicago. Theatrical and elaborate, the fashion show announces Tracy's success as a fashion designer, and contrasts sharply with the second scene that goes back in time to portray an early articulation of her ambitions. Both scenes put Tracy's skill at creating images on display and ask viewers to take it seriously as her fashioning of black feminism.

Before the fashion show begins, white graphic pictographs appear against a black background. As these pictographs begin to move and turn, it becomes clear that they represent bodies moving in fashionable clothing. The calligraphic inscriptions dissolve into a full colour cinematic image and viewers see bodies in costumes arranged on a stair. A red curtain closes over this stylised arrangement and two giant gold dragons slowly drop over the dark red curtains. A male voice announces that this is Mahogany's 'Kabuki finale', and the camera focuses on a procession of women who wear heavy make up that has transformed their faces into masks, deliberately artificial wigs and flamboyant costumes, many of which allude to Asia. Extending far beyond the body's immediate outlines, the costumes are highly imaginative, even fantasmatic. The fabric colours – yellow, silver, orange, purple, red, fuschia, and pink – are bold, bright and eye-catching. Forms of shiny adornment embellish almost every surface, and decorative headpieces, parasols, faux feathers and furs add layers and dimensions to this display of Tracy's sartorial imagination. Exemplifying the key feature of the fashion film, this procession is, a 'ritual parade and twirling models robed in outfits that dreams and stories are made of' (Munich 2011, 260). The models walk on to the round stage with slow and grand gestures as though they are dancing, and they graciously hold out their arms to show the full expanse of the rich fabrics.

Tracy's flamboyant costumes evoke the ancient aesthetic practices of Kabuki theatre, but they also point to disco and glam rock and the influence of Japanese designers on fashion in the 1970s. The work of Kansai Yamamoto brought these elements together. In 1971, Yamamoto became the first Japanese designer to hold a runway show in London and then designed costumes for David Bowie's Ziggy Stardust tour. The geometric shapes and layered density of Tracy's designs also recall the work of Issey Miyake, a Japanese designer who made an impact on western fashion in the 1970s by realising the sculptural possibilities of cloth and expanding normalised ideas of the body's contours and surfaces.

Following from this outlandish procession, Tracy walks on to the stage wearing a modest brown sequined dress. She holds a small mask over her face. When Tracy takes off the mask, she opens her arms to ecstatically receive the applause and shouts of praise from the audience. Though more subdued than the spectacle she has orchestrated, Tracy's mask continues the themes of masquerade she has incorporated into her designs.

Tracy's mask and the Asian themes of her fashion show harken back to what Alys Eve Weinbaum identifies as the *racial masquerade* that was prevalent in the United States during the early decades of the twentieth century. The racial masquerade identifies the ability of modern women to 'consume, put on, and take off racial "otherness"' (Weinbaum 2008, 121). The racial masquerade reflects a bourgeoning consumer culture, directed at women – exemplified by the proliferation of cosmetics and ready-to-wear clothing – as well as the interrelated forms of racism in this period, which includes Jim Crow segregation and anti-immigrant discourses of 'yellow peril' (Weinbaum 2008, 126). As Weinbaum points out, masking was a mechanism for white women to play with images of the primitive and thereby signal their participation in the progress of American modernity. Performing with the masks of racial difference reinforced the idea that women designated as racial others were forever embedded in the past. Weinbaum argues that 'those unable to participate in racial masquerade were perceived as "premodern," "primitive," and/or atavistic members of an outmoded social order that relegated them to traditional roles of wife and mother' (Weinbaum 2008, 121). To illustrate the dynamics of this relegation, Weinbaum analyses Nella Larsen's Harlem Renaissance novel *Quicksand* (1928), which features a biracial woman who attempts to pass and wants to take pleasure in the 'commodified surfaces' of the racial masquerade, but is denied the possibility of 'craft[ing] her modernity and her sense of belonging in the United States' (Weinbaum 2008, 143).

Images that signify Asia have a fraught place in the history of western fashion and it is not wrong to assume that when fashion designers draw upon Asian motifs, a form of what Edward Said identified in 1977 as orientalism is at play. Said's *Orientalism* targets the West's long history of creating images of the Orient to solidify its imperial reach and stabilise the assumption of its superiority (Said 1978). There is no doubt that Tracy's fashion show can serve as an example of this particular form of othering. The costumes indulge in what Anne Anlin Cheng identifies in her essay 'Ornamentalism' as an Orientalist fantasy in which 'opulence and sensuality are the signature components of the Asiatic character; that Asia is always ancient, excessive, feminine, available, and decadent' (Cheng 2018, 425). At the same time, the orientalist themes of Tracy's designs may point to desires for cross-racial identification and a feminist affinity between African American and Asian women (Cheng 2018, 416). Since *Mahogany* is about the impediments a black woman faces as she contests the culturally sanctioned impulse to relegate her ambitions to a domestic role and make her race the ground of her sexual commodification, we could say that Tracy's fashion show participates in fantasies of Asian 'opulence and sensuality' in order to imagine the black female body as an aesthetic surface that cannot be reduced to bare flesh (Cheng 2018, 425). The colourful, shiny, deliberately superficial costumes destabilise the skin as a referent for race and suggest that fashionable clothing can become a passage into a form of visibility that moves out of the denuded forms of commodification inflicted upon the black female body.

The scene that immediately follows Mahogany's fashion show suggests that though Tracy may now have the power to take off the mask of racial difference and can imagine forms of protofeminist identification, she cannot do so with ease. Upon hearing her friend Carolotta Gavina enthusiastically assert that she has become 'a real success', Tracy responds with an expression of deep ambivalence. Her eyes lower with shame and the freeze frame of her face indicates that she is immobilised by fear. Viewers will come to see that Tracy is wary of the sexual exchange she has promised the Italian millionaire Christian for funding the production of this fashion line, but she also may be uncertain about the consequences of displacing her racial identifications with her 'success'. As Thaggert makes clear, Tracy's fears are not hers alone. She could be confronting her own internalised anxieties about black women's achievement in a post Civil Rights United States and enacting the limitations placed on black women's imaginative capacities for self-transformation (Thaggert 2012).

The freeze frame of Tracy's face halts the film's temporal flow and opens on to a flashback in which she is in training to become a fashion designer in Chicago. This scene takes place in a crowded urban classroom that seems a world away from Rome. It begins with a mid range horizontal tracking shot that moves across the backs of students who are seated at a table drawing images of modest, simple dresses. Before we see Tracy, we see, over her shoulder, her drawing of a golden yellow column dress with a pleated chiffon overlay that expands into a half-circle as the figure stretches out her arms and fills the space of the sketchpad.

Tracy's sketch is an expression of defiance. The instructor of the design class, a tastefully dressed white woman, addresses Tracy's resistance to her instruction with a rhetorical question: 'I thought I told you to sketch a simple cocktail dress?' Tracy answers this question with a defiant look. The bell rings and the teacher swiftly steps up to the podium to announce the next assignment: a 'basic swimsuit'. She returns to Tracy's place in the classroom and translates the assignment for her: 'and that means no sequins, no rhinestones, and no ostrich feathers … '. The teacher's list of flashy adornments is meant to connect to Tracy's yellow dress (and probably other designs as well). The teacher is pointing out the fact that Tracy's dress is neither 'simple' nor 'basic' but exemplifies what the teacher sees as the *bad taste* of colourful and ornamental display. And yet, the way Tracy lovingly holds her pens and looks at her sketch again expresses a passion that the pedagogies of white taste cannot erase.

The fact that Tracy's dress resists her teacher's emphasis on the simple and the basic indicates that *Mahogany* is staging a contestation between a streamlined modernist aesthetic and the supposed vulgarities of ornamental design and bright, eye-catching colours. This is to say that the film is alluding to the neoDarwinian ideas that colourful, ostentatious display is an expression of primitive impulses, while also contesting those ideas through Tracy's commitment to her own aesthetic criteria. European and American intellectuals of the late nineteenth and early twentieth centuries bastardised Charles Darwin's treatises on natural and sexual selection and the ideas about sexual and racial inferiority that subtended it – cast in the language of 'sub species' – to stress that excessive colour and ornamentation confirms a person's or a group's low place on the evolutionary ladder. Manifesting residually as 'taste', such arguments have worked with an insidious efficiency to reinforce negative assessments of black women's bodies and make their clothing extensions of the narrow meanings punitively attributed to their skin colour.

Arguments that read ostentatious sartorial display as a sign of the primitive found their way into the 1970s and can be discerned in the many negative reviews of *Mahogany*. Writing about the film in *The New Yorker*, Pauline Kael dismisses the film as a 'garish garbled black version of outmoded white kitsch', which is basically a claim that the film was stuck in a tasteless past, slavish to white styles that had long since become obsolete (Kael [1975] 1982, 354). More recently, in the lead up to the fortieth anniversary of the film, which was celebrated in Chicago with an outdoor screening and a fashion show, film critic

Richard Roeper identifies *Mahogany* as a 'lurid fashion-world soap opera', a description that echoes Kael's accusation of bad taste (Roeper 2015). 'Lurid' is a word often used to describe distastefully bright colours, and the soap opera, which consistently signals the lowest and most feminised form of mass culture, helps to make accusations of bad taste incontrovertible. Roeper's description can be understood as a reactive assessment of the film's deliberate engagement with bright colours ('lurid') that relies upon the sexist assumption that genres and cultural practices associated with women (like the soap opera or fashion) are obviously bad. *Mahogany* is actually staging a black feminist argument against these aesthetic assessments and their link to white cultural dominance. The film reveals how intimately these standards of taste connect to the challenge of making a black woman the centre of a film's visual story.

Set to her popular (but often ridiculed) theme song, 'Do You Know Where You Are Going To?' Tracy leaves class in a crowd of classmates, passes by a long row of dingy school lockers that line a narrow hall, and rides Chicago's 'L' train home. Sitting on the train, she continues to work on her dress design and defy her teacher's aesthetic criteria. Making a connection between the sketch of her dress and black working class street culture of the 1970s is part of this defiance. Tracy sees and becomes inspired by the rainbow graffiti created by two African American boys wearing red knit hats and spray painting the walls of the train platform. After seeing the image they have created through the train window, Tracy waves to them playfully and begins to accent the yellow dress with swathes of rainbow colours.

Since graffiti became a sign of inner city dangers in the 1970s, a shorthand for systemic neglect and racist fears, this scene of Tracy on the 'L' is dense with suggestions about Ross' celebrity image and its connection to the material conditions of racism. The scene may reflect upon Ross' role in the history of Motown, indirectly substantiating Neal's argument that Gordy made Ross a symbol of his 'quest for corporate/social mobility' (Neal 1999, 89). If Ross was a vehicle for Motown's success, this scene with the boys on the 'L' platform serves as an image that helps to cover over the fact that Gordy had, as Neal argues, 'consciously abandoned his working class constituency in Detroit' (Neal 1999, 89). The affective connection that Gordy makes between Tracy's aspirations to be a fashion designer and black working class street culture of the 1970s relies on a gendered separation in which black boys are granted a freedom of movement, an ease of rebellious expression and a public visibility that black women and girls can only participate in from behind glass. Tracy's boyfriend Brian will also embody a visibly intimate connection to urban spaces and the film demonstrates that he needs her confinement within a domestic and heterosexual arrangement to translate that connection into a public life in politics.

Tracy will work on her rainbow dress across the first half of *Mahogany*, and it is compelling to watch it transform from a sketch to a three dimensional form that Ross wears on screen. By following the production of the dress, *Mahogany* asks viewers to reflect on the ways in which colourful and ornamented display figures into this film's attempt to open a space to see the black feminist value of Tracy's aspiration to become a fashion designer. In subtle ways, the film also links Tracy's fashion design to African American women's histories and the multi-faceted role clothing and fashion have played within them.

This connection becomes clear in a scene that begins with Tracy walking swiftly under the 'L' platform and entering a concrete building. Carrying her black drawing portfolio, she wears a tan trench coat, a knit hat, and long red boots. The next shot shows Tracy at the far end of a garment factory, but the image of her body is hard to discern through the rows of women sewing and the piles of fabric and clothing around them. Tracy surprises her Aunt Florence (played by Beah Richards) working at her sewing machine. Seeing the drawing of the dress Tracy has just placed in front of her, Aunt Beah responds with pride and pleasure: 'Hon-ey. You're getting too good for my vocabulary'. Aunt Florence agrees to help her complete the dress but 'at her regular rate,' though Tracy playfully negotiates and asks her for a '25% discount—just for relatives'. Florence goes on praising her niece's designs: 'They're good, child, more than good.' This is a loving collaboration between an aunt and a niece centred on the intergenerational transmission of sewing and design skills.

Aunt Florence and her work as a skilled seamstress index the long history of African American women working with fabric and making clothing: the unremunerated labour they gave to the cotton industry; the work of maintaining clothing (for slaveholders' families as well as their own) on the plantation; their poorly paid work as laundresses and seamstresses during Reconstruction; and the skilled economy of dressmaking, which expanded upon the work women performed during enslavement and allowed women such as Elisabeth Keckley, the writer and dressmaker for Mary Todd Lincoln, a place in the legitimate economy (Camp 2004, 78–89; Jones 2010, 28–29, 38–39). Along with tailoring and millinery, dressmaking was a significant form of work for African American women during and beyond Reconstruction, though whites barred women from the cultural visibility and prestige associated with the occupation. In *Picturing Freedom,* her study of black visual expression in early nineteenth-century American culture, Jasmine Cobb explains that after seeing free black women working with clothing in the urban spaces of Philadelphia, 'whites began to deny "respectable women of color" dressmaker work, even when there was an advertised need, to instead usher Black women into domestic work as cooks and cleaners' (Cobb 2015, 118). Set against this punitive history, black women's pleasures making and wearing clothing can be considered claims to the surplus value of sartorial commodities black women made possible, giving clothing a political significance that has not been fully recognised. The cinematic portrayal of Tracy's passion for dress design continues those pleasures and claims. Reading *Mahogany* this way, it is hard to agree with Neal's assertion that Ross' onscreen performances in the 1970s reflect Gordy's 'proclivity to divorce African American expressive culture from its political and social roots,' and thereby betray the black feminism of that era (Neal 1999, 90). On the contrary, the connection *Mahogany* makes between Tracy's aspirations and her aunt's work as a seamstress aligns with black feminism's emphasis on tracing the material conditions of black women's lives to the histories of colonialism and slavery.

The colour of black feminist resistance

Since African American women have had to contend at every turn with the racism and sexism upon which American culture is built, black feminism has a long and rich history in the United States. It was in the late 1960s and 1970s, when black women confronted the racism within the women's liberation movement and the sexism at work in the civil rights and Black Power movements that black women's resistance became a discernible political and intellectual force that was identified with the name black feminism. One of many texts that announced the emergence of black feminism in the 1970s was Angela Davis' 'The Black Woman's Role in the Community of Slaves,' an essay she published in

1971, the year before she was acquitted of conspiracy charges. 'The Black Woman's Role' exemplifies black feminism's attention to the multiple ways in which in which slavery laid the foundation for imprisoning black women in the fears and fantasies of white American culture. In her preface, Davis points to the discursive visibility and power of the Moynihan report and articulates her commitment to 'shattering' what she calls the 'reified images' and 'grossly distorted categories through which the black woman continues to be perceived' (Davis [1971] 1998, 111). Davis traces the distortions of the Moynihan report back to the particular oppressions black women experienced during enslavement. Pertinent to *Mahogany* and its claim to black femininity is the fact that slave masters inflicted what Davis identifies as the 'deformed equality of equal oppression' (Davis [1971] 1998, 117). That is, black women were subject to the same brutal working conditions as their male counterparts, which gave them an 'equality' that they transformed into a resistant, life- and community-sustaining strength. At the same time, Davis explains they were 'stripped of a palliative feminine veneer which might have encouraged a passive performance of domestic tasks', but this denial of femininity allowed them to become 'capable of weaving into the warp and woof of domestic life a profound consciousness of resistance' (Davis [1971] 1998, 117). *Mahogany* suggests how this 'consciousness of resistance' might have been woven into fashion and clothing.

It is well known that slave masters used coarse and plain clothing as a tool to punitively maintain the boundaries of slavery. As historians Shane White and Graham White explain, 'garments doled out to slaves throughout the American colonies tended to be drab, uniform and limited to relatively few items' (White and White 1998, 9). Crude garments kept slaves identifiable and visually confirmed their subjugation. The use of coarse and bare clothing established the ground for making dressing up in vivid and elaborate clothing not only an act of pleasure and a claim to freedom but an expression of defiance. Discussing the Sunday promenades that took place in urban spaces of the colonial South, White and White speculate that the 'vivid, visual presence [African Americans] established was an emphatic repudiation of their allotted social role' (White and White 1998, 35). Historian Stephanie M. H. Camp highlights the meanings women brought to the act of making and wearing clothing, which reflected the specifically gendered expectations and exploitations imposed upon their bodies. Camp charts how enslaved women 'procured fancy apparel' for themselves and highlights the different ways they created style: 'enslaved women went to great effort to make themselves something more than the cheap, straight-cut dresses they were allowanced. When possible, women cut their dresses generously so they could sweep their skirts dramatically and elegantly' (Camp 2004, 80, 82). These sartorial expressions recalibrated the value to which slavery assigned them. As Camp explains, '[w]omen's style allowed them to take pleasure in their bodies, to deny that they were only (or mainly) worth the prices their owners placed on them' (Camp 2004, 83).

Aesthetic arguments that gained prominence in the late nineteenth and early twentieth century substantiated the impetus to see such expressions of resistance as threatening and distasteful. During this period, the writings of cultural critic Thorstein Veblen, architect Adolf Loos, and feminist Charlotte Perkins Gilman created the intellectual foundation for the argument that vivid and densely ornamented clothing is morally and aesthetically depraved. Drawing heavily from theories of natural and sexual selection, these intellectuals made clothing the focus of their cultural criticism and crafted sustained arguments against bright colours and lavish ornamentation. It is no coincidence that these are the stylistic features that African American women deployed to resist slavery's definitions. Indeed, for these thinkers, vibrant eye-catching display was an irrefutable symbol of the debilitating, feminising barbarism that halted progress toward the beautifully streamlined civilisation many thought members of the white race were obligated to create for themselves. Veblen, Loos, and Gilman articulate many of fashion's familiar criticisms – that it is useless, superficial, and degrading. They bolster this criticism by dismissing femininity and the idea of woman who is instinctually captivated by the showy lures of consumer culture. Moreover, threats of racial degeneracy and images of racial others deepen this dismissal of fashion and highlight the moral stakes of doing so. These writers shared the argument that women's propensity to adorn themselves was a symptom of their debased positions in the process of sexual selection and put them in dangerous proximity to racial degeneracy.

David Batchelor's examination of 'chromophobia' highlights a particular dimension of the arguments against adornment: the suspicion of colour. Batchelor demonstrates that colour has been considered the 'property of some foreign body,' linked to the 'feminine, the oriental, the primitive, the infantile, the vulgar, the queer or the pathological' (Batchelor 2000, 22–23). Signalling civilisation's fall into savagery, colour has been considered dangerous and trivial. We could say that perceptions of black women wearing bright colours synthesise both associations, bolstering the racism and sexism black women confront (Batchelor 2000, 23). Batchelor turns to the work of Charles Blanc, a nineteenth-century cultural critic who perceived colour to be a danger that had to be 'contained and subordinated—like a woman' (Batchelor 2000, 23). Drawing upon formulations such as Blanc's, Batchelor argues that 'colour has been the object of extreme prejudice in Western culture' (Batchelor 2000, 22). Not only has this prejudice remained 'unchecked' and 'passed unnoticed', it is, according to Batchelor, 'so all-embracing and generalised that, at one time or another, it has enrolled in just about every other prejudice in its service' (Batchelor 2000, 22). The prejudice against colour has a particularly strong connection to 'sexual and racial phobias' (Batchelor 2000, 29).

The prejudice against colour has certainly been 'enrolled' to support biases against black women. In her reflections on the infamous red dress, African American studies scholar Karla F.C. Holloway offers a salient example of brightly coloured clothing reinforcing damaging myths about black women's sexuality and its lower value. Holloway writes about her grandmother 'warn[ing] [her] away from red' (Holloway 1995, 16, 15). Her grandmother believed red makes black girls look 'common', and signalled their willingness to be 'passed around' (Holloway 1995, 16). Holloway's memory of these admonitions was provoked by the testimony of Anita Hill and the professional, tasteful attire she wore when she appeared before the Senate Judiciary Committee in 1991. 'A nice girl,' Hill did not wear a red dress for her testimony. She wore instead, as Holloway explains, 'a teal blue suit with a modest row of military-like double buttons down the front,' which mirrored by her 'polite demeanor' (Holloway 1995, 15). Ultimately, however, Hill's clothing did not protect her from sexual harassment or its public re-inscription by either the US senators or the American media (Holloway 1995, 15). Holloway explains that '[f]or all the frank talk about sexual harassment, pubic hair, and pornography, Professor Hill may as well have worn red' (Holloway 1995, 15). In other words, tasteful clothing ultimately cannot defend black women against intrusive forms of sexualisation. In the eye of white American dominance, black women are always wearing brightly coloured dresses and forced to embody the sexual availability the red dress signifies.

Mahogany's consistent focus on the vivid colours of Tracy's dresses is a direct challenge to the deployment of chromophobia against black women. The film stages this challenge by revealing its consequences, but also by highlighting the pleasures Tracy takes in making and wearing clothing of her own design. Indeed, the negative assessments of *Mahogany* should not occlude the fact that the film reflects the new visibility of black fashion in the 1970s and contributed to a vibrant visual culture in which African American women were defying the aesthetic legacies associated with their subordination and asserting their capacity to determine how they were perceived.

There are many reasons to situate *Mahogany* in relationship to the slowly emerging visibility of black women in mainstream American fashion in the 1960s and 1970s. The story of the model and actress Donyale Luna, known as the first black supermodel, has remarkable parallels to both *Mahogany* and Ross' biography. Luna was discovered in Detroit in 1964 and left the United States for Europe in 1965 after 'collid[ing]' with the 'American fashion industry's glass ceiling' (Powell 2011, 82–83). The same year *Mahogany* premiered, Beverly Johnson appeared on the cover of *Vogue*, the first African American model to do so. These resonances are strong, but it is the portrayal of women's fashions in a magazine such as *Ebony* that connect to *Mahogany* in the most interesting ways, as *Ebony* tells a collective story of black striving and success and reveals the role fashion played within it.

Known as the *Life* magazine for African Americans, *Ebony* made fashion part of its work 'visually showcase[ing] and celebrat[ing] the best in black life' (Bivins 2013, 10). Eunice W. Johnson is the reason the magazine highlighted fashion's role in the story of black success. Her role as the magazine's fashion editor was connected to her work producing the *Ebony* fashion fair, an annual tour that showcased both couture and ready-to-wear fashions for African American audiences across the United States. Johnson worked with some of the biggest names in fashion and nurtured the careers of black models and designers. Racism pitted these priorities against each other, but Johnson demanded just representation of African Americans in the fashion industry.

Both *Mahogany* and the *Ebony* Fashion Fair allowed black women to see themselves in fashion's idealising spotlight and on a more subtle level, rewrote the standards of taste that had been used against black women. In his biography, John H. Johnson (Eunice's husband and head of Johnson publishing corporation) explains that '[b]efore the Ebony Fashion Fair, people said Black women couldn't wear red or yellow or purple. The fashion show proved that black women could wear any color they wanted to wear' (quoted in Heaven 2013, 39). *Color Explosion*, the theme Johnson picked for the 1979–1980 season, announced the freedom to wear bright colours quite explicitly and reflects Johnson's penchant, not only for 'selecting garments in brilliant colors' but also her attraction to the 'glamorous, the luxurious, and the dramatic' (Heaven 2013, 40). The *Ebony* Fashion Fair expanded and solidified in the 1970s and perhaps can be considered an extension of the magazine's increased attention to what Toni C. King identifies as *Ebony*'s 'stories about black women's work experience' and the implicitly white standards of taste they were likely to encounter in the workplace (King 2003, 88). Defying chromophobia's link to racism and sexism, Johnson's assertion of a bold aesthetic was not only a protest against the assumption that bright, eye-catching clothes on black bodies are manifestations of bad taste but was also an effort to bring black femininity and its histories into the recognisable definitions of beauty (Bivins 2013, 21).

Since *Ebony* accentuated the black feminist potential of fashion, it makes sense that when promoting *Mahogany*, the magazine emphasised Ross' role as costume designer, almost at the film's expense. The black and white photograph that opens the article suggests a struggle with Gordy. It depicts Ross sitting on the dolly and under the camera looking frustrated and feigning patience. Her portrayal contrasts sharply with the portrayal of the Motown chairman; his stance and profile align with the camera lens as if to highlight the authority and skill he brought to the job of directing. However, the opening sentence of the article undercuts this attention to Gordy: it describes the film 'hit[ting] the screen in a blaze of color—much of it in the *haute couture* gowns Miss Ross designed' and there are large high-quality colour photographs that feature Ross' costumes (*Ebony* 1975, 145). The caption accompanying the photographs details the extent of her work as a designer, stating that she 'personally supervised all operations, from the purchase of special fabrics to coordination of colours to beading and all other finishing techniques' (*Ebony* 1975, 148). This work becomes an expression of Ross' long standing interest in fashion and the article points out that she studied fashion design and illustration in high school and brought this 'passion for creating spectacular clothes' to work when the image of 'The Supremes' was crafted. It quotes Ross explaining that she 'used to talk to the guys who designed our clothes and I'd tell them exactly what I thought we should wear' (*Ebony* 1975, 149).

Like the Supremes, *Mahogany* was made to address both black and white audiences. With its broad, assimilationist appeal, the film could be considered part of the rejection of Blaxploitation films, which attempted to speak directly to African American audiences about racial exploitation and deliberately refused the policing of black people through standards of propriety and taste. Such a distinction does not take *Mahogany*'s immense popularity with African American audiences into account and misses the celebratory attention to clothing and style it shares with Blaxploitation films. While notorious for their raunchy, overtly sexualised depictions of black women's bodies, there is a cluster of blaxploitation films that make feminist arguments about black women's grit, resilience, and self-possession. Bright, flashy, and revealing, the costumes in films such as *Foxy Brown* (1974) hinged sexual liberation to the films' visual assertions of black women's power while also reassuring audiences that black women were not going to upend gender hierarchies completely. To tell Foxy Brown's story of fighting for justice against a drug and prostitution syndicate, Pam Grier wore halter and wrap dresses with deep necklines; her gowns were made of thick, shiny silks and bright, solid colours – lemon yellow, sky blue, orange red. These lavish fabrics and bold colours were not just sexy, they were defying the chromophobia lurking behind white standards of taste.

Mahogany has striking affinities with *Cleopatra Jones* (1973) and *Cleopatra Jones and the Casino of Gold* (1975). In these Blaxploitation films, Pamela Dobson plays 'Cleo', a CIA operative on a crusade to stop the criminal drug trade and its exploitation of African American communities. Dobson creates a striking image for Cleo with a flamboyant, high fashion wardrobe: flowing fur robes; spiked boots and platform heels; large and elaborate gold earrings; large-brimmed hats; bright silk turbans and head wraps that always match the trims and accents of her pantsuits. The article in *Ebony* covering the film begins by addressing women who were tired of the blatant masculinism of Blaxploitation films and argues that *Cleopatra Jones* is made for 'black women's libbers who have sat through the growing procession of *Shaft, Super Fly, Nigger Charley,* and other assorted celluloid sensations of male derring-do with growing impatience for an idol of their own' (*Ebony* 1975, 49). The article goes on to introduce Dobson, her modelling career, her degree in fashion illustration, and her own identification with the character she played: 'The idea that this lady can make a decision and follow up on her point of view is something that compliments my own life pattern' (*Ebony* 1975, 49).

Given this connection between actress and role, it makes sense that Dobson wanted to embody Cleo's strength and performed all the martial arts sequences herself. The less successful sequel, *Cleopatra Jones and the Casino of Gold*, takes place in Hong Kong, which makes the film's debts to martial arts cinema more explicit, and allowed the costume designers to draw upon the imagery and decorative motifs associated with Asia to dress Dobson in even more flamboyant attire. Like *Mahogany*, *Cleopatra Jones and the Casino of Gold* was described as 'lurid,' and similar to Tracy's Asian inspired designs, *Cleopatra Jones and the Casino of Gold* might express the desire for cross-racial identification among women (Ebert 1975).

Clothes between men

My analysis of *Mahogany* has made it clear that fashion is both crucial to Tracy's character and story and points to the film's engagement with and response to the black feminism that emerged in visual culture in the 1970s. Through fashion, *Mahogany* contributes to actively contesting the long-standing arguments against bright and ornamented clothing and refutes the subtle and not-so-subtle ways they have been deployed to police how black women have been allowed to make themselves visible in American cultural life. However, the real plot of *Mahogany* – and by that, I mean the story with which the film is predominantly identified – is put into motion when Tracy meets two men who compete to make her a vehicle of their ambitions: the white, arrogant, slightly queer fashion photographer Sean Mackovy, played by Anthony Perkins with his shrewd, twitchy insight; and Brian Walker, the black grass-roots community organiser and aspiring Chicago politician, warmly embodied by Billy Dee Williams with his all American – and unquestionably heterosexual – good looks. While Sean offers Tracy an entrance into the world of fashion and the promise of success unencumbered by provincial American racisms, Brian represents the pull to racial authenticity and the belief that conservative gender arrangements are a foundation for fighting racial justice. In defiance of Brian's assumption that her career should disappear into his, Tracy takes up Sean's proposal to leave Chicago and move to Rome, only to return to Brian at the film's conclusion.

Brian represents the masculine authority to decide what racial politics are and how they should appear. This authority is on display in a scene in which Brian and Tracy walk through an abandoned Chicago neighbourhood. Thick with clichés, this scene is staged to illustrate the characters' perspectives on collectivity, individualism, and poverty. Through the language of lost feeling, Brian laments that Civil Rights struggles have been undermined by capitalist accumulation (though he does not use those terms). He identifies Tracy's desire to 'get out' and pursue the 'much better life that she wants', aspirations that she is not ashamed of, and asserts himself as the person who will stay and attend to the job of making Chicago's inner city 'a better place to live'. There is a moral heroism in this self-identification that relies upon a judgment of Tracy's individualistic aspirations that Brian never questions as they delve into the plot of their stormy romance.

In the scene that follows, Sean entices Tracy with the prospect of pursuing a modelling career in Rome. He offers her this possibility while photographing her in the rainbow dress she just completed. This scene takes place in the backroom of Marshall Fields, which is littered with the accoutrements of department story display (mannequins, baskets, and ostrich feathers). Transformed from a drawing to a dress Tracy is actually wearing, viewers can now see its details: the gold collar of the chiffon overlay, the form fitted yellow column dress underneath with its high slit up the leg and the row of small yellow buttons placed along the side seam. Aunt Beah accompanies Tracy on this photo shoot and Tracy lovingly identifies her as the 'tailoring department' that helped her make the creation she proudly wears on her own. As Tracy walks among the mannequins and talks about her intentions to sell her designs, Sean expresses skepticism about whether she can do this in Chicago. Aunt Beah asks, 'What's wrong with Chicago?' Beah's rhetorical question gives Sean the opportunity to introduce the possibilities of Rome, where 'pretty things' (like Tracy) are not 'sent out for coffee' that is, where she will not be confined to subservience because she is a black woman. Though Sean has been intermittently photographing Tracy throughout this conversation, the modelling session really begins when Sean turns on music and dares Tracy to 'shine,' 'dance,' and 'move'. Tracy responds by dancing around the mannequins and stretching out her arms in circles so her chiffon overlay swirls around her in a dizzying blurs of ecstatic colour. The department store supervisor, Mrs. Evans – another white middle aged lady, who, like her design teacher, polices Tracy's ambitions – interrupts the photography session to tell Sean that Tracy cannot be the model for this layout: it is against the agency's rules to hire black women as models. Her interruption exemplifies the provincial racisms Sean claims Tracy will not have to encounter in Europe (Figure 2).

This photography session is the last time Aunt Beah appears in *Mahogany*. Her erasure from the narrative can be understood as evidence of Tracy's alienation from African American culture and her steadfast insistence on her own individual success. But it is probably more accurate to say that it is women's work fashioning their places in African American culture from which Tracy becomes alienated. For when Tracy returns to Chicago, it is Brian's political aspirations – not sewing skills – that become her connection to home.

It makes sense that the issues Brian fights for – racial justice and fair housing for the urban poor – take precedence over fashion but what *Mahogany* draws out is the unquestioned assumption that designing and making fashion is a trivial hobby and not a valuable form of work. It also displays the more pernicious idea that woman's identification with fashion is silly, not worth taking seriously. And yet, the film also shows that Tracy's 'visual acumen' can be of value if it is a vital part of the affective labour a woman gives to her partner. In a scene that takes place in his apartment, Brian announces that they will be going out to dinner with a congressman and his wife. This plan conflicts with Tracy's design class and to mark the fact that Brian's career takes precedence over hers, she despondently pins the candidate poster she has been drawing over the sketch of her rainbow dress. Her talents should be put in the service of crafting Brian's image.

This is only a momentary expression of acquiescence, however. In the next scene, which takes place in his campaign office, Brian articulates his assumption that her career does not matter – and Tracy fights back. The scene begins with Tracy answering a number of phones, illustrating the fact that she performs secretarial work for the campaign. With exasperation, she passes the phone to another woman and rushes to leave the office as

Figure 2. Diana Ross and actor Anthony Perkins on the set of the film *Mahogany* in Rome, 1975. Photo by Keystone/Hulton Archive/Getty Images.

Brian enters it. Tracy is on her way to prepare for a design show class, but Brian expects her to be at a dinner for Independent Democrats. He doesn't believe she needs to prepare so thoroughly to present her clothes to designers – 'What's the big deal. They've all said no to you anyway'. This is just one expression of his demand that she relinquish her efforts to create a career for herself. Brian says to her that she 'has gotten herself involved in something really meaningful'. With quick anger she responds: 'Right, your career. You seem to be forgetting mine'. To this, he replies: 'You can't forget about something that doesn't exist'. These statements, and a phone call from Sean inviting her to Rome again, propel Tracy to leave Chicago.

Upon Tracy's departure for Rome, *Mahogany* becomes a story of a struggle over whether Brian or Sean can claim Tracy. As Wiegman argues, by 'moving from black man to white and back again, Mahogany mediates between them, and her image provides the means for a negotiation of power among black and white men' (Wiegman 1991, 316). Indeed, once the film assigns Tracy the role of mediating between Brian and Sean, both of whom want to make her embody their success, the film's attention to her passion for clothing begins to exist on a secondary narrative register, though it does not disappear.

When Tracy defies Sean's authority as the star fashion photographer, Tracy's passion for design reasserts itself. She arrives on set one day wearing one of her own designs, not the ensemble assigned to her. (As a model in Rome, Tracy has only been modelling the designs of other people, not making or displaying any of her own.) Her long dress is bright white and the long sleeves extend out from the wrists into sculpted forms of flowing white fabric. Over the white dress Tracy wears an elaborate neckpiece made of yellow, orange, and turquoise beads that cover her chest and hang over the bodice. She also wears an elaborate headpiece – braids sculpted into wide circular shapes wrapped in red and green ribbons – that extend outward from her neatly coiffed bun. The colours of this ensemble are slightly more muted than Tracy's rainbow dress, but her beaded accessories and headdress are nothing if not ornaments. The ensemble announces Tracy's stylistic affinity with Egypt and the African diaspora.

The timing of this assertion is telling. Tracy decides to wear her design the day after Sean attempted to seduce her. This seduction fails and exposes his impotence, which Perkins skilfully renders with raw humiliation. When Tracy arrives on set, Sean (sitting on top of the dolly) drily takes note of her choice to wear her own clothes and his cool denial of her choice tells viewers that, in his eyes, she is not just breaking the protocol of the photo shoot, but capitalising upon his sexual humiliation. The setting comes to his defense: the vista that looks out onto the Roman architecture, with all its suggestions of Europe and civilisation, becomes Sean's alibi, buttressing his claims to white masculine power and justifying his denigration of Tracy and her designs. Sean tells Tracy she cannot wear the costume she has on, as it is not the 'proper attire'. Sean notes that it is 'wrong for the sequence' and looks out over the vista as if his assessment is obvious. The subtext of Sean's statements is that the Africanist themes of her dress clash with the aesthetic grandeur all around them. Stubbornly, Tracy insists, 'I want to wear it'. In response, he wields the power that this scene has established and rips off the beaded front of Tracy's costume. Sean's punitive restriction extends from this particular shoot to *Mahogany* itself, and I would argue, to African American women's historical relationship to clothing and fashion. And yet, reasserting *Mahogany*'s attention to black feminist defiance, Tracy replies to Sean's exposure by slapping him across the face.

Sean does not allow Tracy's slap to have the last word. He is in the audience of a fashion show for a charity auction in which Tracy surreptitiously wears one of her own designs. Interrupting a sequence of gowns made of sheer and flowing chiffon fabrics and soft, muted colours, Tracy wears a long kimono dress made of a thick tangerine silk. A dragon composed of blue sequins adorns the bodice. This dress has large bell sleeves, and a sharp slit goes up the right side. This is another contestation between a streamlined modernist aesthetic and the supposed vulgarities of colour and ornament. Indeed, before Tracy makes her entrance, the master of ceremonies describes the piece she was supposed to wear: a design of 'classic simplicity, a white silk jersey dress'. When set against the soft, diffuse lines of the other more obviously feminine dresses worn by white models, the hard and sharp contours of Tracy's shiny dress make it look like armour, a defense against becoming an image through which men struggle with each other. Modelling her design with her highly stylised choreography, Tracy receives no bids – only gasps of shock and boos of disapproval – until Sean makes an embarrassingly low bid to highlight her humiliation. This inspires Christian, a wealthy Italian man, to buy Mahogany's design for an enormously high price. This act of rescue transforms into enough support for Tracy to produce a fashion line but she has to pay with sexual subservience, which makes the charity auction echo a slave auction.

Mahogany ends with Tracy fleeing her deal with Christian, which epitomises the sexual and racial objectification she experienced in Europe. She returns home to Brian and Chicago and commits herself to their romance and his career in politics. In the scene of her return, Tracy calls to Brian from within a crowd at the rally announcing his congressional campaign and they come together through a call and response that reaffirms her fluency in black vernacular expression. As David Bogle explains in his sympathetic reading of the film, *Mahogany* 'refuses to let [Tracy] be both successful *and* black' and it is a given that she has relinquished her hope for a career in fashion (Bogle 1994, 255). And yet, the clothing Tracy wears in this scene – a fluffy white fur coat with a wide lapel – indicates that the desires she has attached to fashion have not been completely repressed. Writing about Tracy's final ensemble, Adrienne Munich observes that '[t]he film—and its star costume designer—cannot quite relinquish fashion's allure' (Munich 2011, 277). *Mahogany*'s attachment to fashion is an attachment to the black feminist desire to tell a story about black women fashioning their own relationships to the images their bodies project, without relinquishing an aesthetic claim to black femininity or the historical contestations that claim has entailed.

Disclosure statement

No potential conflict of interest was reported by the author.

References

Batchelor, David. 2000. *Chromophobia*. London: Reaktion Books.
Bivins, Joy L. 2013. "Style and Substance: *Ebony*'s Fashion Fair." In *Inspiring Beauty: 50 Years of Ebony Fashion Fair*, edited by Joy L. Bivins, and Rosemary K. Adams, 10–23. Chicago: Chicago Historical Society.
Bogle, Donald. 1994. *Toms, Coons, Mulattoes, Mammies, and Bucks: An Interpretive History of Blacks in American Film*. New York: Continuum.
Camp, Stephanie M.H. 2004. *Closer to Freedom: Enslaved Women and Everyday Resistance in the Plantation South*. Chapel Hill: University of North Carolina Press.
Cheng, Anne Anlin. 2018. "Ornamentalism: A Feminist Theory for the Yellow Woman." *Critical Inquiry* 44: 415–446.
"Cleopatra Jones". 1973. *Ebony* 28 (9): 48–56.
Cobb, Jasmine. 2015. *Picture Freedom: Remaking Black Visuality in the Early Nineteenth Century*. New York: NYU Press.
Davis, Angela. [1971] 1998. "Reflections on the Black Woman's Role in the Community of Slave." In *The Angela Y. Davis Reader*, edited by Joy James, 111–128. Malden, MA: Blackwell.
Dyer, Richard. 1986. "Mahogany." In *Films for Women*, edited by Brunsdon Charlotte, 131–137. London: British Film Institute.
Ebert, Roger. 1975. "Cleopatra Jones and the Casino of Gold." Accessed December 14 2018. https://www.rogerebert.com/reviews/cleopatra-jones-and-the-casino-of-gold-1975.
Eckert, Charles. [1978] 1990. "The Carole Lombard in Macy's Window." In *Fabrications: Costume and the Female Body*, edited by Jane Gaines, and Charlotte Herzog, 100–121. New York: Routledge.

Fleetwood, Nicole R. 2015. *On Racial Icons: Blackness and the Public Imagination*. New Brunswick: Rutgers UP.

Gaines, Jane. 1988. "White Privilege and Looking Relations: Race and Gender in Feminist Film Theory." *Screen* 29 (4): 12–27.

Gaines, Jane. 1990. "Costume and Narrative: How Dress Tells the Women's Story." In *Fabrications: Costume and the Female Body*, edited by Gaines Jane, and Herzog Charlotte, 180–211. New York: Routledge.

Gordy, Berry. 1994. *To Be Loved: The Music, the Magic, the Memories of Motown: An Autobiography*. New York: Time Warner.

Heaven, Virginia. 2013. "The Power of Fashion: Ebony Fashion Fair." In *Inspiring Beauty: 50 Years of Ebony Fashion Fair*, edited by Joy L. Bivins, and Rosemary K. Adams, 34–48. Chicago: Chicago Historical Society.

Holloway, Karla F. C. 1995. *Codes of Conduct: Race, Ethics, and the Color of Our Character*. New Brunswick: Rutgers UP.

Jones, Jacqueline. 2010. *Labor of Love, Labor of Sorrow: Black Women, Work, and the Family From Slavery to the Present*. New York: Perseus Books.

Kael, Pauline. [1975] 1982. *5001 Nights at the Movies: A Guide From A to Z*. New York: Holt, Rinehart, and Winston.

King, Toni C. 2003. "'Who's That Lady?' Ebony Magazine and Black Professional Women." In *Disco Divas: Women and Popular Culture in the 1970s*, edited by Sherrie A. Inness, 87–102. Philadelphia: University of Pennsylvania Press.

Munich, Adrienne. 2011. "The Stars and Stripes in Fashion Films." In *Fashion in Film*, edited by Adrienne Munich, 260–280. Bloomington: Indiana University Press.

Neal, Mark Anthony. 1999. *What the Music Said: Black Popular Music and Black Popular Culture*. New York: Routledge.

Powell, Richard J. 2011. "From Diaspora to Exile: Black Women Artists in 1960s and 1970s Europe." In *The Migrant's Time: Rethinking Art History and Diaspora*, edited by Mathur Saloni, 78–90. Massachusetts: Sterling and Francine Clark Art Institute.

Roeper, Richard. 2015. "In 1975s 'Mahogany,' Diana Ross timeless, but the attitudes aren't." *Chicago Sun Times*, August 21. https://chicago.suntimes.com/entertainment/in-1975s-mahogany-diana-ross-timeless-but-the-attitudes-arent/.

Ross, Diana. 1993. *Secrets of a Sparrow: Memoirs*. New York: Villard Books.

Said, Edward W. 1978. *Orientalism*. New York: Vintage Books.

"Spectacular New Film for Diana Ross: Mahogany". 1975. *Ebony* 30 (12): 144–146, 148, 150.

Thaggert, Miriam. 2012. "Marriage, Moynihan, and *Mahogany*: Success and the Post Civil-Rights Black Female Professional in Film." *American Quarterly* 64 (4): 715–740.

Weinbaum, Alys E. 2008. "Racial Masquerade: Consumption and Contestation of American Modernity." In *The Modern Girl Around the World: Consumption, Modernity, and Globalization*, edited by Alys Eve Weinbaum, Lynn M. Thomas, Priti Ramamurthy, Uta G. Poiger, Madeleine Yue Dong, and Tani Barlow, 120–146. Durham: Duke University Press.

White, Shane, and Graham White. 1998. *Stylin': African American Expressive Culture From Its Beginnings to the Zoot Suit*. Ithaca: Cornell University Press.

Wiegman, Robyn. 1991. "Black Bodies/American Commodities: Gender, Race, and the Bourgeois Ideal in Contemporary Film." In *Unspeakable Images: Ethnicity and the American Cinema*, edited by Lester D. Friedman, 308–328. Urbana: University of Illinois Press.

Interview with Reina Lewis

Ilya Parkins

This interview with leading fashion studies scholar Reina Lewis discusses the various foci of her research about fashion and visual culture: orientalism, religion (especially Islam), and queer sexualities. The interview highlights the intersection between these strands of Lewis's work. Parkins and Lewis discuss what these intersections might reveal about regimes of visibility for differently marginalized groups, historically and in the contemporary moment. Issues of the gaze, modest dress, online communities, and the commodification of outsider identities are paramount in the conversation.

Reina Lewis has been an influential figure in British cultural studies of fashion for over two decades. She first made her mark with groundbreaking work on fashion and sexuality in the 1990s, as the mainstreaming of 'gay liberation' resulted in the courting of a nascent queer market or 'pink pound/dollar', which was spectacularly reflected in fashion imagery. At the same time, Lewis also began publishing important historical research on the intersections of race, sexuality and gender in the visual cultures of orientalism. Over the last decade, her attention has turned to faith and fashion, as she has considered the burgeoning market for modest, and especially Muslim, dress and clothing. Lewis's work has always been distinguished by its focus on the complex relationships between history, visuality, capitalism and empire. Her insistence on an intersectional lens, and her emplacement of dress and fashion in relation to larger socio-historical shifts and cultural politics, have been critical in ensuring fashion studies' relevance to feminist studies.

Lewis is currently Centenary Professor of Cultural Studies at the London College of Fashion, University of the Arts London. In addition to dozens of essays, she is the author of *Gendering Orientalism: Race, Femininity, Representation* (1996), *Rethinking Orientalism: Women, Travel and the Ottoman Harem* (2004), and *Muslim Fashion: Contemporary Style Cultures* (2015) and co-editor of *Outlooks: Lesbian and Gay Sexualities and Visual Culture* (1996), *Gender, Modernity, and Liberty: Middle Eastern and Western Women's Writings: A Critical Sourcebook* (2006), *The Poetics and Politics of Place: Ottoman Istanbul and British Orientalism* (2011) and *Modest Fashion: Styling Bodies, Mediating Faith* (2013).

Ilya Parkins had a conversation with Reina Lewis on 20 March 2018 to discuss intersections between the various strands of Lewis's work and the insights these might bring to contemporary feminist and queer analyses of fashion and dress.

Ilya Parkins: I was lucky enough to hear you give a keynote last summer that began to get at the connections between the two major areas you've worked on, queer dress and style, and modest fashion. I am wondering if you could talk to us about what's at stake for you in thinking about the relationship between queer fashion and modest dress, how you came to start thinking them together, what insights thinking these two topics in relation to each other can facilitate, and any tensions you might have detected.

Reina Lewis: We met at that wonderful conference on the female gaze at UAL last summer.[1] That was one of several iterations that prompted me to see how these two areas of my research intersect. I'm old enough as an academic to remember that when I started my research career as a graduate student, writing on lesbian, gay, bisexual, trans culture and cultural politics was not a career-enhancing decision.

It so happened that my main PhD research was about the intersection of gender and imperial cultures; particularly I was engaging with the scholarship of Edward Said and those who had responded to his work. So I got into writing about lesbian, gay, queer cultures as a side-line because I was lesbian and people asked me. It was very clear at the time that young colleagues of mine, friends, who were specialising in lesbian or gay or queer topics were finding it really hard on the job market.

It just so happened that I was able to do both of those things. But for quite a long time, they ran along parallel tracks and didn't really, in my written work, intersect very much. When Peter Horne and I were trying to recruit contributors for our book *Outlooks: Lesbian and Gay Sexualities and Visual Culture*, which was published in 1996 – when we were looking for authors in 1993, 1994 – it was really hard. I think it's important to make that point because 1996 when that book came out was really just when, in the UK and in North America, there was a blossoming of publishing in academic queer studies.

Our book came out just at the cusp of that. But at the point when we were trying to recruit contributors, two, three years prior, there were a number of very established, senior art historians who we knew were lesbian, gay, queer, bisexual but who didn't want to write about this because – even though they were already professionally elevated – they thought it would affect their careers. So I think it's important especially for younger scholars and people entering the field now, to point to how things have changed. I think that scholars who work on race and ethnicity, and now also in my other area of religion and religious studies, have sometimes faced similar challenges.

The first time the work came together was in some of the work that I've been doing on contemporary modest fashion when I was looking at the Muslim lifestyle magazines emerging at the turn of the twenty-first century. I was looking at print titles in Britain and North America. I was interviewing the editors, the journalists, the fashion journalists, the publishers. And what I found from the ethnographic material, the empirical data, was that they face many of the same material challenges that the lesbian and gay lifestyle magazines had faced ten years prior to that when I was writing about magazines like *Diva* or *Attitude*, in that the fashion industry and other lifestyle advertisers were either uncertain about giving them product for editorial photoshoots or advertising revenue, or they were downright aversive.

	And that was where I realised that when you're talking about minority cultures or minoritised cultures, dealing with the market can often bring up very similar pattern. Shall I talk a little bit about the gaze?
Parkins:	Please do. That would be lovely.
Lewis:	It was always important for me in both my historical work on nineteenth century imperial cultures and on more contemporary late twentieth and early twenty-first century popular cultures and artistic cultures, to think about representation, not just in terms of the image itself whether on screen, in paint, or in print, but also its conditions of production, how it gets made and how it gets circulated and also its conditions of consumption, the social, physical, personal circumstances in which we read and consume.

And I also then wanted to think about the gaze. So this takes us back to the conference on the female gaze. My work, I think, really started thinking about lesbian visual pleasure, obviously, spinning off from the wonderful work of Laura Mulvey, in relation first to mainstream women's fashion magazines in a piece I did with Katrina Rolley and then in relation to the fashion industry in early lesbian lifestyle magazines like *Diva*.[2]

I had wanted to reframe feminist anxieties about women being constructed as the object of the male gaze, which drove some of the creative and critical responses surrounding what now is called gaze theory in relation to Laura Mulvey's work. I was interested in women as the owner of the gaze – what pleasures could be found in the consumption of, in this case, fashion imagery of women in magazines – and in the pleasures of being the object of the gaze. I wanted to factor into gaze theory the possibilities that women might want to be the object of the, in this instance, female desirous gaze, and that women themselves might exercise a desiring gaze directed at other women. And this gaze didn't necessarily correlate to having an identity as lesbian or as bisexual or as queer; it allowed me to think about the polymorphous perversity of female sexuality.

In this, of course, I was also thinking about some of the excellent scholarship on the female gaze in a number of important collections and articles that had come out that were thinking about 'the female gaze' in relation both to sexuality and to race and ethnicity. Katrina Rolley and I were looking at selected fashion imagery and thinking about the way the desire of that female gaze might be both to *be* and to *have* the woman pictured as an object of overt desire.

I was focusing substantially on the social position of the viewer or the reader and thinking about the cultural or subcultural competencies that particular readers and cohorts of viewers might bring to bear on the reading of the images as onto the visual world in general. So the sense in which we might think colloquially about somebody having a *gaydar*, being able to spot a gay person, male or female or gender indeterminate, on the streets, we also bring that to bear in the way that we look at and read cultural representation. You can easily see parallels to other forms of subcultural competency, whether it's in relation to class communities of visuality or race and ethnicity, or in my more recent work, religious cultures and disposition. So in thinking about the female gaze for this conference which asked me to revisit debates since Mulvey and gave me the opportunity to revisit my earlier work, I had the chance to think not only about race and ethnicity, but also about religious dispositions.

I want to say here that when I talk about the more contemporary work I'm doing on religion and culture, I always try to talk about 'religions', plural rather than singular, and religious cultures rather than religion. I'm not engaging with the holy texts within any given religious tradition. I'm not trained in theology. That's not what I do. I'm interested in the different ways in which people interpret and make use of those texts or find those sources being used to regulate what they do, where they go, how they dress, who they speak to, what they look like, and indeed may themselves use different interpretations. So I find it helpful to think about religious cultures and religious communities plural, even in a context where, sometimes, individuals that I'm speaking to will want to say, 'the Quran says...', 'the Bible commands us...'. I don't challenge those narratives; I draw on approaches from the sociology of religion, and particularly concepts of everyday religion, that conceptualise the daily manifestation of religion as inherently syncretic, changeable, 'messy'. I want to think about the always mobile and contradictory way in which we relate to interpretations of holy sources and community convention.

So at that conference, I wanted to put religion and religio-ethnic dispositions into the mix; to think about another valance of intersectionality in the construction and exercise of the female gaze. And of course, we're never thinking about the female gaze, singular. We're always inevitably talking about a variety of versions of the female gaze. For that paper, and I'm still developing this, I was considering a set of spectatorial relations in relation to what I'm rather clunkily calling the religiously inflected female gaze and body. What variations of identification and desire may operate in the religiously inflected female gaze at the religiously inflected female object, and what dangers and opportunities does a religiously inflected female embodiment present in social relations, on and offline? This involves women, often despite themselves, in being also the surveillor of all other women's embodiment.

Parkins: This really leads in my view to a question about the relationship between past and present, which is something I've been thinking about a lot in relation to insights about the early twentieth century context and their translation into the present. One of the things that strikes me about your body of work is the way that it has taken up multiple eras. And I wondered if you could reflect on whether the perspectives you bring to bear on historical material inform your work on contemporary modest fashion and contemporary queer style cultures. For example, your work on Turkey in the early twentieth century really gets at the complexities of how Islamic dress allowed women to negotiate public space. Now you've taken up similar questions in your newer work on modest fashion. Can you talk about the extent to which you find that those insights can be mobilised and in what ways they don't translate?

Lewis: I really appreciate the opportunity to respond to that. I quite often say that I don't come from a background in sociology, I've trained myself on the job pretty much. Coming from art history and literary studies, I do always take a historical approach to the present. Whereas I used to write about dead people and their books and dead people and their paintings, now, I write about live human subjects and what they design, create, market, wear, and talk about.

And, as for anyone writing about fashion and contemporary fashion – it changes fast. That's part of the nature of it. One of the ways around that when I was working out how to frame my last book, *Muslim Fashion: Contemporary Style Cultures*, was that I had to cast it as a history of the present. Partly, because the present that I was talking about would be history by the time the book was in print and would be a different and further history by the time people read it. (We all hope that our books have a life beyond two months after publication date.) But also, because it's a history of several presents, multiple presents, both in relation to the accelerated cycle of fashion brought about by changes to the fashion industry, what we now think of as fast fashion, and also by the accelerated cycle of change in ICT, Information Communication Technologies. And it is about multiple presents because, of course, different versions of the same present moment are experienced and shaped by human subjects who are coeval – that is, present in the same time – but they're having very different experiences of that moment.

I'm both thinking of it as a history of the present and also wanting to do, in a way, the longue duree of how we come to be where we are now with modest fashion. This is on one level in terms of what might be the obvious genealogy. So, for example, in relation to Muslim modest fashion now, talking about the increase in head covering that developed during the early piety movements in Egypt in the middle of the twentieth century as part of the global Islamic revival, and tracking how that has worked in different geographical locations and different periods and different forms of dress, religious practice and fashion and style and different relationships to the market. That's one thing. But also, going back further and thinking about the ways in which, for example, in my work on women and dress and women's cultural production in the late Ottoman Empire, sumptuary legislation was always only partially enforced. So when we want to think about attempting to control women's religious expression through dress now, we might want to find earlier examples to help us think about that. And indeed, a specialist on Indonesia, like Carla Jones, or on Egypt or on South Asia, would find another set of historical precedents, which no doubt also find ways of linking in.

But that point about how different our experiences of the present are, in a way, takes me back to that question of the gaze and cultural competencies, which isn't only about being able to spot which type of socks are very lesbian in a photograph by Del LaGrace Volcano in the 1990s, but also thinking about what we would now call the different optics of those gazes. When I was preparing for this conversation, it so happened that my partner sent me a really fantastic poem by Maxine Beneba Clarke, the Afro-Caribbean Australian writer and poet. Maxine Beneba Clarke put this out on Twitter on March the 17th, as a reflection on the #metoo movement and the women's marches of 2017 and 2018, and I thought it was just fantastic:

> there are other women
> who want to say
> me too
> but can't
> they sit at home
> minding the children
> of women who march
> & hoping to god
> the husbands
> of those women
> do not arrive home
> first[3]

I thought that was so great because those of us who are historians or who have done women's history and gender history are accustomed to dealing with the reality that many of the white suffrage campaigners had servants, or came from formerly slave-owning families, et cetera. And this poem very powerfully draws out the class and ethnic politics that underwrite the #metoo moment now. Both those sets of women, the women marching and the women who stay at home caring for their children, are in the same moment, but they're having very differential access to it and a very different way of having their voices heard.

So, to come back to your question about the historical and the contemporary, one of the things that really strikes me is the need to historicise the contemporary digital culture that surrounds so many of us. Lots of excellent work on technology, digital humanities, sociology, is already doing this, making the case that we need to look at the local and regional spread and availability of internet infrastructure, for example. You can't send out tweets and say, 'I'm going to reach the world'; not everybody is connected. We have to think about how this allows new forms of participation and the way in which new technology and new mobile digital devices afford different ways of consuming and producing and co-producing images and data and dialogue. This leads both to new opportunities for engagement, which may be very welcome, and new forms of surveillance and regulation which may be less so.

Many of the women involved in modest fashion as designers, creative entrepreneurs, bloggers, and vloggers or digital content producers, may feel themselves to be part of a cross-faith modest fashion 'movement'. Women participating in this online and offline often aim at an ideal of inclusivity and respect for other women's choices. This can be very challenging in relation to intra-religious difference – so, a Muslim woman may feel that the way another Muslim woman is covering isn't within her *own* definition of comfortable modesty, but she would try very hard to be respectful of that different choice. So too there are cross-religious differences and differences across the perceived divides between religion and secularity. And nonetheless, despite this ethos of respect for choice and diversity, women are themselves caught up in surveying and judging other women's bodies and dress online and on the street. It's unavoidable. I think one of the directions for future research, not just in relation to modest fashion but certainly in relation to feminism and thinking about social inclusivity, is to go back to the gaze and think again about surveillance and the surveilling gaze; to what extent might all of us sometimes occupy the centre of the panopticon? I don't yet know how to formulate this, but I am really interested to pursue how new forms of surveillance is built into contemporary society and social media; do you know what I mean?

Parkins: I do.

Lewis: We are always looking, at the same time as we are being looked at, and the technology, the apps invite you to do that. So it might be just liking or sending an emoji, but what does it mean when you withhold your like or when you send direct criticism? And of course, it's been well documented that, certainly, women especially get trolled online; this happens in relation to modest fashion as well. So what we see are social inequalities playing out in terms of who is the most likely target of online hate and the nature of those threats.

Within modest fashion I've seen a transition from the first generation of bloggers who when they started writing 'old-fashioned' blogs it was possible to moderate the comments stream. The volume was small enough that nothing went out without them checking it first; they could take something down if it didn't meet their code of conduct, etiquette. Then along came YouTube and comments became impossible to deal with. Now, with the other social media, the volume of response is uncontainable: the self-appointed guardians of women's morality weigh in with opinion and hatred. When that happens,

	other followers will also weigh in and challenge. But it has caused some people to leave the field or not to enter the field. So again, when we talk about the possibilities of digital communication, not everybody feels equally able to access those possibilities, to take that pressure.
Parkins:	This leads really beautifully into a question I wanted to ask you about the concept of neoliberalism, because what you've just pointed to are both possibilities and foreclosures that have come about as a result of social media. And in some of your work recently, you've taken up in really interesting ways a kind of expansive definition of neoliberalism in which you're attentive to what it generates that might be potentially interesting in terms of dress and fashion, in addition to what it forecloses. I'm wondering if studying dress and fashion and style offers particular insights about neoliberalism that might be used to nuance our analysis of this category.
Lewis:	It is an area of discomfort for me, I have to say, in that I don't think that shopping will bring about world peace. I don't think consumer culture society is an unalloyed good. But I also feel very profoundly that people who have grown up as part of the majority culture often don't understand how hurtful, how alienating, it is if you're from a minoritised culture to find yourself disregarded by prevalent cultural forms. And in the world we live in now, consumer culture is one of those prevalent cultural forms. The example I often give is that here I am speaking to you from my office at London College of Fashion on Oxford Street, London's preeminent shopping boulevard ostensibly full of choice for consumers. But if I want to buy a Ramadan card or a bar mitzvah card, there is not one to be found in any of the department stores or the special stationary stores here. If I want a christening card or a Christmas card, there's millions of them. Sure, I could go to an area of ethnic and ethno-religious clustering and find a card to celebrate Jewish or Muslim religious cultures, but I won't find one in the high street. For modest fashion as a niche market, this is where the internet has been so important; it allowed brands to reach consumers outside their originating religious community.

In a piece of work I did with Emma Tarlo from Goldsmith College in 2010–2011, we looked at online modest fashion retail.[4] Almost all of the brands we were looking at were started by people, mainly women, from within religious communities who could not find what they wanted in a shop, and so they started companies to design, manufacture, and distribute the clothes that they wanted for themselves or their daughters.

We asked them, 'do you get consumers from other religious backgrounds? If you know this, do you welcome it? And do you ever change your offering, your lines, to accommodate it?' And the answer was 'yes, yes, and yes'. That cross-faith commercial activity was possible because of the internet. If what you need is an A-line maxi skirt that isn't transparent chiffon, that has a lining and that doesn't have a slit up to the hip, then you might buy it from a Jewish, Christian, or a Muslim brand. Now, some people didn't want to buy from a brand from another religion because the product is 'contaminated' by association with another religion. And some brands wanted primarily to sell to co-religionists for ideological reasons. But by and large, what we found was an enormous interest in reaching out to other people, to other women, and supporting women from different religious backgrounds who were all engaged in versions of modest fashion. I think commerce offers opportunities, and I think fashion in particular can be a conduit for dialogue as well as for contestation – partly because fashion doesn't always get taken seriously. Because fashion can be so disparaged, you can be under the radar.

I think that there are pluses and minuses to that. I'm certainly very acutely aware in my own life of what happens when queer consumers get constructed as a market segment. Again, this is where I see parallels with my work on religiously related fashion, because now we have Muslims constructed as consumers. Not modest fashion per se but Muslim consumers especially being constructed as a global consumer segment for fashion and lifestyle commodities and services. This is partly because, globally, the Muslim population is youthful and growing, and located in large numbers in parts of the world identified as 'emerging markets' for consumer capitalism.

But it's also because there is now a concerted targeted activity from professional marketers and branders who are creating this category. They're not simply describing an anterior reality; they're creating it as a category and therefore that gets talked up. So now we have statistics which go up exponentially every year of the value of the global Muslim spend on clothing and apparel. You can begin to see where the business case gets made. To bring it back to the way this correlates to queer experience, we might think about Frank Mort, in the 1990s, documented so brilliantly the shift into thinking about the Pink Pound or the Pink Dollar and a move into identity through consumption for queer people that hadn't really been there in the same way before.[5] When I'm talking about this in a Muslim community context, I often draw on this comparison to say, 'be careful what you wish for'.

We find that now, yes, queer magazines or websites can have much higher production value because they're getting advertising revenue; now that we have gay marriage, civil partnership, previously 'straight' wedding venues want to advertise because they want to get the queer wedding business. But on the other hand, as events like Pride move from being based in community to being organised by commerce, do people get priced out of participation? Instead of events being in a park, where if you can't make a donation, you can just attend, now, do you need to be able to buy something in one of the cafes or the shops in order to be there or to feel that you are fully participating? In terms of modest fashion, it is undeniably easier to get dressed when modest aesthetics are having a fashion moment. You walk down the high street, you go into the mall, you can find loads of clothes that will give you different degrees of cover in a stylish way that is actually on trend at the moment. This definitely makes it easier to get dressed in many different interpretations of modest styling and modest fashion. But does that mean then that if you want to go to Iftar meal to break fast each evening in Ramadan, you need to have a new outfit? Now women are getting priced out of piety.

Parkins: This leads to a question about lifestyle, actually. This is the term that's arisen in the last decade or two that fits perfectly with this neoliberal moment. Your work has really usefully taken up 'lifestyle', first with queer consumers in the 90s, as you've just been discussing, and then with modest dress in the last ten to fifteen years. And I thought it was interesting that you point in your work about Muslim lifestyle magazines to some intriguing formulations of lifestyle that might actually move us beyond a kind of kneejerk feminist and queer theoretical dismissal of the term. Can you talk a little bit about how lifestyle is being viewed in more expansive ways perhaps in Muslim 'lifestyle' outlets.

Lewis: I think for Muslims or for other religious cultures, there's partly a generational shift. Muslim women, as with other women from other religious communities, have dressed fashionably and modestly for generations all around the world in many different ways. What is different now is that the younger generation or indeed, two generations, so broadly the under 45, are doing so through participation in mainstream fashion and lifestyle cultures. One of the differences there, particularly in the Muslim minority west where many, though not all Muslims, come from immigrant backgrounds, is that some first and sometimes second generation migrants did not feel comfortable or equipped or welcomed to engage with predominant local, in this case, western fashion norms or cultures. Sometimes, communities want to hold on to so-called 'ethnic' clothing—styles of dress conventional to those communities.

As with other communities, we see forms of fusion fashion emerging often with second, third, and fourth generation women who have a different relationship to conventional community clothing systems. In Western Europe, North America, or Australia, second, third, fourth generation Muslims are very adept at navigating multiple fashion systems. Another factor is that older, previous, generations, may have regarded religion and consumer culture as antithetical, that consumer culture was not something to do with religion. In contrast, women and men of these younger generations have grown up with world music, world food, world fashion, and with consumer culture. I think politically it's really important to point out that this is something they have in common with their global non-Muslim peers. This takes place in context post 9/11 where Muslims are still facing a securitising discourse that positions them as outside of, if not oppositional to, modernity; with modernity understood as a quality of the west rather than understood in relation to the multiple modernities of the Middle East and the Southern Hemisphere.

Forms of religiosity, of engagement with religion, with spirituality, with something beyond the material, have increased amongst many young populations, as amongst older people as well. If you go and you look at the Pew Research Centre's statistics, there's an increase in the number of people who say that they are spiritual not religious, who in some way believe in the immaterial.[6] The secularisation thesis has not entirely come to pass. Religion did not wither away as either an organisation for communities and states in terms of the structure of society, or in the way that individuals understand their life. It's showing in different ways, and it's becoming visible in different ways. Within the sociology of religion this has prompted very interesting debate about the revisibilisation of religion: is it that religion is showing in new ways or that ongoing practices are becoming differently visible? We might come back to this when we think about visuality and the way which the modestly dressed body enters postmodern visuality. We see now a younger generation who have grown up with consumer cultures and expect to be able to explore, express, and articulate many different elements of their selves through participation in global consumer cultures.

Parkins: Another thing that your work on Muslim fashion and lifestyle magazines brings up is the dimension of ethical consumption that they're trying to navigate. Is there a way in which it's possible to make connections between that and other forms of ethical consumption of fashion and style that have emerged from other sets of concerns: environmental concerns, labour, feminist concerns, et cetera?

Lewis: It's absolutely possible to make that connection. And again, this is where participants in modest fashion cultures from a number of different religious backgrounds are exactly like their peers in being concerned with these things. In addition to which, for some, concerns about sustainable fashion are underwritten by religiously inflected spiritual and cultural ethics. You've put your finger on something that is really developing now. I've been tracking this since I started talking to people in the mid 2000s. I would always ask designers and brands, 'is sustainable fashion something that's coming up as an issue from your consumers or indeed for you?'

And I would often hear, yes, more in the UK, less in America, but not as much then as I do now. Previously, it's not something that consumers were asking for so much. I think partly because, at that point, consumers had less money, so the price hike that's often involved in ethical, sustainable, production might have been unappealing. And also, it was still a very new market. As the market has grown, segmented and diversified, it's also allowed different specialisms and different areas of focus to emerge. Plus, there's been a groundswell of concern about sustainability in relation to fashion. This is one of the contradictions of modern life; if you were to stop young women on a high street they'd tell you they care about ethical fashion and then they'd walk into a shop and buy fast fashion. Or they might buy a couple of sustainably produced items and then buy fast fashion. There is no position of moral purity. Even for brands that are trying to produce ethically and sustainably, it's still more or less impossible to track the path of every single commodity that you use or the vehicles that are going to deliver your textile to you or deliver your goods to the retailer and so on.

What we're seeing now is a real increase in sustainability and ethical fashion. And again, 20 years ago, when people talked about sustainable fashionable or eco fashion or ethical fashion, the focus more generally tended to be on environmental stewardship. Now, people are thinking as well about social sustainability, the labour conditions, the impact of production and so on. Partly, that's been galvanised by the terrible events in Bangladesh, with the collapse of the building at Rana Plaza in 2013 with so many workers dead and injured. More recently, discussions about fashion ethics have extended to include fashion imagery and communication; people are concerned with how products are made and also with how they're mediated and marketed. There are now a number of brands and online aggregator portals who would propose that 'it's not enough to say, I'm going to cover my body in particular ways to be modest and to abide by my religious and spiritual convictions if I'm not paying attention to how that cloth, those garments, came to be on my body'. That interface is a growing area and it's also adding to the way in which fashion imagery comes to be created. At the Oscars recently Frances McDormand talked about having an inclusivity rider: I wonder whether we'll see similar demands for ad campaigns and fashion editorial?

There's a really great piece by Danae Clark on queer messaging by stealth in advertising from the early 90s.[7] She looked at how brands, one of them might have been Gaultier, would include just a little hint of same sex interaction in their visual campaigns and their ads, which the queer eye would spot immediately and feel welcomed by. But it wasn't the predominant story and so the non-queer consumer wouldn't be put off. And then eventually we get to a point where queer coding becomes the text rather than the subtext, becomes the overt rather than the covert. Although of course, as we see quite often, brands that do this will still get homophobic pushback from some consumers.

I now see a similar dynamic in the partial incorporation of visible religious diversity. In 2015, Mariah Idrissi, a Muslim Londoner, appeared in a video for H&M. The film, seen on YouTube, was about recycling. The logic of the campaign was: 'break all the rules as long as you recycle'. Wear black with brown, wear white before or after Labour Day, wear a skirt if you're a boy, wear clothes that are 'too young' for you, et cetera, as long as you recycle.

And they imaged this by showing people of visible social diversity, people of visibly different ethnicity – signalled by skin colour – also people of different sizes and different ages; they showed different ability by having somebody with a very highly clearly visible prosthetic limb. And they had Mariah Idrissi wearing a hijab. Well, this went viral within minutes. The entire Muslim and modest fashion blogosphere just hoovered it up and recirculated it. Interesting there was that there had been very few, at that point, campaigns that used religious diversity as part of messaging about social diversity. Arguably, ethnic and racial diversity is still not at all fully integrated proportionately in the fashion industry. Now, we're seeing campaigns about size as well as gender inclusivity. In 2017, Halima Aden, a Somali American model walked on the catwalk and appeared on magazines. So Muslim identity is far more visible. It interests me that when brands use Halima Aden or Mariah Idrissi, both of whom are also not white, they get to double down on showing ethnic as well as religious diversity. And this potentially wins some millennial consumers as well as wooing a Muslim consumer. Campaign strategies like this can appeal to millennial consumers who want to be associated with brands that are 'woke' to religious as well as racial diversity.

I think this is a very interesting moment. And, at the same time, the pushback is constant. So when Nike do their Pro Hijab, they get negative criticism. When Macy's announced a collaboration with the Verona Collection, a Muslim modest fashion line that they're marketing online, they get pushback. It's a very interesting moment which demonstrates that religious inclusivity in fashion industry initiatives is clearly not a straightforward upward trajectory.

Parkins: Brilliant. This discussion of how efforts toward equity and inclusion are playing out in fashion reminds me of this store that I was recently at, called Wildfang, an extremely popular feminist and queer-positive and trans-positive store selling clothes for 'tomboys'—that's how they market themselves. It's based in Portland, Oregon, has a couple of stores there and one opening in New York very soon, I think.[8] Wildfang also has a very, very strong social media presence, especially on Instagram. But its retail presence is not secondary, by any means. With the stores, they're almost trying to fill a community centre role as well as a retail function. This constellation of functions is really interesting to me. And in your work on Muslim fashion, you really take up retail. I'm wondering if you can provide some thoughts about what you make of this kind of venture, about what it can enable and what kind of place it can take for people?

Lewis: I'm looking at their website as we speak. I think we must have a field trip! This looks fantastic. I think it's very important that people can find clothes. It interests me that they're adopting the term 'tomboy' at precisely the moment when some versions of trans activism, and I emphasise some, are overwriting tomboy as a quality of girl and female and woman experience and repositioning it as an experience that is predominantly trans or as proto-trans. I see that Wildfang's website says 'female-founded, women-run'. How are they interpreting female and women?

Parkins: They are very explicitly trans-positive.

Lewis: Because tomboy is an extremely contested category at the moment, as trans politics are so importantly consolidating. I think one of the things that will happen is that trans politics, trans cultures will grow and diversify and segment; in the same way as there are many different discernible versions of feminism. There are different feminist politics. There are different lesbian politics. There are different bisexual politics. It will become easier in time to distinguish different trans political and cultural affiliations. And that will help clarify, 'oh, it's this sort of approach' rather than, this is the only way of understanding and storying this. So it's very interesting to me that this company is starting now because they are doing something that, to me, looks very wonderful. And they're doing it at the same time as they're having to navigate gender identities and politics in particular ways. I don't know the people involved [in Wildfang]. I don't know what their social formation is and what their groups and their allies are. So I'm not at all presuming that they're struggling with this. I think it's coming at a really interesting moment.

I also think there is an enormous need for clothing for masculine-coded bodies, including women who are masculine-coded, because it's really hard to find product that works. I used to offer personal shopping service for the 'lesbian nation' (aka my mates), and one of my assignments was taking butch women to buy bras. I saw butch dykes dealt with as the body of horror in department stores. Any woman can find bra shopping a horrible experience and traumatic – including heterosexual, female identified, ultra-normative women, for want of a better phrase. But if you're someone who gets told, 'this is the bra department and you have no right to be here', or who has a very unhappy relationship to your breasts and to female-coded parts of your body, then it can be even worse.

So I think it sounds really fantastic that they're doing this. I would be really interested to see what happens and also what sort of aesthetic there is. I'm working on a piece at the moment about so-called 'plus size' and modest fashion, so I am thinking a lot about design resolutions for under-served consumers. For the plus-size, or 'curve' market, it's not just a case of scaling up. If you want to make something into size 24, you have to tailor the whole thing differently. If Wildfang do manage to produce garments aimed at this overlap, tailored clothing for all bodies and for different sized bodies, I should think the clothes will walk off the shelf.

Parkins: Absolutely. I'm just wondering if my assumptions, as somebody in my 40s, haven't caught up really with the way that they're thinking of it, the way that the term tomboy is even signifying? Whether the break between a kind of trans politic and a lesbian and feminist politic is just being reconfigured in ways that are almost undetectable to someone over a certain age. There's something generational here that we don't even understand yet.

Lewis: Absolutely, there's generational change, and I'm older than you and neither of us dress the way we dressed in our 20s, although those may have been formative years in terms of our style. But gender codes are changing out there in the 'heterosexual' world as well. We've now got two generations of men who are using skin cream and exfoliating, which, when I was a teenager, was unheard of. In those days, any man that paid any attention to his skin or his clothing was either gay or has to be comfortable with being presumed to be gay. Otherwise, you couldn't do it.

When I look online at these clothes, yes, there's lots of them that if they were styled differently with a pair of stilettos and full makeup and girly-girly hair, would just be regular fashion. So I think it's really interesting because the boundaries of what counts as butch or tomboy also change. And the boundaries of what counts is recognisable butch have changed. And, of course, these distinctions are also marked by ethnicity and the specifics of the body that sports the clothes. A tall body with pronounced shoulders and narrow hips is going to look one way inside these clothes, and a short, portly body with large breasts is going to look another. As we speak, I'm scrolling through their imagery to see the body types that they're putting garments

	on, because if you are short as many women are, and you've got breasts and a stomach and curves, then some of these clothes are going to look very different. A buttoned-up vest over large chest is going to give a very different look than over a skinny frame with small breasts. Well, you tipped me on to something fabulous. We definitely have to go on a shopping trip.
Parkins:	Absolutely. There are some great things there.
Lewis:	Yes. What did you buy?
Parkins:	I bought a floral blazer.
Lewis:	Okay. I'm liking the bomber jacket with the floral trousers.
Parkins:	It's great.
Lewis:	And they're all wearing Doc Martens style shoes like we used to wear or like I used to wear!

Notes

1. *Revisiting the Gaze: Feminism, Fashion and the Female Body*, was organised by Morna Laing and Jacki Willson and held at the Chelsea College of Arts, University of London, 28–29 June 2017. Information available at https://revisitingthegaze.wordpress.com/. Accessed June 5, 2018.
2. Lewis and Rolley 1996; Lewis 1997.
3. Maxine Beneba Clarke, untitled poem posted on Twitter, March 17, 2018. Twitter: @slamup.
4. Lewis and Tarlo 2011.
5. Mort 1996.
6. Lipka and Gecewicz 2017.
7. Clark 1991.
8. The New York store opened in early May 2018.

Disclosure statement

No potential conflict of interest was reported by the author.

References

Clark, Danae. 1991. "Commodity Lesbianism." *Camera Obscura: Feminism, Culture, and Media Studies* 9 (1–2): 181–201.

Lewis, Reina. 1997. "Looking Good: The Lesbian Gaze and Fashion Imagery." *Feminist Review* 55: 92–109.

Lewis, Reina, and Katrina Rolley. 1996. "Ad(dressing) the Dyke: Lesbian Looks and Lesbians Looking." In *Buy this Book: Studies in Advertising and Consumption*, edited by Mica Nava, 178–190. London: Routledge.

Lewis, Reina, and Emma Tarlo. 2011. "Modest Fashion: Faith-based Fashion and Internet Retail." Project Report. Accessed June 5, 2018. http://ualresearchonline.arts.ac.uk/4911/1/LCF_MODEST_FASHION_ONLINE.pdf.

Lipka, Michael, and Clare Gecewicz. 2017. "More Americans Now Say they're Spiritual but not Religious." *Pew Research Center*, September 6. Accessed May 18, 2018. http://www.pewresearch.org/fact-tank/2017/09/06/more-americans-now-say-theyre-spiritual-but-not-religious/.

Mort, Frank. 1996. *Cultures of Consumption: Masculinities and Social Space in Late Twentieth-Century Britain*. London: Routledge.

Digital Fashion Engagement Through Affect, Personal Investments and Remix

Rosa Crepax

ABSTRACT
As the fashion scene becomes progressively digitalised, new dynamics emerge between consumers, content, and fashion professionals. Reflecting on forms of online interaction, this article explores contemporary audience engagement in the context of mainstream androgynous fashion. First, I consider the effects of the digitalisation of fashion communication in terms of the particular role played by sentiments and emotions. Due to the brevity, immediacy and informality of online communication, I argue, affect emerges as an increasingly crucial component of the fashion discourse. I then turn to an assessment of both the dangerous implications and the positive potential of such phenomenon. On the one hand, I explore cases where members of the public interact directly with fashion intermediaries on social media and highlight how direct engagement leads audiences to internalise the scrutiny of professionals and make emotional investments in their implicit promises. On the other, I examine *Tumblr* blogs as an example of forms of indirect audience engagement with fashion. In this context, acquiring a distance from fashion mediation, consumers are able to engage in practices of creativity and semantic alterations of the dominant aesthetics.

Introduction

The increasing digitalisation of the fashion scene has resulted in the ongoing transformation of important dynamics that tie together fashion content, consumers and professionals. Linked to the globalisation of fashion flows, the expanding interconnectedness of the fashion scene, enabled by new digital communications, has emerged as a main focus in contemporary fashion scholarship (Entwistle 2016). Blogs have established themselves as key sites in the aesthetic production of feminine identities (Rocamora 2011; Titton 2015), and their ambiguous position in relation to questions of legitimacy and value within the fashion industry has fascinated contemporary scholars (see Rocamora 2012; Pham 2013; Pedroni 2015; Laurell 2017). The digital has entered the fashion world so pervasively that, beyond communication, wearable technologies now blur the lines between sciences, aesthetics and the human body (Wissinger 2017). Moreover, thanks to new social media platforms like *Facebook, Instagram, Tumblr* and

Twitter, the roles of fashion audiences and consumers are more fluid than ever before. Digital means have blurred the lines between production and consumption, transforming audiences into (inter)active media producers and content creators (David and Burrows 2010; George and Nathan 2010; Duffy 2015).

Reflecting on such a shifting and intricate landscape, this article explores the impact of the digitalisation of fashion communication, while also considering whether the instruments offered by this transformation are able to open up spaces where engagement with mainstream fashion can escape its normative standards. To do this, I focus on the case of styles that play with the boundaries of femininity and masculinity, or, in other words, the trend of androgyny[1], styles which gained particular prominence in the 2010s. As part of my broader research, I have identified androgynous mainstream fashion as producing ideals that are paradoxically defined against groundbreaking gender nonconformity, and maintain intact both white upper/middle class privilege and the gender binary. While the trend for androgynous styles may appear as a progressive response to an increasing interest in non-normative gender roles and sexualities in contemporary popular culture, it was in fact found to paradoxically reinforce traditional ideals of femininity.

In particular, the article provides a discussion of audience engagements with this fashion trend, focusing on the specific features of online interaction.[2] Special attention, in this regard, is given to the affective component of contemporary digital fashion communication. I highlight how affectivity is significantly embedded in the relationship between contemporary fashion, social media and blogs, and consider what kind of affective dynamics arise from this encounter.

After exploring this phenomenon, I delve into the question of how members of the audiences relate affectively to mainstream representations of fashionable androgyny on the internet. First, I focus on particular cases in which there is a direct engagement between the public, fashion communication professionals and the product of their work, and, second, looking for an alternative perspective, the article explores forms of indirect engagement, where audiences are able to make sense of, and experiment with, the fashion trend, using the materials filtered through by intermediaries without, however, directly interacting with them.

The affectivity of contemporary fashion communication

The turn to affect has been a marked tendency in feminist research. The diverse set of queer and feminist works associated with what has been defined as the 'affective turn' (Clough 2007) in cultural studies forms a highly variegated field, comprising many different strands, and stemming from different theoretical traditions, from engagements with psychology (see for example Sedgwick and Frank,1995 and Wilson 2010), to the Deleuzian influences on the writings of feminist thinkers like Braidotti (2013), Probyn (1995) and Grosz (2008). Despite the different models for thinking about affect and emotions, the sum of these approaches can be seen as a materialist reaction to, and critique of, the representational, textual, semiotic, discursive and linguistic emphasis within poststructuralism, guilty of overlooking the affective realm of sensations. As a relational and fluid entity, affect circulates between bodies, shaping them, and represents thus a highly significant concept for understanding bodily experiences in relation to ideas of interaction and sensation, and outside of the dominant structures of representation.

The first thing that is important to underline, when using the concept of affect to approach the study of a phenomenon like a fashion trend, is the conception of emotions as social and political rather than as a mere expression of individual states. Ahmed (2004) argues that emotions are 'relational' and 'feelings do not reside in subjects or objects, but are produced as effects of circulation' (Ahmed 2004, 8).

> [E]motions are not something 'I' or 'we' have. Rather, it is through emotions or how we respond to objects and others, that surfaces or boundaries are made: the 'I' and 'we' are shaped by, and even take the shape of, contact with others. (Ahmed 2004, 10)

According to Ahmed, moreover, emotions are capable of bringing people together as well as against each other, due to their positions in terms of value and ideology, history and context. For instance, reactions of hate and disgust and experiences of shame become attached to particular bodies, which, through the reiteration of such emotional responses, are then turned into, and recognised a priori as, objects of hate, disgust and shame:

> [S]ome words stick because they become attached *through* particular affects. [...] The circulation of signs of hate involves movement and fixity; some bodies move precisely by sealing others as objects of hate. (Ahmed 2004, 60)

The line between positive and negative forms of affect is often blurred. For example, in queer theory, feelings of shame have been interpreted in terms of their productive and transformative force by scholars like Sedgwick (2003) and Halberstam (2005). Similarly, as we are about to see, in some cases the pursuit of positive emotions, such as particular forms of happiness and good feeling, can hide negative implications.

Ahmed (2010) argues that there are different forms of happiness, the distinction between which is based upon a moral judgement. '[S]ome forms of happiness are read as worth more than other forms of happiness, because they require more time, thought, and labor' (Ahmed 2010, 12). 'Ideas of happiness', Ahmed continues, 'involve social as well as moral distinctions insofar as they rest on ideas of who is worthy as well as capable of being happy "in the right way"'(13). Although every human being optimistically and dutifully wishes to be happy and is fundamentally concerned with the pursuit of happiness, this quest, rather than being personal and individual, is very much entangled with wider social mechanisms. In this regard, Ahmed underlines the performative quality of this kind of affectivity and explains that, once positive emotions are believed to be found in particular objects, they gradually turn into universally recognised 'happy objects', promoted as being good and sought after for their goodness. The industry of happiness, and the logic behind it, thus, produce it as only attainable through proximity to specific objects.

This discussion is especially relevant when dealing with the field of fashion, tied as it is to myths of self and life-improvement and aesthetic transcendence. 'Selling dreams' is a phrase often associated with the business of fashion magazines, fashion advertising and the fashion industry in general. Fashion images construct emotional narratives of hopes and fantasies by promoting consumer goods, while offering glimpses into the 'perfect' lifestyles of 'perfect' people. Coleman (2013) expresses this well talking about how, across popular culture, images appeal to those who are not satisfied with their present, through affective promises of a future 'better life'. Expectation and anticipation, Coleman argues, are key ways in which images operate in contemporary capitalism, and their pervasive power is to be found in the intense affective nature of their action. Within fashion, which Roman Meinhold defines as 'a manifestation of the human striving for the beautiful and the better' (2013, 67), he describes how '[t]he fashion myth [...] makes consumers believe that they can acquire a style or life or even an art of living via consumption or lifestyle' (66). Featherstone (2010) further examines the relationship between clothing and emotions, arguing for the affective importance of adornment in terms of a 'look good: feel good' dynamic. Beside functioning as a means of communication, fashion provides 'an outward image which seeks confirmation in the returned glances of others, for the inner narrative of what one feels one should be' (Featherstone 2010, 198), resulting in the construction of individual fictions and wider narratives of self-actualisation. In this regard, Ruggerone (2017) brings attention to the gendered dimension of feelings associated to the clothed body and claims that femininity is particularly related to negative, positive and aspirational experiences with the 'right' and 'wrong' use of clothing.

Even in spite of accepting and pursuing the accepted ideas of the good life, acknowledged by dominant social discourses, not everyone is ultimately capable of finding happiness in the 'right' way. Berlant (2006) describes this condition in wider terms by introducing the idea of 'cruel optimism' intended as a 'relation of attachment to compromised conditions of possibility' (Berlant 2006, 24). When people invest their hopes for happiness in dreams of an idealised 'good life' that is nevertheless unobtainable, they get attached to particular objects with a desire that is both optimistic and cruel at the same time, as those very objects turn eventually into obstacles to the realisation of their fantasies.

In terms of fashion, for example, economic limits often stand in the way of fulfilment. As Arnold (2001) states, 'fashion advertising and magazine images constantly hold out the promise of the attainment of such ideals, yet for all but the very wealthy the products contained are unobtainable' (14). We can then see how the fashion industry can often be interpreted as enabling and even fuelling cruel relationships of attachment through its trade of sparkling and unreachable dreams, presented as leading to a happy, worthy and aesthetically superior way of life. Often, we care very little whether these objects, for which we make sacrifices, do not actually hold the power of making us happy, and, on the contrary take us further away from happiness, or even that this happy ending we pursue is in reality the dream of the dominant society and the privileged few, rather than our own.

Before moving to an analysis of the different kinds of online audience interactions, it is useful to pinpoint the specificities of contemporary fashion communication, which, as I am about to argue, is strongly connected to affective practices. Alongside, and inextricably connected to ubiquitous social media, the blogosphere represents a key channel for today's fashion conversations. In the past few years, the phenomenon of fashion blogging has gained a significant prominence to the extent that bloggers now sit in the front row at catwalk shows, are photographed for the covers of magazines and can even achieve a celebrity status. Regardless of particular commercial interests, or professional aspirations that may motivate their owners, blogs traditionally resemble online diaries, characterised by the personal and intimate sharing of opinions and an affective kind of fashion communication, based on a colloquial and informal tone and emotional language. In their posts, the dominant fashion discourse is remediated through affect by interacting with it at the autobiographical level of sentiments and emotions, which range from extreme enthusiasm to lack of confidence:

> Every time I wear a trouser suit I ask myself, 'why the hell don't you do this more often!?' There's something about androgynous tailoring that just makes you feel like the coolest, most nonchalant person on the planet. (*La Petite Anglaise* 2014)

> Every day I find myself trawling through Instagram (I love it ok) and I'm always coming across the most beautiful girls wearing the most beautiful clothes, which inevitably leads me to feeling as if I need to run into Zara A$AP Rocky and grab myself some new knitwear (*The Little Plum* 2015).

Beside the broad segment of independent blogs, run by dedicated fashion enthusiasts without necessarily any connection with the fashion industry, a significant number of corporate blogs has emerged. These include blogs by fashion brands and PR agencies, and linked to print magazines. Adopting blogs' distinctive mode of communication and fashion mediation, they feign an affective, friendship-like bond between writers and their readers. *Topshop's* blogger for example writes:

> We love how you wear *Topshop*! That's why we always keep a close eye on #topshopstyle to see which pieces you're loving and how you're styling them (Topshop.com/blog, December 18, 2017).

On the other hand, *Anthropologie's* blogger frequently starts posts by addressing readers directly, through friendly questions, and by sharing what appear like personal tastes, experiences and opinions:

> How do you prepare for summer? If you're like us, you already have a couple (or more than a couple) new bathing suits […] (blog.anthropologie.com, April 5, 2017).

> We'll admit it—we have a cacti crush (blog.anthropologie.com, April 28, 2017).

Emotions of thrill and excitement, in particular, have become standard patterns used in digital fashion communication to engage audiences at an affective level. On their blogs and social media channels, fashion brands and magazines abandon their professional distance and impersonal demeanour. News and announcements are delivered though a hyperbolic language often paired with emojis. Everything is extremely exciting, a new skirt is something the *Topshop* team cannot get enough of and garment details are described by *Vogue* as divine:

> We LOVE this look on you!!! (@RiverIslandPR on *Twitter* July 29, 2016)

> Meet the new-in skirt we simply cannot get enough of [hearts emoji] (@Topshop on *Twitter* July 31, 2017)

> DID YOU SEE? All the divine details from #CoutureFashionWeek (@BritishVogue on *Twitter* July 12, 2017)

Cultural intermediaries have opened up to an emotional language that is closer to everyday life conversations among ordinary people. Their public approach to fashion products themselves increasingly mirrors the more visceral reactions of the wider public. On the one hand, this is linked to today's means of digital communication with their heightened informality and immediacy, on the other hand, of course, it is also part of broader marketing and PR strategies to engage audiences and consumers. Nevertheless, it is impossible to ignore how emotional reactions are playing an increasingly crucial role in the shaping of fashion communication, transforming the traditionally elitist fashion world into a hyperconnected scene, intertwined with dynamics that tie together the industry, the public and the sphere of affect.

In the time of social media, members of the audience are able to make the formerly exclusive fashion world an ordinary part of their daily experience. Official social media channels offer the possibility to see and comment on fashion shows in live streaming, keep up to date with the latest events through pictures and videos, and express feelings and opinions on announcements, new advertising campaigns, or daily celebrities' outfits. Audiences can gain (digital) access to areas previously restricted to fashion insiders only (e.g. through live updates from the backstage, or from the front row at the shows) and be connected with the fashion world 24/7 through their own PC, phone or tablet. Regardless of the commercial interests behind this phenomenon, it is important to recognise the extent to which the existence of contemporary fashion and its trends is now increasingly connected, and also dependent upon, affective interaction with the public. As a consequence of social media's mode of interaction, characterised by brevity, simplicity, affectivity, immediacy and informality, responses published by members of the public on fashion social media pages tend to be short, straightforward and communicate a range of emotions provoked by such representations, from passion to shocked enthusiasm and disgusted outrage.

> Angelina looks INCREDIBLE. That androgynous look. FIT!! #BAFTAs (@FrankiMarie on *Twitter* 2015)
>
> I have a serious girl-crush on CD (Rachelle on *British Vogue* 2014)
>
> Horrible (Gabriela on *British Vogue's Facebook* page 2014)
>
> I adore her so much! (speendecouture on *Harper's Bazaar UK's Facebook* page 2015)

During the 1970s and 1980s, with the emergence of theories of active audience (such as McRobbie 1991 and Morley 1992), the study of audiences was complicated by critical new works about the public's active involvement in making sense of cultural texts and resisting existing meanings. In the contemporary context, characterised by the spread of social media as tools for the exchange of opinions and feelings in the form of user-generated content, it is also necessary to take a further step in the conception of the media/audience relationship. Instead of inhabiting the role of passive receivers of cultural messages, or even playing an active, and possibly oppositional, part in their interpretation, members of the audience have now the potential to act as key figures in the actual mainstream shaping of those very messages and cultural phenomena. The new audiences, enabled by contemporary technological means, can engage in public, informal and affective exchanges with communication professionals, and get their voices heard. Today, members of the audience cannot be simply and straightforwardly associated with the act of consumption. '[A] series of recent social changes, especially those associated with the internet and Web 2.0 (briefly, the user-generated web, e.g. *Facebook, YouTube, Twitter*),' Ritzer and Jurgenson (2010) argue, 'have given [the entanglement of user production and consumption] even greater centrality' (14). In this kind of scenario, audiences can also gain enough visibility and popularity to take up roles that are increasingly similar to those of cultural intermediaries.

Of course, on the other hand, it would be naive to think about the social media revolution simply in terms of democratic mass participation in cultural production and mediation, and ignore the more complex dynamics of interest that still shape interactions. With this premise in mind, I will now move to an exploration of the particular ways in which the androgyny trend developed, and continues to develop, in relation to the affective engagement of the new audiences.

Direct engagement and the audiences' imagined audience

Bashing and judging

Facebook comments on pictures of androgynous outfits worn by it-girl Alexa Chung and top model Gisele read:

> Eeww her feet! (Sarah on *British Vogue's Facebook* page 2015)

> She looks like a man! Sorry Tom [Brady, Gisele's husband]! (Judy on *British Vogue's Facebook page* 2014)

> Omg! That woman has no boobies. Man chest (Belinda on *British Vogue's Facebook page* 2014).

Instead of criticising images in terms of the particular features of mainstream androgynous fashion, a major part of the audience shows feelings of indignation at the particular way in which androgyny is embodied by models and celebrities. They are attacked for not displaying the right kind of composed body associated with the trend, or for not being able to find the appropriate balance between masculinity and femininity. Moreover, the way in which, for example, top model Gisele Bündchen is accused of lacking femininity through an expression of sympathy for her husband, contributes to highlight the patriarchal framework within which such judgements are formulated.

Comments do not denounce what is wrong with mainstream androgynous dressing, which I have interpreted elsewhere (Crepax 2017) as reproducing normative aesthetics and identities. Rather, negative reactions from the audiences appear instead to criticise the published images in terms of the very standards set by this kind of fashion itself. Or, in other words, rather than judging the trend, commenters seem to judge other women *through* the trend. Rather than being celebrated for their androgyny, bodies that are perceived as gender-ambiguous are affectively reproduced as repulsive objects of hate (Ahmed 2004), and gender nonconformity as a source of shame. Through the comments, in fact, androgynous fashion emerges as being quite straightforwardly about not only femininity, but a femininity that is constructed around normative ideas about heterosexuality and traditional gender roles.

A particularly interesting case is represented by *Grazia* magazine's regular online feature, where readers are asked to judge celebrity and street style outfits on *Grazia's Facebook* page. Let us consider comments on two outfits[3] worn by singer Rita Ora:

> she wears it well but it is less 'sartorial take on masculine styling' and more 'hot girl dressing as a man and getting away with it' (Gillian on *Grazia's Facebook* page 2014, commenting on the first outfit)

> It's achingly cool but sadly not very flattering. Swap the shorts for a feminine skirt and we might be onto something (Genna on *Grazia's Facebook* page 2014, commenting on the second outfit)

> A beautifully cut androgynous outfit, that could have really done with a hint of femininity. (Emily on Grazia's *Facebook* page 2013, commenting on the second outfit)

The emphasis is placed upon the right equilibrium between masculinity and femininity. Comments stress how a high degree of normative and heterosexual femininity is seen as a requirement in order to succeed in incorporating masculine elements and embodying the trend of androgyny in the right way. Ora is accused of sporting an outfit that is simply menswear, instead of being androgynously fashionable, and of only being able to successfully embody it by balancing it with her feminine and attractive appearance. Having learnt their lesson from fashion intermediaries, who instruct about how to give a feminine touch to otherwise too masculine ensembles in order to look fashionable and androgynous (reference deleted to maintain the integrity of the review process), members of the audience reproduce normative expectations of gender by connecting a perceived lack of femininity to inappropriateness and lack of elegance.

> Mistakes in embodying the fashionable androgyny are also overlaid with class connotations:

> It's very white! The trousers look a touch too 'sailor' with the amount of gold buttons. And white shoes as well? But the coat is amazing, stops it being too costume[4] (Raychel on *Grazia's Facebook* page 2014)

> Something went horribly wrong in the styling here. That suit is incredible but looks almost cheap. It's too cluttered with necklaces and neck tie[5] (Meshenda on *Grazia's Facebook* page 2014)

> I hate those chavvy phone case bags. Makes a sophisticated outfit look cheap[6] (Kristie on *Grazia's Facebook* page 2014)

> clown trousers they are! (devinnora on *British Vogue's Instagram* page 2015)

Through the words of commenters, negative affect, expressed in the form of loathing, contempt, bewilderment and disappointment, is associated with aesthetic surplus. In spite of the fact that this surplus is constituted by expensive designer items, excess is interpreted as the cheapening of a good outfit. In contrast to middle-class aesthetic standards based on restrained elegance and chic minimalism, varied aesthetic assortment and the overload of visual signs are defined in relation to vulgarity, and bad taste. Moreover, class is brought directly into the picture by comments in which eye-catching details are described as 'chavvy', and blamed for making otherwise sophisticated outfits look cheap. Linked to middle class derision of, and disgust for, white working class people, chav style is commonly associated with obsession with brands and the flaunting of (fake or authentic) luxury items in contrast with the overall outfit. In the words of Tyler and Bennett (2010), celebrity chavs are described as 'systematically reproduced as abject, gauche and excessive tragi-comic figures' (Tyler and Bennett 2010, 376). Through the description of certain designer items as 'chavvy', and inconsistent with the elegance of androgynous fashion, mainstream androgyny becomes an instrument in the class ridden judgement of celebrity fashion. The question is: why does this happen?

Skeggs and Wood (2012) underline how, in reality TV, including fashion-centred shows, viewers are invited to cast judgement on ordinary people, who are in turn judged by 'experts', as a pretext to stimulate the assessment of 'failing' working class characters. Although *Grazia* places instead models, actors, singers and other celebrities as objects of critique, this kind of audience engagement can be seen as a further example in which audiences are induced to stand next to entitled 'experts' in the war against bad taste. In the field of popular media, Tyler (2006) stresses the power that negative affects, and in particular class disgust, hold in creating a shared sense of community:

> Popular media can be effective means of communicating class disgust and in so doing, work to produce 'class communities' in material, political and affective senses. [...] class disgust is performed in ways that are community-forming. (Tyler 2006)

The way in which audiences use social media to make affectively-charged negative comments on androgynous fashion, with reference to its classed dimension, can thereby be interpreted in terms of a particular presentation of the self for the sake of community bonding. Moreover, it is crucial to recognise how the community that is thus formed relates to the context in which it emerges. As Marwick (2013) argues:

> [I]dentity expression is influenced by the perception of audience. Posting to a community of close friends is different from the sprawling mass of contacts most people amass on Facebook, and will affect how people present themselves. (358)

Online 'bashing', in the form of heated attacks on web content and other internet users, often linked to fandom and celebrity culture 2.0, can be seen as a distinctive feature of the era of virtual communities and user-generated content. Discussing this phenomenon in the context of social interaction between American teenagers, Marwick and boyd (2014) observe two key things about their particular kind of communication: first, it presupposes an 'active, engaged audience' (Marwick and boyd 2014, 5) to be performed in front of, and second, it is characterised by conflict. Drawing from Goffman's (1990) seminal text, *The Presentation of the Self in Everyday Life*, Marwick and boyd (2011) stress the deep influence of the space in which a conversation takes place, with its norms and expectations, on socialisation both online and in real life: people adjust their presentation of the self in relation to particular contexts, and speak to an 'imagined audience'. Since they cannot positively know who will actually read their words, social media users write for an ideal audience that they construct in relation to the wider context. In the case of direct engagement between members of the audience and exponents of mainstream fashion media, this phenomenon acquires a particular significance. The audience's imagined audience is inevitably constituted by people working in mediation and communication, and thereby, the fashion experts themselves. This is even explicitly stated in the particular instance of the *Grazia* feature, where it is explained how the judgements of the public are, in turn, to be judged by actual professionals. In other words, intermediaries attract the responses of the segment of the audience that is already socially integrated within the dominant discourse reproduced by androgynous fashion, while, at the same time, they also set up the conditions in which the remaining ones are brought to adhere to that very discourse. As a consequence, spaces of first-hand interaction among members of the industry and the wider public emerge as arenas for the affective reproduction of normative messages.

Investing

> I am wearing a suit. If it wasn't for the boobs I could be Tilda Swinton androgynous! (@Braintree_ on *Twitter* 2014)

Audience responses to mainstream media portrayals of mainstream androgynous fashion —both complimentary, and, as we have just seen, critical—predominantly seem to approve and be in agreement with the aesthetic model created by the trend. In fact, they predominantly adopt its terminology and comment on its representations in terms of its themes.

It is possible to interpret this phenomenon in terms of a general tendency to invest in the trend's ideals and the promises of a better, more glamorous and more accomplished life, inherent to the whole fashion discourse. Interestingly, instead of highlighting the irreconcilability between the luxurious androgynous dressing of celebrities and fashion insiders and the economic means of ordinary people, social media comments draw the line between those who have the means to embody the androgynous look, and those who have not, in terms of a moral duty to set the good example.

> Rita slipping up with the footwear! This is what my dad looks like putting the bins out on a Thursday morning [4] (Chloe on *Grazia's Facebook* page 2014)

> an outfit she should only wear popping to the petrol station for milk at 1am [7] (Marie-Louise on *Grazia's Facebook* page 2013)

> This could be any commuter. Lily looks like a normal person! Nope [4] (Michelle on *Grazia's Facebook* page 2014)

> Does anyone think she looks like she should be working in airport security? When a Chanel bag doesn't save a look its bad! [5] (Mikaela on *Grazia's Facebook* page 2014)

> Lily goes incognito in this yawnsome suit. Looks like a headmistress! [5] (Marie-Louise on *Grazia's Facebook* page 2014)

> At least if the acting dries up Demi can find work as a British Gas man ... [8] (Laurel on *Grazia's Facebook* page 2014)

The androgynous outfits of actresses and singers are harshly criticised for being too average and normal. Amanda (*Grazia's Facebook* page 2013), for instance, judges a look to be unacceptable, describing it as 'shapeless', in opposition to the androgynous trend's signature sharp and structured silhouettes, and both 'plain' and 'thoughtless', in contrast to the exquisitely calibrated elegance that the trend prescribes. Moreover, negative criticism juxtaposes the glamorous world of celebrities to images of ordinary life, using the latter for vilification. 'Lily [Allen] looks like a normal person!' exclaims an outraged commenter (*Grazia's Facebook* page 2014), who compares the singer to just another commuter. Others evoke the squalor and the mediocrity of ordinary life, by imagining detailed scenarios, such as waking up early to take out the trash on a weekday morning, or shopping at a service station at night, which they perceive to be in contrast with the kind of life associated with the right kind of androgynous fashion. Furthermore, failed attempts at an androgynous look are often criticised with ironic reference to the field of labour, and in particular to humble jobs such as an airport security guard or gas engineer. Audiences seem to be attached to an ideal world, populated not by ordinary people, but rather by fashionable individuals who are extraordinary, superior and impeccable in terms of both aesthetics and style of life.

This investment in an idealised version of reality, as well as in the promises set by the mainstream mediation for those able to conform to the standards of fashionable androgyny, can be best understood with reference to Berlant's (2011) concept of cruel optimism, intended as a vicious attachment to normative forms of happiness, despite the impossibility of fitting the dominant dream.

In this context, audience investments in the ideal of fashionable androgyny become especially problematic, since such an ideal appears to be produced precisely in terms of detachment from everyday life and its remoteness from ordinary people. The direct interaction between the fashion media and the public induces the latter to optimistically entrust its hopes to a cruel object, which is tainted by social exclusion at its core. Mainstream fashion communication professionals invite audiences to play the role of mainstream androgyny's aspirational jury, turning the allegedly democratic and affective space of social media engagement into yet another means for the reproduction of taste-based social distinction and normative identities. With the prospect of gaining access to the glamorous and impeccable world featured in representations, members of the public, ranging from readers of more elite publications to those of inexpensive weeklies, appear to pursue the path indicated by those holding the authority on the matter, and adjust their expectations to the legitimate mainstream ideal.

The above-described phenomenon of induced judgements and investments, however, should not be taken to imply that, in spite of how social media interaction is formulated through active participation and the expression of sentiment, audiences respond in passive accordance to the norm. In fact, if spaces of direct audience engagement are too haunted by the ghost of their prospective audience, for the emergence of any alternative and oppositional reaction, indirect engagement offers instead more freedom and possibilities for the re-appropriation and modification of mediated contents.

Indirect engagement and semantic alterations

In the era of Web 2.0, culture and media production have witnessed an increasingly active and first-hand participation of audiences and consumers. 'User-generated content' is now a widespread phrase, which mirrors how the boundaries between producers and consumers of media and cultural content have become increasingly blurred. According to Borschke (2015), an important shift has occurred 'from the passive consumers of the broadcast era […] to the active participants of Web 2.0' (Borschke 2015, 107), which has led many scholars to consider the new audiences' possibilities for empowerment and resistance. boyd (2010) argues that social network users and the networked public in general, participate in common daily practices of copy, alteration, remixing and recontextualisation of digital texts, which result in the blurring of boundaries between those who create content and those who consume it.

The particular relationship between affect and emotion on the one hand, and practices of cultural remix on the other, has been investigated in terms of the creative channelling of emotions through the assemblage and sharing of visual content. Steyerl (quoted by Papenburg and Zarzycka 2013) notes how 'the digital archive is nowadays charged with affect as it requires active user participation. Users upload, rip, remix and share existing materials' (Papenburg and Zarzycka 2013, 219), which are thus shaped through informal emotional labour. Popular image archives and networks themselves can be seen as non-linear and ever-changing visualisations of affective experiences (Cho 2017). Reflecting on queer communities, moreover, Cho (2017) identifies practices of remix on *Tumblr*, where content is reblogged rather than created, as key sites for the study of how affective dynamics circulate in digital culture.

Tumblr is a social network site and a microblogging platform founded in 2007 and counting, as of January 2018, more than 391 million user blogs (www.statista.com, accessed on March 1, 2018). Differently from other blogging platforms such as *Blogger* or *WordPress*, *Tumblr* is not based on the creation and upload of original content; on the contrary, its users follow other blogs and engage in practices of reblogging. *Tumblr* blogs, in this sense, basically consist of archives of videos, gifs, quotations, music, but predominantly images, that users find meaningful enough to reblog. In contrast to traditional fashion blogs, which often mimic fashion magazines and where content is posted for an audience and from a position of relative authority, based on the distinction between blogger and blog followers, *Tumblr* communities are constituted by circles of, often anonymous, peers. Usually without any pretension of professionalism or desire for fame, they reblog material from secondary sources for entertainment purposes.

While responses of the audiences on official social media pages represented a form of direct engagement, approaches to online fashion content such as *Tumblr* blogging are instead indirect and do not presuppose any kind of first-hand contact with cultural intermediaries, or the fashion industry. As a consequence, looking at the way in which *Tumblr* users consume representations of mainstream androgynous fashion, we can investigate how affective responses to fashion, enabled by the digitalisation and the focus on the immediacy of its contemporary experience, are used to make sense of the trend outside of the influence of professionals in the field, as well as of dominant structures of meaning.

After browsing *Tumblr* in search of pictures associated with the androgyny trend as defined in my previous research (Crepax 2017), I focused on four particular *Tumblr* blogs: *A Cultural Boneyard, Bad Hearts Club, Wink, Pout, Ask Me Out* and *Poison and Butterflies*. While being adequately representative of its representation in the *Tumblr* community, in terms of both themes and aesthetics, these are able to illustrate the main patterns emerging from their study.

In several *Tumblr* collections, images of fashionable androgyny are reblogged alongside pictures of the naked female body. *A Cultural Boneyard* posts plenty of pictures that were probably originally obtained from mainstream fashion media outlets (e.g. we see shots taken from ad campaigns, catwalk shows and editorials published in magazines). We see tall, thin and long-limbed models sporting androgynous coats and suits. There are sportswear-inspired outfits, oversized, structured and minimalist silhouettes, crisp whites and pristine monochrome pastels. Androgynous shapes are balanced by feminine high heels or exposed legs.

In my previous research (Crepax 2017) I have stressed, how, in mainstream androgynous fashion, following the representational patterns of dominant fashion, female sexuality frequently takes the form of a tension between the images of the virginal and angelic respectable woman, and the sophisticated and elegantly sensual *femme fatale*. This way, it ends up embodying middle class ideals of femininity and normative expectations of gender. On *Tumblr*, this kind of imagery is put side by side with pictures of high erotic impact. Although most of these are still professional shots of white, slim models, they stand in contrast with the androgyny trend's elegant sexual restraint. Instead of the composed, controlled and disciplined bodies that are usually shown embodying mainstream androgynous fashion, the *Tumblr* users' choice of putting androgynous fashion side by side with pictures of undressed women in languid, sensual and provocative poses appears as an attempt to reclaim the open expression of female sexuality. The focus is largely placed on breasts and cleavage, which Tyler and Bennett (2010) highlight as a signifier of working class glamour, and are thereby concealed in mainstream representations of androgyny. The contrast also appears clearly from *Tumblr* feeds (e.g. *A Cultural Boneyard*, or *Bad Hearts Club*), where pictures of exposed breasts and erotica are placed next to portrayals of flat-chested women whose breasts are modestly concealed by high necklines and oversized and structured garments.

It should also be noted how contemporary mainstream androgynous fashion is often characterised by the refined minimalism of monochromatic white and pale colours. *A Cultural Boneyard*, for example, features several images of models wearing pastel-coloured coats characterised by a clean and sharp cut, while, in *Bad Hearts Club*, similar coats are shows side by side with images portraying sleek white shirts, tops and trousers. The predominance of clean shapes and spotless white as a prevailing colour can be seen as hinting at a cultural dynamic with dangerous implications in terms of race, but also class. As Dyer (1993) highlights, in representational dichotomies, white often becomes a positive symbol of cleanness, hygiene and rationality, as opposed to black's associations with dirtiness, danger and disorder. Through reblogging, however, *Tumblr* users combine such imagery with ethnic inclusion. Images from popular culture are used as symbols of racial diversity. *Bad Hearts Club*'s feed shows a set of emojis with different skin tones (this was reblogged before diverse emojis were officially released with *Apple's* iOS 8.3 update in 2014), and a digitally manipulated picture, where white blonde Venus is replaced by black actress Lupita Nyong'o, in Botticelli's *Primavera*. In *Wink, Pout, Ask Me Out*, moreover, we find pictures of black women in whimsical artistic makeup, inconsistent with the minimalism and the barely-there makeup of mainstream androgyny, which emerges from adjacent pictures. In *Poison and Butterflies*, photographs of clean-cut, androgynous fashion are cropped on the face of the black model with vitiligo who is wearing it. It should also be noted that the number of non-white women present in this kind of visual archives is much higher than that of mainstream fashion content, where, too often, diversity still means one or two token black models (Murray 2017).

The remixing of mediated material also emerges as linked to personal expression. The way in which the majority of fashion pictures reblogged on *Tumblr* does not show the faces of the women portrayed, suggests their use in an affective process of shaping of the self, where images become means through which the users are able to negotiate understandings of female bodies and identities in relation to their own. The self is also articulated through quotes and messages intended to be motivating and empowering. For example, alongside visual material, the blogger of *A Cultural Boneyard* shares bits of text through which she defines herself in terms of her intelligence, and ridicules misogyny, reblogging a sexist phrase quoted as a 'Male proverb'.[9] Others (*Wink, Pout, Ask Me Out* and *Poison and Butterflies*) instead use references to popular culture (e.g. out-of-context still images from TV shows), everyday life (e.g. a screenshot of a text message[10]) and everyday aesthetics (e.g. a DIY motivational plaque made with glitter letters and sticker gems[11]), to share snappy comebacks and words of self-affirmation.

According to Ahmed (2004, 2010), through the reproduction of meanings and narratives, particular emotions stick to particular bodies, such as black bodies or queer bodies, which are thus affectively produced as problematic, and stuck in networks of negative attachments. This happens due to the political and communal quality of emotion, in the form of a phenomenon which Ahmed calls 'affective economy'. In *Tumblr's* aesthetic narratives, such patterns of affective attachments linked to bodies that are frequently problematised in dominant sociocultural contexts, are reversed. The collages invite a positive affective reading of traditionally 'unhappy' bodies, which is informed by other images that are part of the same mix, that is, images which convey emotional power, and free self-expression.

Manovich (2015) underlines the sociality linked to active audience' practices of sharing and remixing in the contemporary digital age. In fact, a further common theme in *Tumblr* blogs that remix the contents of androgynous mainstream fashion can be found in concepts of friendship and sisterhood. A considerable number of the bloggers use the social network to create a community based upon female friendship, placing links in their home pages to the *Tumblr* blog of their digital, or IRL (in real life) friends, indicated, for instance, as 'BFF' (i.e. best friend forever) or 'partner in crime'. This is also reflected at the level of the meanings that emerge from the reblogged images: we find popular-culture pictures portraying scenes of friendship among women, such as still images from TV shows *Sex and the City* (Wink, Pout, Ask Me Out), *Orange Is the New Black* (Poison and Butterflies) and teenage witch film *The Craft*, as well as as an embroidery piece with hearths and the words 'best' and 'friends' (Wink, Pout, Ask Me Out). Even among images representing dominant androgynous fashion, the bloggers often pick those featuring groups of models in more spontaneous poses resembling genuine friends hanging out.

Glitter and stickers, often applied to the body, can be very frequently found in feeds, alongside pictures of notebooks, scrapbooks, DIY projects and paint. Although the practice of browsing *Tumblr* from a digital device and reblogging pictures could be perceived as passive entertainment without much value, its content appears instead to be linked to notions of imagination and creativity. It is especially significant how the kind of imagery that emerges from such blogs does not simply conform to the traditional aesthetics of dominant fashion culture that can be observed in magazines. Rather, this more playful and crafty aesthetics, driven by emotions, can be associated with Willis (1990) concept of 'grounded aesthetics':

> The received sense of the 'aesthetic' emphasizes the cerebral, abstract or sublimated quality of beauty. At times is seems to verge on the 'an-aesthetic' – the suppression of all senses. By contrast we see grounded aesthetics as working through the senses, through sensual heightening, through joy, pleasure and desire, through 'fun' and 'the festive'. (23-24)

In this regard, we can observe how fashion audiences and consumers negotiate the meanings of androgynous mainstream fashion on an aesthetic level. Its minimalism and refined elegance are here juxtaposed with visual excess, found for example in the kitsch hot pink neon silhouettes of a naked female body (*A Cultural Boneyard*) and a feminine pout (*Wink, Pout, Ask Me Out*), colourful collages, bold rudimentary graphics, and bodies adorned with paint, glitter, stickers and temporary tattoos. In a previous section of the article, androgynous fashion's taste for restrained elegance emerged through its association with the superiority and refinement of the affluent classes and as defined in contrast to working class vulgarity and excess. Here, it is remixed with allusions to a semantically opposed scenario, and so are its aesthetic claims of legitimacy based upon hierarchical notions of beauty. In fact, such aesthetic pastiche also reallocates the meaning of excess, making it shift from bad taste to empowerment. For instance, besides opposing the clean and subdued style of mainstream androgyny, the collages reblogged in *A Cultural Boneyard,* and in particular those portraying a female hand with varnished nails holding a handful of tiny planets, and a giant naked woman against a galaxy background overlooking a scene of swimming pool bathers, communicate ideas of feminine power that are expressed through grandeur rather than aesthetic minimalism and restraint.

In terms of aesthetics, furthermore, the way in which visual overload creates a contrast with fashionable androgyny's severity can be linked to the reclaiming of girly style as serious and valid. Traditionally girly colours such as pink and fuchsia, symbols such as tiny stars and hearts, hobbies such as embroidery or scrap-booking, and again, stickers and glitter, are used to remix the dominant aesthetic. Kearney (2015) argues that, through its link to creativity and affectivity, glitter and the 'sparklefication' of girly popular culture hold a potential for the subversion of patriarchy. In addition, White (2015) highlights glitter's complex association to 'lower-class values, sexual promiscuity and gender nonconformity' (White 2015, 162) and links it to the reappropriation of girly culture in the context of nail-polish bloggers. Similarly, this analysis shows how, instead of merely constituting silly and frivolous consumption, girly culture and a broader aesthetics of pastiche can be seen as representing an attempt in reclaiming a space for ethnic, gender and social diversity through everyday creativity.

Conclusion

This article has examined the multifaceted relationship that exists between direct and indirect forms of digital audience engagement and the dimension of affect, in the context of the particular trend of mainstream androgynous fashion.

It should be noted that the concept of androgyny, so popular in the fashion field, is now almost exclusively used in aesthetic terms to talk about a particular look or style, rather than an identity. While in the Western classical world the androgyne first emerged as an intermediate category between the male and the female, today the term, even as an adjective, is rarely used in discussions of sexual and gender identity. Contemporary popular interest in alternative gender roles and sexualities is instead directed towards concepts like gender fluidity, non-binary identities, transgender, and pansexuality.

My analysis further underlines how the ubiquitous trend of androgynous fashion is not ultimately as concerned with gender ambiguity or alternative gender identities as it is with the affective reproduction of standards of femininity. In this sense, the research uncovers important implications in terms of a feminist reading which links digital engagement with the androgyny trend to wider dynamics of affective manipulation, which reproduce traditional gender roles on the internet. Characterised by immediacy and informality, the interaction between audiences and commercial fashion content on the internet has been found to be guided by emotional stimuli and responses. The analysis highlights how mainstream channels of fashion communication appear to use contemporary means of affective audience engagement to reproduce normative understandings of appropriateness, in relation to gender, clothing and fashion consumption. The androgyny trend does not use gender ambiguity to expose the artificiality of conventional ideals about gender. Instead, digital engagement is used to affectively reiterate dominant narratives of gender and, thus, to reproduce normative and unthreatening standards of women's fashion. In this sense, the emotional triggering which characterises this kind of audience interaction can be seen through the lens of the wider dynamics of affective capitalism. In the form of management and mobilisation of affects, fashion intermediaries' emotional labour (Hochschild 1983, 7), frames a particular kind of affective reception, which, in contemporary digitalised communication, takes the form of further emotional and immaterial labour (Lazzarato 1996; Wissinger 2009), which sees consumers affectively participating in the cultural promotion of aesthetic objects. Moreover, not only does the elicitation of emotions serve to create visceral connections between fashion products and potential consumers, but the emotions elicited this way also work towards the reproduction of the gender binary, a key tenet of both capitalist consumption and the patriarchal society.

On the other hand, indirect engagement with representations of androgynous fashion, for example practices of reblogging on *Tumblr*, was found to open up possibilities for semantic alterations, reappropriation and remix. Manovich (2015) stresses how, within remix, meanings and aesthetics are deconstructed, reassembled and reimagined to reflect new perspectives, and defines it as 'a composition that consists of previously existing parts assembled, which is edited to create particular aesthetic, semantic, and/or bodily effects' (142). In this context, mainstream androgynous fashion is transformed, through indirect forms of affective audience participation on the internet, into an opportunity to talk about a variety of issues such as ethnic and racial inclusion, feminism, women's representation, and include them, through consumption, into mainstream fashion's imagery.

This article has thus underlined the complexity of the relationship between contemporary fashion communication and the affectivity that emerges from its increasingly digital character. If, on the one hand, a heightened emotional involvement can give rise to problematic dynamics, on the other hand, it has also an interesting potential. In fact, every step away from cultural intermediaries and their work, is a step towards more opportunity for resistance and re-workings, where affectivity takes the form of interpersonal bonds, inclusivity and creative joy.

Notes

1. Deriving from the union of the Ancient Greek words for man (ἀνδρ, anēr, andrós) and woman (γυνη´, gynē, gynaikós), androgyny refers to the combination of feminine and masculine traits in a same object or subject, as well as to an intermediate entity between the feminine and the masculine. Before becoming what I analyse as a distinctive trend in contemporary fashion, androgyny has been a constant in Western culture, travelling in and out of dominant society, finding moments of mainstream appeal, but mostly living at the margins as subculture or counter culture.

    A critical foundation for the exploration of androgyny in relation to style and clothing, can be found in Butler's (1990, 1993) theorisation of gender performativity and gender trouble. Thanks to the concept of performativity, which sees sex and gender as created through their reiterated enactment, not only we can question the nature of current gender models, but we can also interrogate the daily practices that bring them into being. These, as Butler acknowledges, are written on the body, to the extent that gender can be defined as a 'stylization of the body' (Butler 1993, 43), for example, through clothing and adornment.

In his analysis of female masculinity, Halberstam (1998) argues that although masculine clothing is accepted in girls, who are labelled as unthreatening tomboys, gender non-conformity starts being problematised when they enter adulthood. With regard to mainstream culture, moreover, Halberstam (2005) draws attention to the gap that exists between authentic, real-life and potentially unsettling gender identities, and, on the other hand, the watered-down and inoffensive representations fit for the dominant public.

The literature on gender ambiguous dressing underlines thus a critical dynamic not so much between a simple femininity/masculinity dichotomy as between tensions of mainstream normativity versus the radical potential of its opposite.

2. The analysis, conducted between 2013 and 2018, and focusing on contemporary fashion communication from the year 2010 onwards, examined the category of new digital media. The investigation addressed the digital practices of both media producers, spanning from emerging independent intermediaries to established ones, and their audiences. In particular, on the one hand, I looked at a sample of 87 blogs, managed by either independent fashion enthusiasts or professionals (e.g. blogs associated with fashion magazines, brands or PR agencies). On the other hand, I analysed blog content side by side with content found on social media outlets (e.g. their corresponding pages on *Instagram*, *Facebook* and *Twitter*). Finally, after mapping the key themes, terminology and aesthetic patters emerging from the analysis of blogs and social media content, I used them as search parameters on *Tumblr*, in order to find independent responses to them, which have been later examined through a comparative analysis.

3. The first outfit is a classic black suit, worn oversized and with a masculine cut. It is coupled with a large-fitting white shirt, a simple black tie, and black leather shoes. While the first look is a formal one, the second one consists of an ensemble of baggy sportswear by *Adidas*. The whole outfit is made of honeycomb mesh fabric in neon colours: a neon yellow jacket worn over a neon orange tank top and neon green, baggy, knee-length shorts. To complete the look, Ora wears white football socks and white flip flops.

4. The picture shows an all-white look worn by Jennifer Lopez, which consists of high-waisted, boot-cut white trousers, white stilettos, a white shirt, a gold clutch bag and an oversized white coat draped over Lopez' shoulders. Both the trousers and the coat are adorned with golden buttons which give them a nautical look.

5. Singer Lily Allen wears a grey tweed suit with a simple white shirt and white crocodile skin stilettos. She also wears a blue neck scarf, a matching blue matelasse leather handbag, three small necklaces and a bracelet.

6. In the picture, *Vogue* Japan's editor-at-large Anna Dello Russo sports a sleek black suit, with a ballroom white shirt and a black bow tie. The look is accessorised with black stilettos, a transparent *Chanel* box bag, and an *iPhone*, also worn as a small bag, thanks to a strap attached to its case.

7. The picture shows singer Rihanna wearing a large-fitting grey hooded tracksuit with grey trainers and a dark baseball cap.

8. Actor Demi Moore wears a long-sleeved denim jumpsuit with the legs rolled up, paired with a simple black handbag, black sunglasses and white ballet flats.

9. 'Hey sexy, nice tits. Whoa, why are you so upset? It's a compliment. I'm only being nice to you, you stupid bitch. Male Proverb' and 'The sign of intelligence is that you are constantly wondering. Idiots are always dead sure about every damn thing they are doing in their life'.

10. The text message reblogged in *Wink, Pout, Ask Me Out* shows a pictures of a trampoline along with the text 'Here you go. Since you love jumping to conclusions so much'.

11. The plaque reads 'Fuck everyone who has ever hurt me'.

Acknowledgements

I would like to thank my PhD supervisors Bev Skeggs and Beckie Coleman, and the editors of *Australian Feminist Studies*, Lisa Adkins and Maryanne Dever, for their support. My thanks also go to guest editor Ilya Parkins and the two anonymous reviewers for their thoughtful comments on the manuscript.

Disclosure statement

No potential conflict of interest was reported by the author.

References

Ahmed, Sara. 2004. *The Cultural Politics of Emotion*. New York: Routledge.
Ahmed, Sara. 2010. *The Promise of Happiness*. Durham: Duke University Press.
Arnold, Rebecca. 2001. *Fashion, Desire, and Anxiety: Image and Morality in the 20th Century*. New Brunswick, NJ: Rutgers University Press.
Berlant, Lauren. 2006. "Cruel Optimism." *Differences* 17 (3): 20–36. doi:10.1215/10407391-2006-009.
Berlant, Lauren. 2011. *Cruel Optimism*. Duke University Press: Durham.
Borschke, Margie. 2015. "The Extended Remix: Rhetoric and History." Chap. 7 in *The Routledge Companion to Remix Studies*, 104–115. Abingdon: Routledge.
boyd, danah. 2010. "Social Network Sites as Networked Publics: Affordances, Dynamics, and Implications." Chap. 2 in *Social Network Sites as Networked Publics: Affordances, Dynamics, and Implications*, 39–58. London: Routledge.
Braidotti, Rosi. 2013. *The Posthuman*. Cambridge: Polity Press.
Butler, Judith. 1990. *Gender Trouble: Feminism and the Subversion of Identity*. London: Routledge.
Butler, Judith. 1993. *Bodies That Matter: On the Discursive Limits of 'Sex'*. New York: Routledge.
Cho, Alexander. 2017. "Default Publicness: Queer Youth of Color, Social Media, and Being Outed by the Machine." *New Media and Society*. 20 (9): Online. doi:10.1177/1461444817744784.
Clough, Patricia. 2007. *The Affective Turn: Theorizing the Social*. Durham: Duke University Press.
Coleman, Rebecca. 2013. *Transforming Images: Screens, Affect, Futures*. London: Routledge.
Crepax, Rosa. 2017. "The Aesthetics of Mainstream Androgyny: A Feminist Analysis of a Fashion Trend". PhD. Diss., London: Goldsmiths University of London.
David, Beer, and Roger Burrows. 2010. "Consumption, Prosumption and Participatory Web Cultures." *Journal of Consumer Culture* 10 (3): 3–12. doi:1469540509354009.
Duffy, Brooke. 2015. "Amateur, Autonomous, and Collaborative: Myths of Aspiring Female Cultural Producers". *Critical Studies in Media Communication* 32 (1): 48-64. doi:15295036.2014.997832.
Dyer, Richard. 1993. *The Matter of Images: Essays on Representation*. Abingdon: Routledge.
Entwistle, Joanne. 2016. "The Fashioned Body 15 Years On: Contemporary Fashion Thinking." *Fashion Practice* 8 (1): 15-21. doi:10.1080/17569370.2016.1147693.
Featherstone, Mike. 2010. "Body, Image and Affect in Consumer Culture." *Body and Society* 16 (1): 193-221. doi:10.1177/1357034X09354357.
George, Ritzer, and Jurgenson Nathan. 2010. "Production, Consumption and Presumption: The Nature of Capitalism in the Age of the Digital 'Prosumer'." *Journal of Consumer Culture* 10 (1): 13–36. doi:1469540509354673.

Goffman, Erving. 1990. *The Presentation of Self in Everyday Life*. London: Penguin.
Grosz, Elizabeth. 2008. A. *Chaos, Territory, Art: Deleuze and the Framing of the Earth*. New York: Columbia University Press.
Halberstam, Jack. 1998. *Female Masculinity*. Durham: Duke University Press.
Halberstam, Jack. 2005. *In a Queer Time and Place: Transgender Bodies, Subcultural Lives*. New York: New York University Press.
Hochschild, Arlie Russell. 1983. *The Managed Heart: Commercialisation of Human Feeling*. Berkeley: University of California Press.
Kearney, Mary Celeste. 2015. "Sparkle: Luminosity and Post-Girl Power Media." *Continuum* 29 (2): 263–273. doi:10.1080/10304312.2015.1022945.
Laurell, Christofer. 2017. "When Bloggers Become Designers: On the Role of Professions in a Fashion System Undergoing Change." *Fashion Practice* 9 (3): 310-328. doi:17569370.2017.1358420.
Lauren, Berlant. 2011. *Cruel Optimism*. Durham: Duke University Press.
Lazzarato, Maurizio. 1996. "Immaterial Labor." Chap. 10 in *Radical Thought in Italy: A Potential Politics*, 133–150. London: University of Minnesota Press.
Manovich, Lev. 2015. "Remix Strategies in Social Media." Chap. 9 in *The Routledge Companion to Remix Studies*, 135–153. Abingdon: Routledge.
Marwick, Alice E. 2013. "Online Identity." Chap. 23 in *Companion to New Media Dynamics*, 355–364. Malden, MA: Blackwell.
Marwick, Alice E. and danah boyd. 2011. "I Tweet Honestly, I Tweet Passionately: Twitter Users, Context Collapse and the Imagined Audience." *New Media and Society* 13 (1): 114-133. doi:10.1177/1461444810365313.
Marwick, Alice E. and danah boyd. 2014. "It's Just Drama: Teen Perspectives on Conflict and Aggression in a Networked Era". *Journal of Youth Studies* 17 (9): 1187–1204. doi:10.1080/13676261.2014.901493.
McRobbie, Angela. 1991. *Feminism and Youth Culture: From 'Jackie' to 'Just Seventeen'*. Basingstoke: Macmillan.
Meinhold, Roman. 2013. *Fashion Myths: A Cultural Critique*. Bielefeld: Transcript Verlag.
Morley, David. 1992. *Television, Audiences, and Cultural Studies*. London: Routledge.
Murray, Daisy. 2017. "This Model Has Had Enough Of The Industry Not Being Able To Handle Her Afro." Elle UK, April 19. Accessed 1 March 2018. http://www.elleuk.com/beauty/hair/news/a35072/fashion-industry-cant-handle-her-afro/
Papenburg, Bettina, and Marta Zarzycka. 2013. "Introduction." In *Carnal Aesthetics: Transgressive Imagery and Feminist Politics*, edited by Bettina Papenburg, and Marta Zarzycka, 1–20. New York: I.B. Tauris.
Pedroni, Marco. 2015. "Stumbling on the Heels of My Blog: Career, Forms of Capital and Strategies in the (Sub)Field of Fashion Blogging." *Fashion Theory* 19 (2): 179-199. doi:175174115X14168357992355.
Pham, Minh-Ha T. 2013. "Susie Bubble is a Sign of The Times: The Embodiment of Success in the Web 2.0 Economy." *Feminist Media Studies* 13 (2): 245-267. doi:14680777.2012.678076.
Probyn, Elspeth. 1995. "Queer Belongings: The Politics of Departure." Chap. 1 in *Sexy Bodies: The Strange Carnalities of Feminism*. New York: Routledge.
Ritzer, George, and Nathan Jurgenson. 2010. "Production, Consumption, Prosumption." *Journal of Consumer Culture* 10 (1): 13–36. doi:10.1177/1469540509354673.
Rocamora, Agnes. 2011. "Personal Fashion Blogs: Screens and Mirrors in Digital Self-Portraits." *Fashion Theory*. 15 (4): 407-424. doi:175174111X13115179149794.
Rocamora, Agnes. 2012. "Hypertextuality and Remediation in the Fashion Media: The Case of Fashion Blogs." *Journalism Practice* 6 (1): 92–106. doi:17512786.2011.622914.
Ruggerone, Lucia. 2017. "The Feeling of Being Dressed: Affect Studies and the Clothed Body." *Fashion Theory*. 21 (5): 573-593. doi:10.1080/1362704x.2016.1253302.
Sedgwick, Eve Kosofsky. 2003. *Touching Feeling: Affect, Pedagogy, Performativity*. Durham: Duke University Press.
Sedgwick, Eve Kosofsky and Adam Frank, eds. 1995. *Shame and Its Sisters: A Silvan Tomkins Reader*. Durham: Duke University Press.

Skeggs, Beverley and Wood, Helen. 2012. *Reacting to Reality Television: Performance, Audience and Value.* Abingdon: Routledge.

Titton, Monica. 2015. "Fashionable Personae: Self-Identity and Enactments of Fashion Narratives in Fashion Blogs." *Fashion Theory* 19 (2): 201-220. doi:175174115X14168357992391.

Tyler, Imogen. 2006. "Chav Scum: The Filthy Politics of Social Class in Contemporary Britain." *M/C Journal* 9 (5). http://www.journal.media-culture.org.au/0610/09-tyler.php

Tyler, Imogen and Bennett, Bruce. 2010. "Celebrity Chav: Fame, Femininity and Social Class". *European Journal of Cultural Studies* 13 (3): 375–393. doi:10.1177/1367549410363203.

White, Michele. 2015. *Producing Women: The Internet, Traditional Femininity, Queerness, and Creativity.* London: Routledge.

Willis, Paul. 1990. *Common Culture: Symbolic Work at Play in the Everyday Cultures of the Young.* Milton Keynes: Open University Press.

Wilson, Elizabeth A. 2010. *Affect and Artificial Intelligence.* Seattle: University of Washington Press.

Wissinger, Elizabeth. 2009. "Modelling Consumption: Fashion Modelling Work in Contemporary Society." *Journal of Consumer Culture* 9 (2): 273-296. doi:10.1177/1469540509104377.

Wissinger, Elizabeth. 2017. "Wearable Tech, Bodies, and Gender." *Sociology Compass* 11 (11). doi:10.1111/soc4.12514.

Cindy Sherman in a New Millennium: Fashion, Feminism, Art and Ageing

Pamela Church Gibson

ABSTRACT
If feminism and the fashion industry were once seen as adversaries, given how the strictures of Simone de Beauvoir in *The Second Sex* (1949) permeated so much of second wave feminism, a consideration of 'fashion' is now central to contemporary feminist scholarship. But just as the earlier critique of fashion seemed finally to have been supplanted, certain basic arguments around dress and makeup nevertheless resurfaced within contemporary feminism. The current neoliberal climate has led to the ever-increasing consumption of 'fashionable' goods, provoking unease and encouraging the contested 'protectionist discourse' within feminism to shield young women from just such excesses. Meanwhile, the fashion world itself, arguably more powerful than ever, has across the last twenty years continued a process of legitimising itself through its various modes of alliance with the art world; it has even hijacked elements of feminist practice in the pursuit of publicity. This article suggests that the fashion industry and contemporary feminism are nonetheless alike in one significant respect: neither have properly engaged with the needs of an ageing population. It is an omission that this article will seek to examine through a discussion of the recent 'portraits' of Cindy Sherman, an artist of great interest to feminist scholars, in whose earlier work there was a discernible 'anti-fashion' element. Now 'fashionable' herself, a leading figure in the global art world, she has collaborated with the fashion industry in rather different ways. Her 'portraits' of 2012, in which she reconfigured herself as imaginary Manhattan socialites in or beyond middle age, and a later series, exhibited in 2016, where she appears as a series of ageing, anonymous 'movie stars', reveal more general ideological tensions surrounding the representation of women, the ageing process and the fashionable ideal. It is the dissection of these tensions that underpin this article, for while Sherman's work has been the subject of academic debate across a forty year period, her use and critique of the 'fashionable ' image has not been examined alongside an exploration of the expanding activities of the fashion industry itself; nor have her recent images of ageing women been examined within this more general context.

Introduction: fashion, feminism and an ageing population

Simone de Beauvoir, in her extraordinarily influential discussion of 'the woman of fashion' (1949/1997, 543–550) was actually protesting against the overly-feminised, physically restricting clothes inspired by Dior's 'New Look' of 1947, which influenced high street fashions for the next decade. But if these particular criticisms of fashion were firmly dismantled in Elizabeth Wilson's *Adorned in Dreams: Fashion and Modernity* (1985/2003, 125–6), they have gradually resurfaced in rather different ways. First, there is a growing concern with the over-consumption of 'fast fashion', cheap clothes made in ways that are far from eco-friendly and which can only be consigned to landfill; the fact that they are made by women across the world who work under appalling conditions seems not to affect their overall sales. Second, there are divisions within feminism around sexuality and dress (see Lynch 2012; Dines 2010) driven by a desire to shield younger women from the excesses of fashion and sexualised dress. For, of course, many contemporary young women, in their daily lives, embrace both the delights of fashion and the idea of 'post-feminism'. This particular term, suggesting as it does that the feminist project has either been superseded or is complete, has of course been hotly contested (see Negra and Tasker 2007; Negra 2009; McRobbie 2008); Hilary Radner has also written persuasively of 'neofeminism' (2010) but argues for a different 'time-frame' here (Radner and Smith 2013). However, despite debates around the adequacy of terminology and the role of fashion within a culture of neoliberalism, fashion itself has also become an accepted part of feminist scholarship. Angela MacRobbie has interrogated the industry itself, with its largely female workforce and discriminatory working practices (McRobbie 1997; 1998) while other feminist scholars have sought to bring out some of the theoretical issues at stake for feminism in the study of fashion cultures (Church Gibson 2000; Parkins 2008).

This interest has occurred at a time when the fashion industry itself flourishes as never before; it now has extraordinary power on a global scale, achieved and assisted by excessive, endless internet activities and its profitable alliance with 'celebrity culture' (see Church Gibson 2012). According to a Congress Joint Committee report of 2015, the industry had become 'a 1.2 trillion dollar global industry' which managed to survive the difficult economic period following the global economic crisis of 2008 and grow even stronger worldwide (McKinsey/Business of Fashion 2018). And well-known artists—including Sherman herself—have seemingly been seduced by a relatively new form of patronage, the commercial collaboration with a well-known fashion house. Some designers of course have proclaimed their own 'feminist' credentials, producing couture tshirts emblazoned with feminist slogans; in February 2018, fashion designer Tom Ford showed off a range of 'Pussy Power' handbags at New York Fashion Week. 'Feminism' has arguably been hijacked by fashion today precisely because it is now seen as something very different from the dour spectre of the last century. However, while the fashion industry and 'feminism' may be seen to have forged a new alliance, they may also both be seen to reveal a problematic relationship to the realities of the ageing process. The fashion world has voiced its pride in the older models on the catwalk and in certain high-fashion advertising campaigns, which have included women from outside the industry, often carefully selected for their cultural capital. However, this has involved a celebration of a particular form of *successful* ageing in the form of glamororous, financially and socially empowered high-profile women. In January 2015 not only was eighty year old writer Joan Didion employed to advertise Céline sunglasses, but seventy plus singer Joni Mitchell became the new figurehead of the St Laurent press campaign. In 2018 actress Isabella Rossellini, at sixty-five, returned to work for the cosmetics company Lancôme—interestingly, twenty years earlier they had dismissed her from her post as 'brand ambassador' on account of her age. But despite these various—and arguably tokenistic—high-profile appointments—which have recently seen Jane Fonda and Helen Mirren making catwalk appearances for L'Oreal—the fashion industry has remained dependent on images of youth and beauty, while at the same time having little or no interest in the provision of clothing for an ageing population. Even feminist activist Barbara Macdonald, although totally uninterested in fashion and dress, described in her polemic, *Look Me in the Eye: Old Women, Ageing and Ageism*, the difficulty of actually acquiring any new clothes, noting the disbelief of shop assistants when she appeared before them (1983, 74). While there is a burgeoning body of academic writing on fashion, there has been very little on the subject of ageing and fashion. There are a handful of essays (see, for example, Jermyn 2016; Church Gibson 2000, 2013) as well as Julia Twigg's monograph, *Fashion and Age: Dress, the Body and Later Life* (2013), which employs an ethnographic approach, but overall this topic does not seem to generate much scholarly interest.

Despite changing demographics, feminist work within the field of cultural studies overall has also paid insufficient attention to the process of ageing, which is still largely the provenance of sociologists, gerontologists and scholars such as Kathleen Woodward (1999) who arguably belongs to a discipline of 'age studies'. There is of course a degree of feminist writing on the subject, including books written by some second wave luminaries—Friedan (1993), Steinem (2006) and Greer (1992)—together with Lynn Segal's rather different investigation, *Out of Time* (2014). Interestingly, this last book has on its cover an image of Simone de Beauvoir, who surely began this thread within feminist writing in her book - *The Coming of Age*, 1970/1996. Unlike recent feminist authors, de Beauvoir directly addressed, exhaustively researched and graphically outlined the problems of poverty and physical frailty that are faced by many in their old age; she described the plight of both men and women equally. Perhaps she was setting out to counter the way in which, in her novels and her volumes of autobiography, women's physical ageing is so often portrayed as abhorrent—the loss of looks and sexual allure are graphically described. Two years later, Susan Sontag demanded in the American press that women challenge exactly that fear—what she called 'the double standard of ageing' (Sontag 1972, 29–38). In some of the recent memoirs, the feminist authors may write of loneliness and ill-health, but from the perspective of those in a social and financial position to counter them. However 'Age Studies' is surely a separate discipline, while much of contemporary feminist writing is concerned with issues that concern younger women.

The *practical* demands of second wave feminism, articulated in the 1960s and 1970s, did not include a call for help with the demands of extreme old age—illness, fragility, a need for care and possibly for assisted living. Certainly, in England, most of the women who marched in the 1960s and 1970s to demand equal pay, free childcare, contraception and abortion, were relatively young at the time and so these were their central concerns. Ironically, as these women now face ageing themselves, many might wonder why nothing was said, in those early days, about the problems faced by ageing women, so many of whom have to join the flotilla of unpaid 'carers' for their elderly parents—until the day when they may need such care themselves, with noone necessarily on hand to provide it. There is still a silence; there have been recent high-profile feminist campaigns and many demonstrations, but these are often organised around rather different issues—#MeToo and Slutwalk, for instance, although the Women's March Against Trump unsurprisingly attracted older women. The 'Grey Panthers', an American initiative formed to address the concerns of an ageing population, has focused on issues such as inadequate nursing-home care and enforced retirement, but it does not attract the kind of media attention generated by gatherings involving large numbers of much younger women.

Art, fashion and celebrity culture

Artist Cindy Sherman has interrogated and recreated ideas of the 'fashionable' image for nearly forty years. This, together with her acclamation by feminist scholars, her growing fascination with the ageing process—she herself is now in her sixties—and her new 'celebrity' status, mean that a reflection upon her work is highly illuminating for a discussion of the intersection of art, fashion and feminism and the tensions that these reveal. For while Sherman's work has been the subject of academic debate across a forty year period, her use and critique of the 'fashionable' image has not been examined alongside an exploration of the expanding activities of the fashion industry itself; nor have her recent images of ageing women been examined within this more general context. By attempting to look 'across' rather than *along* the different platforms of contemporary visual culture (see Church Gibson 2012, 11) the following discussion will examine Sherman's work over the past forty years as an illustration of the new convergence of art, celebrity and fashion that reveals both a changing relationship to feminism and a growing anxiety around ageing that has been registered elsewhere in the culture but as yet inadequately discussed.

Sherman, whose first exhibition was held in 1980, is now an extraordinarily successful and widely respected artist. One of her 'Centrefolds' series from the 1980s, offered for sale in 2012, commanded the third-highest price ever paid for any photograph—and the highest-ever for a woman photographer. Her recent work, described towards the end of this article, can be seen online; the pictures are all there to be consumed, but an academic press could hardly afford to reproduce too many of them. For after nearly four decades, Sherman is still at the centre of an increasingly competitive, highly lucrative 'art world'. In 2012, her 'Retrospective' exhibition held in New York's Museum of Modern Art drew large crowds; the global display of her newer work in 2016 attracted attention in each and every location. She has also joined the stable of well-known artists who have accepted commercial work from the luxury fashion brands; they include Jeff Koons, Takashi Murakami, Richard Prince, Yayoi Kusama, Tracey Emin and the Chapman Brothers, among others.

The extension of fashion's tentacles—in search of cultural capital—means that international art fairs and high-profile gallery openings increasingly act as fashion showcases (Schieren and Sich 2011; Thornton 2009) while luxury brands continue to build galleries and museums and fashion entrepreneurs collect expensive art (see Thornton 2009; Ryan 2012; Pedroni and Volonté 2012). The ever-strengthening links between art, fashion and celebrity go deeper still. For across the past three decades, fashion houses and their designers have not only sponsored shows and individual artists, but have themselves been the subject of increasingly successful exhibitions, culminating perhaps in the extraordinary 'blockbuster' show of Alexander McQueen's designs at the Metropolitan Museum of Art in 2011 (see among others Church Gibson 2012). Now, too, the fashion idustry tempts selected artists, including Sherman, into overtly commercial collaborations. The handbags, trunks and monographs created for the Louis Vuitton brand are probably the best-known, owing to Jeff Koons' most recent work for them. In 2018, he created two collections of handbags, bearing both his own initials and the Louis Vuitton logo, but in fact featuring the paintings of canonical artists of the past. Leonardo da Vinci, Titian, Turner, Monet and Van Gogh were among the artists Koons coopted posthumously and whose works were used to decorate bags costing thousands of dollars. For those who might argue that this new form of patronage is no different from working for Renaissance Popes and Princes, the answer might be not only that the artists of the Quattrocento were paid rather less, but more importantly, that many of their commissions were designed for sites where they could be freely consumed by the public.

Sherman herself, in recent years, created for Louis Vuitton a special edition of the brand's historic 'steamer trunk' and a corresponding series of advertisements, while, in 2012, she created images to advertise a new makeup range for the international brand, MAC. These partnerships are among the indications that Sherman herself is now very much a part of the artist-as-celebrity pantheon. She is now one of the lionised artists invited to endless functions and—in her case—to sit in the front row at fashion shows. Her new celebrity status actually inspired a disgruntled boyfriend, Paul Hasegawa-Overacker, to direct a film, *Guest of Cindy Sherman* in 2008. This was prompted by his being exiled to an outer table at a celebrity dinner while Sherman herself was seated at the top table with other well-known figures. She is of course attired today for such occasions in designer clothes, many offered to her by fashion houses anxious for yet another opportunity to acquire cultural legitimacy and artistic capital. Yet for so long the face of Sherman herself was hardly known, for of course it was transformed and reconfigured for each artwork, while interviews with her were invariably illustrated by the latest reworkings of her appearance. Now she is often pictured in her own clothes, usually casual designer outfits, as 'herself' rather than as artistic recreation.

Andy Warhol, of course, whose face was instantly recognisable through his own effective self-publicising, designed dresses for the New York boutique, Paraphernalia, as long ago as the 1960s (Church Gibson 2012) and the liaison created between art, fashion and music in New York was described by Elizabeth Currid as the 'Warhol Economy' (2008). But now fashion can happily swallow up and even transform what was once deliberately subversive—and overtly feminist—artwork. This is perfectly exemplified in the purchase by Selfridges, London's fashionable department store, of Barbara Kruger's famous anti-consumption billboard artworks. The best-known of these, bearing the slogan 'I shop therefore I am' was used, instead, to coax visitors into the shop's annual sales while another billboard slogan, 'Buy me—I'll change your life', was hung above displays of luxury goods, all ironies lost in the translation from anti-capitalist artwork to in-store advertising. It is unsurprising that Kruger herself, a contemporary of Sherman in what was nicknamed the 'Pictures Generation' group of the 1980s and an avowedly 'feminist artist', has been consistently unwilling to comment on this deal with Selfridges, and the consequent reinterpretation of her artwork.

Kruger has however continued to create slogan pieces that question consumption, gender and politics—and most notably interrogated the fashion industry directly in a performance piece, 'The Drop', in 2017. As part of Performa, the biennial performance art festival held in New York—which received the profits made by her work—a store in Soho, on a street housing well-known fashion boutiques, was given over to 'The Drop'. This was a parody of the weekly dropping–off of previously publicised new designs that characterises the contemporary fashion industry. The 'audience' obediently queued outside the shop as if waiting for fashion goods; when admitted, they entered a space designed to look like a skatepark, selling branded T-shirts, hats and skateboard decks, created by Kruger. In 2018, in an ironic contrast, Sherman herself entered into collaboration with real-life skatewear and streetwear company Supreme, a global behemoth who create 'real' queues across the world and who appropriated for its branding the typeface and colour always used by Kruger in her artworks, without permission. Now two of Sherman's 'Grotesques' series from the 1980s will be used for very expensive skateboards as part of their 'Artists' series—which includes Damien Hirst and Basquiat. And through her most recent fashion partnership, with New York's Dover Street Market shop in New York in 2018, it is possible to buy highly-priced sweatshirts printed with images from her very first exhibition, of the 'Untitled Film Stills 1977–1980', which excited art critics and feminist scholars alike.

Sherman and feminist criticism

> The work is what it is and hopefully it's seen as feminist work, or feminist-advised work. But I'm not going to go around espousing theoretical bullshit about feminist stuff. (Sherman, quoted in Cain 2016)

If Sherman's earlier work directly interrogated gender and identity, her later 'portraits' show us women engaged in more problematic modes of 'dressing-up'. From the start, feminists were fascinated by Sherman's work, for here was a woman artist, always photographing only herself, but recreating this 'self' quite differently in every image. By totally transforming and disguising herself in each photograph through makeup, dress, and hair-styling, her work reflected current feminist ideas of dress and makeup as 'masquerade'. But as the quotation above suggests, Sherman sought to resist 'theoretical bullshit' even as she sought the accolade of 'feminist work'. Sherman, born in 1954, is of course close in generation to many second wave feminists—but if the scholars among them consistently praised her work, they also had to 'fly in the face of her own expressly non-theoretical, even anti-theoretical gaze' (Mulvey 1991, 138).

Her first exhibition was held in 1980, just as feminism itself had successfully moved from counter-culture to centre-stage and feminist scholars were taking their place within the academy; her unsettling images of women were heralded as feminist art and her questioning of the fashionable ideal applauded. The imaginary films from which these sixty-nine 'stills' might have been 'taken' are varied; they seem to be from 1950s and 1940s B-movies in the main, with some referencing of film noir and European art cinema. There are images in which she presents herself so as to resemble particular film stars, but in many others she 'becomes' a young, vulnerable, anonymous woman seen in a lonely urban space, or a domestic interior made strange. Crouching on a kitchen floor, lying on a bed, waiting with a suitcase at the side of a lonely road, or solitary and surrounded by skyscrapers, so many of these women are vulnerable in some way, despite their defences of carefully applied makeup and becoming dress—or undress. Laura Mulvey wrote of this series:

> The accoutrements of the feminine that struggle to conform to a façade of desirability haunt Sherman's iconography. Makeup, high heels, back-combed hair, respectable but eroticised clothes are all put on and 'done'. Sherman, the model, dresses up into character while Sherman, the artist, reveals her character's masquerade. (Mulvey 1991, 141)

These particular photographs were created when Sherman was still a part of what was nicknamed the 'Pictures Generation' group, who were exploring mass media images—films, advertisements, television—at the time when second wave feminists were themselves developing new theories around the ways in which women were traditionally portrayed, posed and adorned in the media. They were unsurprisingly fascinated by Sherman's work since here was a young woman artist directly interrogating traditional, accepted images of women and their accepted modes of self-presentation. Judith Williamson published an essay in *Screen*, a journal which played a significant role in developing new feminist discourse (Williamson 1983, 102–116). She praised Sherman for the fact that her 'pictures force upon the viewer that elision of image and identity which women experience all the time' (102).

Laura Mulvey's intervention in 1991 discussed not only the 'Untitled Film Stills', but later work which includes her first fashion—or 'anti-fashion'—images. Mulvey invokes not only her own concept of 'the male gaze', which she sees Sherman as subverting, but also the feminist reconfiguration of 'the abject'. Her essay covers Sherman's work across the ten year period from 1977 to 1987 and therefore includes the 'Centrefolds' series of 1981, commissioned by the influential magazine, *Artforum*, which rejected them for publication, and her very first 'fashion' commission of 1983. These photographs too—disturbing and deliberately grotesque—were also spurned by the designer who had extended the invitation.

It would be interesting to see what Williamson and Mulvey might make of her recent work, not only the two series which portray much older women, but also her later fashion work, created as it arguably is from the position of a knowing *insider* rather than a rebellious young woman outsider. If in the 1980s and 1990s, she chose to critique fashion just as so many feminists had done, now she—like the second wave feminists—is ageing herself and her perspective has seemingly shifted. This is seen as vital in an understanding of her recent work by feminist art historian Abigail Solomon-Godeau. She chose to call her most recent essay on the artist 'The Coming of Age: Cindy Sherman, Feminism and Art History' (2017), now published in the book *Photography after Photography: Gender, Genre, History* (2017). This is not only a nod to de Beauvoir's seminal text of 1970, but a reference to Sherman's move from young, overtly feminist artist to an establishment figure with what appears to be a complex attitude to ageing. Solomon-Godeau, who has written consistently about Sherman's work, discusses the 'ageing' of feminism alongside that of Sherman herself. Solomon-Godeau argues that the 'society portraits' of 2008 are, contrary to most critical assumptions, 'problematic both for feminism itself and for women more generally' (2017, 203). This essay, first written in 2014, could not, of course, discuss the 'ageing film stars' series, unveiled in 2016. Solomon-Godeau, however, does not deal with Sherman's changed and changing attitude to *fashion* and her possible cooption; nor do other of her critics note, or chart, this process.

Sherman's work of the 1980s and 1990s continued to reflect various feminist preoccupations. The 1981 'Centrefolds' showed her as clothed, vulnerable, often distressed young women in the kind of poses familiar to us from men's magazines. In 1985, she explored the more unpleasant aspects of 'fairytales' in a sequence of the same name, and in the 'History Portraits' (1988–1990) she presented grotesque images of herself, seemingly created by high-canonical 'old masters'. Even the—inaccurately titled—'Sex Pictures' (1989–1992) pleased some women. Confounding any expectations, here the artist herself disappeared entirely from the frame, to be replaced by objects: prosthetic body parts, a limbless torso where sausages protrude from a vagina, a severed head sprouting a penis, grotesque sex dolls with missing limbs, all parodying pornographic images. Lastly, of course, there are the 'fashion photographs' of the 1980s and 1990s, as critical of fashion as the most censorious of second wave feminists might wish.

Fashion images: from critique to collusion?

> I really started to make fun not of the clothes, but much more of the fashion. I was starting to put scar tissue on my face to become really ugly ... I'm disgusted with how people get themselves to look beautiful. (Sherman, on her 1983 fashion shoot, quoted in Mulvey 1996, 70)

In February 2016, in an interview given to an issue of *Harper's Bazaar,* for which she created both a fashion feature and a cover shoot—both very different from her earlier 'fashion' work —Sherman explained that she had always been fascinated by fashion photography. Shea Spencer, writing in *Artforum*, suggests that, for artists, 'fashion photography is unique, in that it is the only applied photography that consistently allows for fantasy and personal imprint' (Spencer 2016, 240). So it was unsurprising that when in 1983 Sherman accepted a commission from designer Dorothée Bis, the images that she created were rejected, since they did indeed bear her unmistakable 'imprint' of that time, that of the grotesque. These photographs showed her transformed into women with curiously arranged and sometimes bloodied limbs, scarred or bruised or puffy faces, contorted or deadened expressions, distorted teeth and even—in one shot—a seemingly-blackened eye. This image, 'Untitled 137', shows us a woman, naked but for a red coat, who could be a victim of domestic violence; her face is utterly devoid of expression, there is bruising around her eyes and her hair is standing on end. Sherman explained in interview at the time:

> I've really got to do something to rip open the French fashion world. So I wanted to make really ugly pictures. The first couple of pictures I sent to Dorothée Bis they didn't like at all. That inspired even more depressing, bloodied, ugly characters. (Sherman interviewed in 1984, quoted in Respini, Sherman and Burton 2012)

Mulvey championed these images, published in *Interview* magazine that year, saying that Sherman 'parodies the kind of feminine image ... geared to erotic consumption and ... turns upside down conventional codes of female allure and elegance' (Mulvey 1996, 143). Ten years later, when *Harper's Bazaar* asked for an 'artistic contribution', Sherman chose once again to produce a set of fashion images, using clothes provided by well-known designers; in this rather different context of 'art' as opposed to 'fashion', the still-challenging pictures were completely acceptable to the magazine (see Loreck 2002, 258–9).

Since designer Dorothée Bis had rejected her pictures, Sherman then opted to work with designers whose own 'fashion' was rather different and who welcomed her confrontational approach to fashion imagery. In 1994 she created a series of advertisements for designer Rei Kawakubo of Comme des Garçons, whose own designs always challenge convention. For Kawakubo herself has consistently interrogated gender, even reshaping the female body completely through a series of humps and bumps in her controversial collection for Spring 1997. In the 1990s Sherman was still involved in a clear critique of conventional fashion; in 2002, Hanne Loreck published an essay on her 'fashion photographs' as feminist activity (Loreck 2002, 255–276). But this would be difficult to do today, since the overall context of fashion photography has changed considerably. Fashion photographers themselves have increasingly deployed sensational images, in attempts to generate publicity: bloodied models, cleaver-wielding models, fashion shoots constructed around murder and mutilation. Even in 1993, Sherman's idea of using a model whose underwear was stained, seemingly with the blood of her own menstrual flow, was happily received by *Harper's Bazaar* (see Loreck 2002, 270). Magazine publishing itself has also changed; many of the new titles that emerged twenty or more years ago—*Tank*, *Purple* and *Acne* among others—give equal status in their pages to fashion and art.

Sherman's later 'fashion images', too, are much less confrontational, especially in a climate of unconventional, innovative fashion photographs; she has also dispensed with blood, bruising and scar tissue. Her unusual images are now sought after by leading fashion houses. In 2006, she worked with designer Marc Jacobs and leading fashion photographer Juergen Teller, who himself appeared alongside Sherman in a advertising campaign that resembled bizarre family portraits. Asked by Balenciaga for a series of photographs in 2008, she created pictures in which, even though some of the 'women' she becomes may look worn, tired or even slightly manic, they are all recognisable fashion *types*, employees, spectators or simply hangers-on, a kind of industry in-joke seemingly relished by the French fashion house. For the cosmetic company, MAC, in 2011, she created three images—a ditzy 'heiress', a demented 'cheerleader' and a pink-wigged clown; the brand's executive director revealed in interview that this collaboration was 'a good thing to do', generating as it did a positive response across the worlds of art and fashion, even if its effect on sales was less successful (James Gager interviewed in *Popsugar*, 2016). In 2010, the glossy magazine *Pop* commissioned a 'zine insert' from Sherman and here she took up an earlier offer by Chanel to use anything she wished from their archive. In each of the resulting pictures Sherman becomes an unsmiling sombre-faced woman, without glamour, wearing a strange and usually unbecoming mixture of vintage designs and recent styles, standing in a sunless, sombre landscape and seemingly ill-at-ease. If some saw the images as unattractive, the house of Chanel used the pictures quite happily. Sherman herself said: I was conscious about the choices I was making with the pieces, to select things that didn't read 'fashion'—I was looking for things that had some other kind of quality' (Sherman, quoted in Slater, July 2016). In 2016, *Harper's Bazaar* again asked her to collaborate with them, on a fashion shoot, four different cover images and an article, all entitled 'Project Twirl'. The feature article-cum-interview began: 'Sherman and *Bazaar* have been plotting. The idea: a satire of that storied—well, snapshot—species, the street style star' (Brown 2016). This cosy, conspiratorial tone was obviously acceptable to Sherman, who herself seemed critical of 'famous-for-being famous' women and their social media activities:

I was physically repulsed after looking at some of these accounts—thinking how this person travels with hair and makeup and a photographer and is just going to visit her sister in LA. They're not even selfies, they're set-ups. Then some of them get paid to wear the clothes? I guess it makes sense—it's business, but there's just something so dead about the whole thing. It's so self-involved. (Brown 2016)

Yet she then says, quite unselfconsciously, in the very same interview: 'Stores call me and say, "We've got this for you". When I say I'm too busy, they *send* them' (Brown 2016). And the cover story has details of Sherman's personal life—spa visits, for example—of the kind that accompany most fashion-celebrity stories. Interestingly, most of the 'Project Twirl' images show smiling, perfectly attractive women, looking very like some of the older 'street style stars 'who many journalists dislike for their interference with 'fashion dissemination'—but who have nevertheless been appropriated, for maximum publicity, by the industry. There is nothing 'grotesque' here.

Socialities and movie stars: ageing, ambivalence and dressing up

At the age of sixty-two, following a four year hiatus, Sherman returned to her work of photographic portraiture. Given her own recent anxieties about ageing, which she has discussed quite openly in press interviews (see Eckardt 2016; Adams 2016) some of these 'portraits' of imagined older women do show a sense of distaste, which can also be seen in the 'Headshots' series of 2000 (see Solomon-Godeau 2017). Despite the avowals of Sherman herself, in endless interviews, as to her admiration for these supposed 'movie stars' (see Eckardt 2016; Slater 2016) we should not only take into account the 'intentional fallacy' (Wimsatt and Beardsley 1946) but also be alert to the workings of the unconscious. In her interviews, she has talked of having had Botox herself, and has wondered aloud if she should 'go further' (Adams 2016; Eckardt 2016). Yet, at the same time, she also speaks admiringly of the English Classics Professor and television presenter, Mary Beard, consistently vilified for her uncompromising appearance, her long grey hair and her sagging face. In response, Beard famously declared: 'This is what fifty-nine year old women who have not had work done look like' (Adams 2016).

In the work displayed in the exhibition of 2016, the new 'portraits' of Sherman disguised as ageing Hollywood stars, all seemingly trapped in the dated clothes and makeup of their youth, and posed in the quasi-seductive manner demanded by production stills, were shown for the first time. Alongside them were the 'society portraits' first shown in 2008, in which Sherman creates other imaginary older women, of the kind regularly shown off by Ari Seth Cohen in his blog *Advanced Style*. Here she poses as these rich, ageing 'socialites', before backdrops signifying wealth and status, all in a veritable armour of expensive, ornate clothes, lavish jewellery, elaborately coiffured hair and heavily applied cosmetics—which, in some of these images, inadvertently reinforces the signs of surgical 'intervention'. Both sets of 'portraits' were even larger in size and scale than her earlier work.

The images in the 'society portraits' series are designed to emphasise that nothing in the privileged habitus of these rich, powerful women can protect them. They are rich and empowered, certainly; their clothes and jewellery are evidence of great wealth. But their money and their status do not seem to have made them happy, nor are they at all relaxed in these 'portraits'. Only one—slightly younger than the other—manages a

Figure 1. Cindy Sherman, *Untitled #465*, 2008. Chromogenic color print. 70 × 63.5 inches, 177.8 × 161.3 cm. (MP# CS–465). Courtesy of the artist and Metro Pictures, New York.

tremulous half-smile. The others return the gaze of the camera with expressions varying from stoicism to near-distaste (Figure 1).

Here the images have once again that hint of the grotesque which was evident in many of the 'Headshots' series from 2000–2002. Here women from humbler backgrounds were posed as longing to project youth and beauty—and are cruelly exposed. Abigail Solomon-Godeau argues that here and in the 'society portraits', there is a radical divergence from all the artist's earlier images of women:

> … in both of these 'portrait' series, which feature only female subjects who are either the approximate age of Sherman or older, there is a significant change from Sherman's earlier imagery … where earlier work demonstrates that femininity is an empty signifier, such as to imply that there is not and cannot be a 'real woman' in the image, these other series imply that these are indeed in some fashion 'realistic' representations of a certain type of woman. (Solomon-Godeau 2017).

Therefore, when we look at these images and criticise them as we are invited to do, we are implicitly criticising 'real' women for their efforts in self-presentation. And some of the settings for the 'society portraits' are 'realistic' too, computerised images of the sort of places where similar rich women may be found—including the Cloisters, a part of the Metropolitan Museum of Art, and the Upper East Side. We might ask if it is just the very rich and over-privileged we are invited to scrutinise and to judge, or whether such scrutiny could extend to all older women who take such elaborate pains with their appearance. It is this possible shift to a wider judgment—based around an ageing femininity—that makes these images potentially troubling.

One of these images, 'Untitled 466', used in publicity material, shows Sherman as a woman of late middle age standing in 'the Cloisters'. Her eyes are slightly bloodshot and suspiciously taut, her glistening mouth heavily outlined. She wears a shimmering kaftan, peacock blue with heavy gold embroidery; her elaborate gold earrings hang to her shoulders. She looks as if she resents the intrusive gaze to which she is subject. 'Untitled 470' is even more unsettling; here, Sherman-as-socialite stands in what seems to be a carefully-restored castle, with a deep embrasure behind her. She has carefully arranged, obviously dyed brown hair; her bright-red lipstick has been fastidiously selected to match exactly the colour of her silk dress, with its cut-out neckline. Her jewelled earrings reach her shoulders, while the fan she holds is not posed to deliver a coquettish gesture—rather, it is held against her body in seeming self-defence. Sadly, her eyes are red-rimmed to match both dress and lipstick, while the harsh lines beside her mouth register both discontent and unease. Her apparent unhappiness might arguably be mitigated by her wealth and presumed prestige, but she is unhappy nevertheless and her discontent—like her age—is all too clearly displayed. It is the kind of portrait that a male photographer—or an artist of the past—might perhaps make of an ageing woman, were he sure that there would be no repercussions from husband or family, or wanted to ignore for once the need to flatter a patron. It does not show 'feminist' sympathies; it is the work of someone disturbed by the fact of ageing, fascinated by the ways in which some women try to ward off its ravages, and determined to render them visible.

In another image,'Untitled 465', Sherman presents herself as a woman in late middle age standing in a formal garden, at the foot of a massive stone staircase. She is facing slightly away from the camera and turns over her shoulder to confront the lens, a parody of a traditional provocative pose. She wears a black evening dress, and her back, shoulders and arms are bare. Her hair—again, harshly dyed—hangs loose over her shoulders. Her ears are decorated with sizeable pearls, as is her neck: her gaze is stony, her mouth pursed, her eyes reddened. But the most disturbing 'portrait' is, perhaps, 'Untitled 468'. Here Sherman, as a much older woman, stands in front of a massive mock-Gothic apartment building. Her brown hair, cut in a defiantly youthful fringe, seems slightly askew and might easily be a wig. Her face is lined, her teeth prominent, her cheeks over-rouged, her expression anxious. Her hands in their kid-leather gloves are clasped defensively across her waist, so emphasising the slightly prominent stomach below— another sign of extreme old age. Her red jersey, black velvet jacket and opulent silk scarf are seemingly chosen in a spirit of defiance. This, like all these portraits, is notable for what seems to be a hostility to the subjects, the coldly observed signs of expensive dress and ornament, where coiffed hair and bright makeup emphasise rather than mitigate the effects of the ageing process.

Michelle Meagher has written enthusiastically of these images, ranging them alongside very different self-portraits by ageing women artists (2014, 101–43). She seems not to diffentiate particularly between Sherman's images and the other works she discusses. What pleases her here is the making visible of the ageing process itself. Although she does emphasise the fact that Sherman's 'socialites' are struggling and failing in their attempt to ward off the ageing process, nothing at all is said about the complete lack of sympathy on display here.

Yet Sherman insists these are 'the most sincere things that I've ever done—that aren't full of irony, or caricature, or cartooniness—since the film stills series' (Gopnik 2016). Like Gloria Swanson as the retired, reclusive, ageing actress in the film *Sunset Boulevard*, directed by Billy Wilder in 1959, who is recreated in one of these images, the 'film stars' she creates for us are all dressed and made up in the styles of their heyday; it might perhaps be remembered—even if Sherman champions these 'stars'—that the Swanson character is lonely, delusional and descends into madness. There are rouged cheeks, elaborate curls, turbans and—most unsettling—pursed mouths carefully painted into the style known as a 'Cupid's Bow', popular in the late 1920s and early 1930s. If she is serious, that these women are to be admired, we are compelled to ask why they all cling so carefully to the clothes, makeup and hairdos of their successful youth. She has not talked of this in interview; strangely, no one has even asked her about this most notable and noticeable element within these portraits. One interviewer (Adams 2016), asked her if she had been influenced by the series of photographs that the late Eve Arnold took of Joan Crawford in 1959. Here, the ageing actress is seen in her underwear, applying makeup and curling her eyelashes, transforming herself from a woman in late middle age into 'Joan Crawford, movie-star'. But the clothes Crawford puts on at the end of the series of pictures are in the style of 1959: she does not don the Adrian designs, the padded shoulders and biascut dresses of her earlier film career. She is seen as carrying out her toilette carefully, so that she will emerge an elegant older woman, not a 1930s star pickled in aspic, as she appeared in the film *Whatever Happened to Baby Jane?* directed by Robert Aldrich in 1962. One or two of the 'movie stars' she creates for this series call to mind this latter film.

Her 'stars', she said in the same interview, are 'trying to maintain some dignity as they're ageing' (Gopnik 2016). This might be true of certain images: a Gloria Swanson lookalike in her striped dress and turban stares grandly at an imaginary audience, another woman with bobbed hair leans on the back of a bentwood chair, casually holding a bouquet of dark red roses to complement her outfit, while a third, looking very like Mae West in her Hollywood heyday, poses regally in an elegant black dress. And certainly none of them have the reddened eyes, or the signs of cosmetic surgery, so notable in the 'society portraits'. Nor do they look cold, or challenging.

The idea of women trying to 'maintain their dignity' is, however, belied by certain other portraits. In one of them Sherman becomes an actress with long crimped hair—as worn by Mary Pickford and the Gish sisters—who twirls a lock of this hair seductively as she looks sideways out of the frame. She wears a peach negligée, and her parted lips are painted into the 'Cupid's Bow' of the late 1920s. It is an image redolent of a Lorelei on a rock, disturbing and unsettling. In another, what seem to be four ageing child stars are grouped under a tree, like young girls who have just picknicked in the country. They all have short hair that has been 'Marcel-waved', another style from the late 1920s; they too have pursed carefully painted Cupid's Bow mouths. A woman in white evening dress with a trimmed cape sports the white hair-ribbon of a young girl in her bobbed hair. Other women wear flapper dresses, one a Clara Bow type headband. This is surely why it is possible, as suggested earlier, to invoke the 'intentional fallacy' and highlight the apparent discrepancy between an artist's stated intention and the clearly legible connotations of their work (Figure 2).

To wear the fashionable dress of a past era is to make a statement, one usually confined to young fashion students; designers continually recycle the past, but with careful modifications to suit changed tastes. But for a woman to preserve and to wear the styles of her

Figure 2. Cindy Sherman, *Untitled #570*, 2016. Dye sublimation metal print. 56 1/4 × 48 inches, 142.9 × 121.9 cm. (MP# CS–570). Courtesy of the artist and Metro Pictures, New York.

own successful youth is rather different; despite the claims Sherman herself makes, it is nevertheless possible to read these images as having about them something of Freud's 'uncanny' (1919/2003). This suggests that there are significant unaddressed questions around these images. Both series use dress and makeup in very different ways; the rich 'socialites' seem to be blamed for their attempts to use their wealth in the vain pursuit of elegance, while the 'movie stars' are defiant in clinging to the styles of their youth. Both series seem to encapsulate different tensions and anxieties around ageing, fashion and ideals of femininity; both display a type of 'performance' using the tools of self-adornment which differs radically from that seen in the earlier work and which elicited so much praise from feminist critics.

Conclusion

The realities of ageing can create multifold anxieties for individual women, but these have not been properly addressed by feminist scholarship which, I have argued, has focused, in the main, on issues that concern younger women. Meanwhile 'fashion' imagery seems simply to present a difficult-to-achieve idea of 'successful ageing', whether in magazines or in the 'blogosphere'. 'Successful' ageing, using the tools of the fashionable trade, and arguably epitomised by Sherman herself, is perhaps what Sherman's 'socialites' and 'movie stars' would like to think they have achieved; her work reveals their failure to do so. What I have suggested here is that her recent work has made the anxieties of ageing women explicit but without fully acknowledging the processes involved or the tensions revealed. There are important issues here for an ageing population but feminist scholarship, the fashion industry and Sherman the artist have yet to engage fully with them. It is therefore time for the academy and the industry to acknowledge and address these social changes.

Interestingly, Sherman has now taken happily to Instagram where she posts images using the 'Facetune'app—designed to make the poster's features in a 'selfie' more conventionally attractive—in quite another way. She uses this and other 'apps' to turn her own face and body into grotesque images, where distorted faces are smeared with wildly applied makeup, evocative of her much earlier artwork. Here of course she reaches an entirely new audience. In April 2018, she posted several images from the retrospective exhibition of Dior couture garments in Paris. Most of the responses she received involved a flurry of enthusiastic superlatives and far too many heart-shaped emojis. But one follower commented tartly: 'Ladies who lunch have never changed the course of history'. The 'poster' here is referring, of course, to those rich women who wore the Dior couture of the past. Another, too, 'found it highly depressing … rich ladies—who did nothing—wore expensive dresses—once. Who cares, honestly?'

Sherman 'cares', obviously, offering her followers elegant clothes and grotesque images side by side—just as she has done in the recent portraits. What this also reveals is indicative of the complex way in which her attitudes towards fashion and the representation of women have altered. This is not only the result of her changing relationship with the fashion industry and celebrity culture but also her artistic negotiation of the realities of women's ageing, very different from her own 'successful' personal strategies; this in turn of course is symptomatic of a more general trend within feminism which needs to be addressed in scholarship and hopefully in the wider world.

Disclosure statement

No potential conflict of interest was reported by the author.

References

Adams, Tim. 2016. "Cindy Sherman: 'Why am I in these Photos?'" *The Observer*, July 3.
Brown, Laura. 2016. "Cindy Sherman: Street-Style Star." *Harper's Bazaar*, February 9.

Cain, Abigail. 2016. "A Brief History of Cindy Sherman and Feminism." *Artsy*, June 2. https://www.artsy.net/article/artsy-editorial-is-cindy-sherman-a-feminist.

Church Gibson, Pamela. 2000. "Redressing the Balance: Patriarchy, Postmodernism and Feminism." In *Fashion Cultures: Theories, Explorations, Analysis*, edited by Stella Bruzzi and Pamela Church Gibson, 349–363. London: Routledge.

Church Gibson, Pamela. 2012. *Fashion and Celebrity Culture*. London: Bloomsbury.

Church Gibson, Pamela. 2013. "Fashion, Fears and Ageing: Contradictions and Complexity Across the Media." In *Fashion Cultures Revisited*, edited by Stella Bruzzi, and Pamela Church Gibson, 322–339. London: Routledge.

Currid-Halkett, Elizabeth. 2008. *The Warhol Economy: How Fashion, Art and Music Drive New York*. New York: Princeton University Press.

De Beauvoir, Simone. 1949/1997. *The Second Sex*. London: Vintage Books.

De Beauvoir, Simone. 1970/1996. *The Coming of Age*. London: W.W. Norton and Co.

Dines, Gail. 2010. *Pornland: How Pornography Has Hijacked Our Sexuality*. Boston: Beacon Press.

Eckardt, Stephanie. 2016. "Cindy Sherman's Latest Guise: Extreme Vulnerability." *W Magazine*, May 3.

Freud, Sigmund. 1919/2003. *The Uncanny*. London: Penguin Books.

Friedan, Betty. 1993. *The Fountain of Age*. New York: Simon and Schuster.

Gager, James. 2016. "Interview." *Popsugar*, October 21. https://popsugar.com.au

Gopnik, Blake. 2016. "Cindy Sherman Takes on Aging (Her Own)." *New York Times*, April 21.

Greer, Germaine. 1992. *The Change: Women, Ageing and the Menopause*. London: Penguin Books.

Jermyn, Deborah. 2016. "Pretty Past-it? Interrogating the Post-Feminist Makeover of Ageing, Style, and Fashion." *Feminist Media Studies* 16 (4): 573–589.

Loreck, Hanne. 2002. "De/Constructing Fashion/Fashions of Deconstruction: Cindy Sherman's Fashion Photography." *Fashion Theory: The Journal of Dress, Body and Culture* 6 (3): 255–275.

Lynch, Annette. 2012. *Porn Chic: Exploring the Contours of Raunch Eroticism*. London: Bloomsbury.

Macdonald, Barbara. 1983. *Look Me in the Eye: Old Women, Ageing and Ageism*. San Francisco: Spinsters Ink.

McKinsey/Business of Fashion. 2018. *The State of Fashion* 2018. https://cdn.businessoffashion.com/reports/The_State_of_Fashion_2018_v2.pdf.

McRobbie, Angela. 1997. "Bridging the Gap: Feminism, Fashion and Consumption." *Feminist Review* 55: 73–89.

McRobbie, Angela. 1998. *British Fashion Design: Rag Trade or Image Industry?* London: Routledge.

McRobbie, Angela. 2008. *The Aftermath of Feminism: Gender, Culture and Social Change*. London: Sage.

Meagher, Michelle. 2014. "Against the Invisibility of Old Age: Cindy Sherman, Suzy Lake and Martha Wilson." *Feminist Studies* 40 (1): 101–143.

Mulvey, Laura. 1991. "Phantasmagoria of the Female Body: the Work of Cindy Sherman." *New Left Review* 188: 137–150.

Mulvey, Laura. 1996. *Fetishism and Curiosity: Cinema and the Mind's Eye*. London: BFI.

Negra, Diane. 2009. *What A Girl Wants*. London: Routledge.

Negra, Diane, and Yvonne Tasker. 2007. *Interrogating Postfeminism: Gender and the Politics of Popular Culture*. Durham: Duke University Press.

Parkins, Ilya. 2008. "Building a Feminist Theory of Fashion: Karen Barad's Agential Realism." *Australian Feminist Studies* 23 (58): 501–515.

Pedroni, Marco, and Paolo Volonté, eds. 2012. *Moda é Arte*. Milan: Franco Angeli.

Radner, Hilary. 2010. *Neo-Feminist Cinema: Girly Films, Chick Flicks and Consumer Culture*. London: Routledge.

Radner, Hilary, and Natalie Smith. 2013. "Fashion, Feminism and the Neo-Feminist Ideal." In *Fashion Cultures Revisited: Theories, Explorations, Analysis*, edited by Stella Bruzzi and Pamela Church Gibson, 275–287. London: Routledge.

Respini, Eva, Cindy Sherman, and Johanna Burton. 2012. *Cindy Sherman*. New York: Museum of Modern Art.

Ryan, Nicky. 2012. "Patronage." In *Fashion and Art*, edited by Adam Geczy and Vicki Karaminas, 155–169. London: Bloomsbury.

Schieren, Mona, and Andrea Sich, eds. 2011. *Look at Me: Celebrity Culture at The Venice Art Biennale*. Nűrnberg: Verlag fűr Moderne Kunst, Nűrnberg.

Segal, Lynne. 2014. *Out of Time: The Pleasures and Perils of Ageing*. London: Verso.

Slater, Meghan. 2016. "Cindy Sherman Embraces an Invitation from Fashion House Chanel." *Qagoma*, July 1. https://blog.qagoma.qld.gov.au/cindy-sherman-embraces-an-invitation-from-fashion-house-chanel/.

Solomon-Godeau, Abigail. 2017. *Photography After Photography: Gender, Genre, History*. Durham: Duke University Press.

Sontag, Susan. 1972. "The Double Standard of Ageing." The Saturday Review, September 23, 29–38.

Spencer, Shea. 2016. "The New Look: Art and Fashion Photograhy." *Artforum International* 9 (54): 240–271.

Steinem, Gloria. 2006. *Doing Sixty and Seventy*. San Francisco: Elders Academy Press.

Thornton, Sarah. 2009. *Seven Days in The Art World*. Cambridge: Granta.

Twigg, Julia. 2013. *Fashion and Age: Dress, the Body and Later Life*. London: Bloomsbury.

Williamson, Janice. 1983. "Images of 'Woman'." *Screen* 24 (6): 102–116.

Wilson, Elizabeth. 1985/2003. *Adorned in Dreams: Fashion and Modernity*. London: I.B.Tauris.

Wimsatt, K. W., and M. C. Beardsley. 1946. "The Intentional Fallacy." *The Sewanee Review* 54 (3): 468–488.

Woodward, Kath. 1999. *Figuring Age: Women, Bodies, Generations*. Bloomington: Indiana University Press.

Fashionable 'Formation': Reclaiming the Sartorial Politics of Josephine Baker

Jennifer Sweeney-Risko

ABSTRACT
This article historicises Josephine Baker's use of fashion in terms of contemporary black stage performers, particularly Beyoncé Knowles-Carter's evolving black feminist politics. It examines Beyoncé's references to Baker as an inspiration for her own black feminist art and argues that they offer an opportunity to re-examine Baker's legacy in our own contemporary moment. Using Beyoncé's arguments about Baker as a starting point, the article examines Baker's fashions and costumes and argues that she used them to manipulate her relationship to the models of white supremacy that attempted to structure her identity and relationship to the public sphere. Using contemporary black feminist criticisms of respectability politics, it argues that Baker's fashions produced a politics of disrespectability, where clothing and body worked together to carve out space for black feminist experimentation. By constantly changing the terms through which her audiences and the public read her, Baker carved out a subjective space where she could *become* in relation to her clothes without restraining herself to the identity categories normatively allotted to black women.

During the 2006 Fashion Rocks live television broadcast, Beyoncé Knowles stepped onstage in a sparkling banana skirt. The skirt, consisting of a fitted waistband and a series of stuffed, sequined bananas, clearly referenced Josephine Baker's famous 1926 skit at the Folies Bergère. In the costume, Beyoncé danced a remixed version of Baker's routine and sang a song from her new album, *B' Day*, entitled 'Déjà vu'. As if the skirt and the song's title weren't enough, images of Baker's face, flashed across the backdrop, directly signaling Beyoncé's homage to the 1920s dancer (Figure 1).

In an interview before the Fashion Rocks concert on *Good Morning America*, Beyoncé outright proclaimed her desire to live and perform such as Baker. She said, referencing the creation of *B'Day* and 'Déjà vu', that 'I wanted to be more such as Josephine Baker because she didn't – she seemed such as if she was just possessed, and it seemed such as if she just danced from her heart, and everything was so free' (quoted in Francis 2007). Beyoncé imagines and commends Baker's seeming ability to possess her own body, to control her image despite the racial contours of the lens through which her

Figure 1. Beyoncé performs at the 3rd annual 'Fashion Rocks' concert at Radio City Music Hall, 7 September 2006. Image: Timothy A. Clary/AFP/Getty Images.

audience read her. As scholar Terri Francis argues about the interview, 'Beyoncé sought to capture Baker's dance practice, which is characterised by total movement, a sense of possession … and unpredictability, controlled with her own bodily intelligence' (Francis 2007).

That Beyoncé chose to reference the banana skirt and Josephine Baker's dancing as inspiration for her own quest for personal and performative freedom in the *Good Morning America* interview indicates that we may want to take a second look at the controversial dancer. Critics of Baker have been quick to point out that her performances allowed her to profit off of racist stereotypes by creating fantasies of white colonial encounters.[1] Her costumes, such as the banana skirt, and erotic dancing did invoke primitivist visions of an imagined African Jungle. Yet, perhaps, as Beyoncé alluded to in her interview and performance, Baker also offers new ways to imagine black feminine freedom. As Anne Anlin Cheng argues, Baker's public persona changed how Europeans viewed and interpreted racial difference (Cheng 2013, 4–5). This version of black femininity, informed by the racial categories imposed by European imperialism, in part produced the mania for all things considered 'black' that infected the western world during the 1920s and 30s.

Primitivism, a white supremacist ideology popular in Europe at the height of Baker's celebrity, characterised her as savage, overly erotic and unable to fully adapt to the speed and complexity of modern, Western life. The ideology more generally interpreted black bodies and cultures in terms of a 'primitive' African past, one that was innocent of the horrors of modern, industrialised living categorised by events such as World War I and the rise of industrialisation. As Marianna Torgovnick explains, primitivism produced an Other westerners could use to re-imagine themselves. Primitives were 'children ... mystics, in tune with nature, part of its harmonies. They exist at the "lowest cultural levels ... "' (Torgovnick 1990, 8). In creating such a dichotomy between white and black, civilised and savage, primitivism allowed white Westerners to indulge in what they saw was freeing in black culture, including a more open model of sexual expression. Audiences enjoyed Baker's topless dancing and references to Africa in her dance routines because they considered the supposed culture she portrayed to be both backward, yet more in tune with the body and the earth.

However, as Beyoncé's comments in her interview reference, Baker's dancing and costumes do more than just reiterate primitivism for mass consumption. Viewed through Beyoncé's homage, they represent a styling of black femininity that can free itself from the constraints historically placed on black women. Taking a second look at how Baker dressed on and off stage indicates that her relationship to her clothing shifted the terrain of signification through which her identity could be read. Her off-stage fashions and interactions with the fashion industry, coupled with her often improvised, syncopated dancing and outrageous costumes, produce what Brittney Cooper names a politics of 'disrespectability' (Cooper 2017b, 184). Disrespectability politics acknowledge that respectability politics, the black strategy for equality based upon conservative, middle class white values, damages black women's ability to express themselves fully. Beyoncé's comments allow us to re-imagine Baker's use of her attire and costumes as intervening in the way in which black respectability politics and white primitivism traditionally viewed black femininity. Baker's act constantly shifted the terrain through which her audiences and the public read her, giving her more space to more freely express herself.

Viewing Baker's fashions and dancing through the lens of Beyoncé's comments opens space for us to re-examine her legacy in our own contemporary moment, a moment where black feminism has assertively entered the mainstream media. Celebrities such as Beyoncé have begun to use their platform to speak out pointedly against the oppression that black women have historically suffered under white supremacy. Using Beyoncé's references to Baker and her own development of a radical style of black feminism later in *Lemonade*, this article re-examines Baker's legacy in terms of the potential strategies for black feminine expression it offers. That Beyoncé sang on tour with the word 'Feminist' emblazoned across the stage and then did the same with Baker's face and costumes speaks to how Baker's freedom of movement and sartorial risks inspire black women in the contemporary present. Beyoncé's homage asks us to rethink our understanding of Baker, and more radically, the way that the sartorial can refigure damaging perceptions of the black feminine body.

Get in formation: Beyoncé and Baker's black feminist performance

Before re-examining Baker's fashions and costumes, it is important to note just how she inspired Beyoncé. As a global pop phenomenon, Beyoncé's articulation of black feminist thought offers a great indicator of how, more generally, the public experiences and comprehends issues of gender and sexuality. As Hobson (2017) explains, celebrity articulations of feminism – such as Beyoncé's – theorise 'critical issues pertaining to gender and its intersections with race and class for a mass audience' (1000). Beyoncé's repeated conversations about feminism determine and are determined by the ways in which the mass media express the fight for gender equality. Just as she is inspired by people such as Baker, the media and audiences who consume her music are in turn affected by her message. The worldwide platform through which Beyoncé speaks offers her a unique position through which to voice and explore issues of gender and sexuality, making her comments and tributes to Baker an important part of the larger conversations about black feminism that are happening right now.[2]

Given Beyoncé's centrality to these conversations concerning black feminism, it is important to follow her evolving understanding of the movement. Her 2006 homage to Baker demonstrates her progression into a radical version of black feminist politics that can be traced back to her work with Destiny's Child and early solo albums.[3] However, her 2016 music video for 'Formation' shows most notably the growth of her black feminist thought. In the video, Beyoncé responds to the media's worries about the blackness of her daughter's hair and nose and draws a firm affiliation to her black and creole Southern heritage. Beyoncé's unapologetic declaration of her love for her daughter's afro and husband's facial features loudly stands against the media's racism and speaks to a larger stance against white supremacist interpretations of black bodies.[4] Black feminist Griffiths (2017) explains that 'Formation' acts as a rallying call for black women to acknowledge unapologetically the beauty of their bodies. For Griffiths, the song indicates a progression of Beyoncé's legacy of fusing together black bodies, fashionable aesthetics and black feminist politics.

Moreover, that Beyoncé's 'Formation' video is set in New Orleans speaks to her emerging dedication to working class, Southern black culture. Images of the city's impoverished black neighbourhoods and spaces cut across the different scenes in the video, with a camera surveillance style of filming that makes the viewer feel like an outsider. Amidst images of dilapidated buildings, flooded out streets, and a large police presence alluding to Hurricane Katrina, Beyoncé sits on top of a drowned police car and announces her pride in her Southern heritage: 'My daddy Alabama, momma Louisiana, You mix that negro with that Creole make a Texas bamma' (Brown, Hogan, Will Made It, Knowles-Carter 2016). In this scene, she unapologetically proclaims her black womanhood from a position of power normatively ascribed to white men, police. Even when the car inevitably sinks into the flood waters, Beyoncé's body indicates her agency. She spreads out her arms and legs over the cruiser and holds her breath as if to push the car – the police state – under. The car and her body sink, but her body's position signals to the viewer that it is she who drowns the vehicle.

The mise en scène of 'Formation' with the drowned cruiser acts to remix primitivism for contemporary politics, more specifically, the politics of racial primitivism that informed descriptions of the suffering of the black community in Katrina. For journalism scholar Hemant Shah, the news media's coverage of the hurricane depicted black citizens with language akin to that of late nineteenth and early twentieth century primitivism, the same ideology that framed Baker's rise to fame. He argues that 'the easy confluence the [conservative news media] see between the terms *breed, creatures*, and *law of the jungle* with notions of primitive violence and lawlessness evokes Hegel's formulation of the "savage Negro" as "animal-man"' (Shah 2009, 8). The media's language echoes the types of descriptions early twentieth century primitivism used to define black populations: backward, savage, and less evolved than the whites around them. For example, news coverage after the levees broke in New Orleans characterised its black residents as a 'different breed' from the white Americans who fled the oncoming storm ("Take Back New Orleans" 2005, 2). Black citizens of New Orleans were characterised as less evolved and therefore less human in comparison to the whites who left the city before the flood.

However, Beyoncé flips the script on the media's primitivist readings of New Orleans' black community in the 'Formation' video, making the city a place where black femininity flourishes because it is categorised as primitive. For example, split between the scenes of drowned houses and the police car is one where Beyoncé and her backup dancers dance in unison in a disused swimming pool. The pool appears closed, with darkened lights that indicate that the women might be trespassing. However, instead of demonstrating the women's criminality, the pool's emptiness instead draws attention to the space it creates for them to express themselves outside of the devastation. The women's dance and costumes further demonstrate how the scene flips primitivist tropes about Katrina on their head. They dance in formation in Gucci jumpsuits, showing off their bodies and hair. It is as if, within the history of colonising discourse associated with discussions of the hurricane, the women find a way to express themselves positively, even going as far as to show that they too have the means to indulge in designer clothing despite the devastation around them.

Even beyond the Gucci jumpsuits that Beyoncé and the other dancers wear in the pool, the clothing she wears when standing on top of the police cruiser further demonstrate the radical version of black feminism she is working through in the video. On the car, Beyoncé wears a red shirt dress and clean black boots, which speak to the control she has over herself and the community. More specifically, the outfit seems to reference the Student Non-Violent Coordinating Committee, or SNCC. Created in the 1960s, the SNCC consisted of students who would travel through the American south planning freedom rides, sit-ins, voter registration drives, etc. According to Ford (2015), SNCC members began to wear blue jeans and simple dresses while working in the South in order to replicate the attire of the black working class (68).

The SNCC's simplified uniform flew in the face of the black middle class's strategy of black respectability politics, where black women were expected to behave and dress in line with the white middle class. Evelyn Brooks Higginbotham defines respectability politics as an African American ideology that imagines a route toward racial liberation through the values and morals of white middle class culture (Higginbotham 1995, 16). If, respectability politics insists, black communities would just imitate the morals and beliefs of their white middle class counterparts, they would be treated with more respect. Black women are supposed to, for example, dress modestly, perform the duties of a model housewife, and refrain from sexual activity outside of marriage. Like Beyoncé in the video, however, the SNCC chose not to follow the gendered tenets of respectability politics. Instead, they chose their attire to show solidarity with the black poor of the American South.

It is important to note that the SNCC and Beyoncé herself are not members of the black working class. Although Beyoncé grew up in Houston and some members of the SNCC came from the South, their middle to upper class lifestyles starkly separate them from those with whom they claim solidarity. Beyoncé was not drastically affected by Hurricane Katrina and the SNCC could always take their jeans off if they wanted to blend back in with the black middle class. Even more starkly, the dress Beyoncé wears on top of the police cruiser, like the jumpsuit she wears while dancing in the pool, is a Gucci design (Carlos

2016). Even within the lens of 'Formation's' celebration of the South's black poor, Beyoncé stands apart because of the massive wealth that she has acquired.

However, we need to measure Beyoncé's celebrity and wealth exemplified in the Gucci clothes that she wears in 'Formation' through the history of racial and gendered oppression that she alludes to in the video. Yes, Beyoncé has class privilege that those who suffered during Hurricane Katrina did not. Her celebrity affords her a public platform that other less privileged black women do not have. Yet, given the many allusions to slavery in 'Formation', Beyoncé's wealth must be interpreted through the history of African American oppression. For example, spliced between the cop car scene stands a few others, most notably that of a Southern plantation. Dressed in a style that pays homage to the American antebellum period, Beyoncé sits respectfully in what appears to be a parlour room filled with other, similarly well-dressed people. Her attire and the location of this scene reminds us that for vast periods of American history, and still today, black women were and are still considered objects that can be acquired in the capitalist marketplace. Saidiya Hartman explains that, as slaves, black women could not accrue wealth themselves but became fungible symbols of capitalist accumulation (Hartman 2008, 2). So, when Beyoncé dresses in the Gucci dress or jumpsuit, she does so with the knowledge that she herself can accumulate wealth, that the civil rights movement made it possible for her to become wealthy, instead of an object of wealth made for white ownership.

Tracing Beyoncé's aesthetics – from her allusion to Baker at Fashion Rocks to radically proclaiming her black, Southern womanhood in 'Formation' – enables us to see her development of what Brittney Cooper calls 'ratchet acts' (Cooper 2017b, 218). She explains that 'ratchet acts are meant to be so over-the-top and outrageous that they catch your attention and exceed the bounds of acceptable saying' (218). They throw disrespect in the viewer's face and revel in the negative reaction such an act elicits. Beyoncé's reveling on top of the drowned cruiser or flaunting her body in the empty pool offers an example of a ratchet act as she celebrates her power over the white police state.

In her analysis of ratchet politics, Cooper argues that ratchet representations of black womanhood such as Beyoncé's take a stand not only against models of white supremacy, such as primitivism, that seek to silence black women but also against the history of black respectability politics that forces black women to take subordinate positions in the fight for racial equality (Cooper 2017b, 219). In response, Cooper advocates for a politics of 'disrespectability', where black women,

> must consider the potential in the space between the diss and the respect—the potential (and the danger) of what it means to dis(card) respectability altogether. This space between the disses we get and the respect we seek is the space in which Black women live our lives. It is the crunk place, the percussive place, the place that makes noise (and music), the place that moves us, the place that offers possibility in the midst of two impossible extremes. (184)

Disrespectability politics acknowledge that the black community's trust in respectability has left black women vulnerable to violence. It also acknowledges that abandoning the ideology will require them to expose themselves to potentially more violence as they engage in more radically open challenges to white supremacy. A disrespectable black feminist embraces the ratchet, snaps respectable notions of black femininity, and celebrates the disturbance despite the potential for violent backlash.

Cooper attributes Beyoncé's disrespectable, ratchet politics in 'Formation' to her choice to draw from and celebrate her Southern, black and Creole heritage. However, Beyoncé's allusion to Baker may speak to another inspiration. That Beyoncé pointed to Baker's freedom of movement and vibrant fashions as an inspiration for her album, *B'Day*, shows how she studied the dancer in the evolution of her politics in 'Formation'. In 'Formation', Beyoncé shows the freedom of expression that she read in Baker's fashions and dancing. For Beyoncé, Baker assertively commanded her audiences on and off the stage with her dancing and fashions. Perhaps, using Beyoncé's references and allusions to Baker as a guide, we might say that Baker too created a politics of disrespectability that allowed her to claim her own place in the public sphere.

Baker's ratchet: rethinking primitivism through disrespectability politics

Through the lens of Beyoncé's reading of her, we might argue that Baker's dancing and fashions provided her with a means to exist in between the diss(respect) black women often received in terms of Europe's history of colonial racism and the respect she desired (and often acquired) as a talented black dancer. Born in St. Louis, Missouri, in 1906, Baker travelled to Paris in 1925 to escape the violence of US segregation norms.[5] Once in France, she quickly became one of the most highly paid celebrities in Europe as her white audiences couldn't get enough of her personality and performance style. She used her immense salary and celebrity to accumulate couture fashions and was often seen walking in the latest trends down the Champs-Élysées with her cheetah, Chiquita. In doing so, Baker took advantage of Europe's obsession with Africa and black peoples to carve out a public identity for herself that black women could not normally perform.

Baker's route to fame progressed along the lines of the transatlantic network of black artistic production that developed during the beginnings of the twentieth century. As Europe and the US developed into industrialised economies, white populations began to rely on primitive images of blackness to combat the objectifying logic of modern, global capitalism. As Archer-Straw (2000) argues, the French in Paris, in particular, developed what she coins 'negrophilia,' or 'a love for black culture' (9). For Negrophiles, the primitivist fantasy was that blackness embodied what the modern world had lost: a collective life governed by sensual instincts instead of a bureaucratic life driven by technologies of efficiency and profit. Baker's dancing offered one of these outlets – many reviews of her performances emphasised the natural blackness of her body's motion. For example, in Andre Levinson's review of La Revue Nègre, Baker's first show in Paris, he compared her dancing and costumes to the 'magnificent animality' of 'Negro sculpture' (quoted in Rose 1989, 31).

In representing Africa as developmentally regressive and morally vacant, primitivism placed it in a time lag behind the West. As Sieglinde Lemke explains, the ideology froze the continent into antiquity (Lemke 1998).[6] Separated by geography and the ugly contours of scientific racism, primitivism imagined Africa as a space where white Europeans could go to let loose and fulfil fantasies normally barred by European norms and morals.

The apparently freeing aspects of primitivist interpretations of Africa and black cultures for white cultural consumers hinged on the portrayal of black women as sexually exotic, with an animal-like eroticism. For Sharpley-Whiting (1999), primitivism encouraged white populations to view black women as having pre-modern sexualities because it allowed them to enjoy and consume black culture while still adhering to the racial dichotomy that separated whites from blacks (24–25). Baker's banana skirt offers an example of primitivism's depiction of black femininity. Topless on stage, her gyrating body, in part, represented the primitive sexuality and availability of black women. White audiences could enjoy her erotic display without exposing themselves in the dark theatres where she performed.

While many cultural and economic sectors, such as the entertainment industry, promoted primitivist interpretations of black femininity, fashion played a prominent role. The streamlined, drop waist aesthetic most often depicted as popular 1920s fashions encapsulated by the designs of those such as Coco Chanel, Madeleine Vionnet and Jean Patou after World War I demonstrate fashion's relationship to the ideology.[7] Historian Victoria Rovine (2009) explains that the fashion industry actively pilfered from the French colonial imaginary during the interwar period to produce its depictions of the chic, fashionable New Woman. According to Rovine, New Women could use fashion's primitivist representation of black femininity to fuel their own sexual liberation.

Desiring a way to construct their bodies and live beyond the confines of Western, industrialised society, New Women turned to primitivist fashions because they represented the allure of Africa, encapsulated by black women's supposed animalistic sexualities. By returning to an imaginary past symbolised in primitivist representations of Africa, the trend allowed white women to feel ultra-modern. For example, according to fashion historian Susan Hannel (2005), the 1920s signature drop waist, fringe style dress looks remarkably like a stereotypical African grass skirt (71). These skirts were famously seen at French colonial expositions, such as the one held in Paris in 1925, the year that Baker would break into her first 'Danse Sauvage' in La Revue Nègre.[8] A cover of *Life* magazine from 15 July 1926, offers an example of the relationship between the New Women's shortened skirt and primitivist interpretations of Africa. In the forefront of the picture, a woman with cropped hair and a drop waist, pleated skirt dances the Charleston. The background portrays a repeated image of a primitivist rendition of an African warrior, complete with grass skirt and spear. The warriors dance in the same manner as the flapper and repeat the movements of her body. As Hannel argues, the repetition between the black men and the white woman in the picture emphasises the relationship between her fashionable attire and unleashed primitive allure (70) (Figure 2).

The repetition between the white woman and black men in the *Life* cover also represents the New Woman's gendered liberation. Not only does she perform a sexually alluring dance in front of black men, but those men step in line with her, mimicking her movements. In doing so, the image shows how the new women used primitivism to fight for gender equality as well as sexual liberation. The men stand in the background, emphasising the white woman's movements but do not join her. They must be content to dramatise the backdrop of her rise to prominence – it is she who dances the Charleston at the forefront.

Although *Life* magazine is an American publication, the way that the cover represents popular style shows how European primitivism and American racism worked together to create the New Woman's sexually and gendered liberated representation on both sides of the Atlantic. The dress style depicted in the image, reminiscent of a Coco Chanel dress, demonstrates that French fashion migrated across the Atlantic into American

Figure 2. Cover of *Life* magazine, 15 July 1926.

understandings of style.⁹ Furthermore, the image represents blackness in terms of its primitivist connotations but the dancing itself emerged out of an African American context. The white woman in the picture dances the Charleston, which was first popularised in the hit Broadway musical *Runnin' Wild*. However, the image also references European primitivist representations of Africa with its repeated drawings of black men in grass skirts. The combination of primitivist motif and the African American dance throws into relief the ways that the fashion industry sidestepped America's history of racism and slavery in its representations of black culture in preference for a more exotic rendering of African American and African art.

By connecting popular African American dance culture to orientalist motifs already made famous by those like Poiret in the 1910s, 1920s designers such as Chanel, Patou and Vionnet popularised African American dance culture for white audiences while simultaneously severing such a promotion from any liberating potential.¹⁰ Following larger social trends, the fashion industry instead equated diasporic black communities to Europe's African colonies and, in so doing, erased any geographical particularity from representations of black culture. This helped the 1920s primitivist trend gain popularity among white women. It allowed them to engage in the sexual promiscuity primitivism attributed to black femininity without forcing them to identify with the realities or histories of black oppression, giving them, in turn, access to the type of gendered empowerment that made them feel superior to black men.

The *Life* cover's conflation of African American music culture with European primitivism helps to explain Baker's immense popularity in Europe. Baker first gained popularity in France in La Revue Nègre, first performed at the Théâtre des Champs-Élysées in Paris in

1925. The show was modelled after African American vaudeville reviews and was meant to introduce the French to American theatrical portrayals of black culture. Caroline Dudley Reagan, its producer, commissioned the performance because she wanted to bring an African American Broadway musical, such as the popular *Shuffle Along*, to the French stage. However, when Reagan's chosen performers, pulled from Harlem and New York City, began practising in Paris, she quickly realised that French audiences would not appreciate the racial stereotyping that American audiences enjoyed. There was too much minstrelsy and not enough of the sexual promiscuity that the French had begun to associate with black culture.

To adjust the show's American slant closer to a French one, Reagan called in a new director, Jacques Charles, who 'translated' the review for a French audience. Although there are conflicting accounts about Charles's role in Le Revue Nègre and the amount of authority he had over production, most historians agree that he did work to reinscribe the skits with primitivist ideas. Henry Louis Gates and Kate Dalton, for example, explain that Charles made the show more 'African' by 'placing less emphasis on tap dancing and spirituals and more on Josephine Baker's phenomenal ability to dance suggestively' (Gates 1998, 913). In doing so, Charles added the 'Danse Sauvage,' a highly eroticised number where Baker and her partner, Joe Alex, danced to 'jungle music' clad in feathered loincloths' (913). La Revue Nègre would also be the first time Baker appeared barebreasted, at Charles's recommendation.

Charles's primitivist alterations to La Revue Nègre propelled Baker to Parisian stardom as audiences flocked to see her perform. Her celebrity and representation in popular culture, in turn, encouraged France's designers to pay attention to her, hoping to use her image to advertise their primitivist designs. Many, such as Vionnet, gave her extravagant gifts of couture clothing to wear to public events to further advertise their current lines (Jules-Rosette 2007, 144). Jules-Rosette explains that in 1926 alone, Poiret gifted Baker 285,000 francs worth of clothes and furs (143). Poiret's slowly diminishing popularity, coupled with his already vested interest in the global south marked by his Orientalist designs, made Baker the perfect model for his clothes; he hoped to use her to bolster sales.

As Beyoncé alluded to in her Fashion Rocks performance and interview, Baker's own interest and participation in fashion speak a different message than that of white interpretations of her. Although her performances did enact a primitivist stance, like Beyoncé, her choreography and choice of attire on and offstage rearticulated the ideology to make space for subjective movement. Baker's unconventional, often improvised (one could say ratchet) dancing style allowed her to prevent any totalised image of her from taking hold.[11] As Daphne Brooks argues, Baker 'was able to turn the static body of black female sexual exploitation into a dynamic, mobile enterprise' (2007) by using improvised dancing and humorous body movements to consistently prevent her audience from stereotyping her. For Brooks, Baker's comedic rendering of the primitive allowed her to create not only parodies of primitivist understandings of black femininity but also gave her the means to carve out her own space to imagine herself in the public sphere. Set between the racist disrespect she experienced in Europe and the United States and the respect she longed for as a professional dancer, she used her clothes and costumes to create a disrespectability politics that gave her the space necessary to explore her identity on her own terms.

The banana skirt that Beyoncé alludes to in her 2006 Fashion Rocks performance in and of itself demonstrates the line that Baker walked between diss and respect. As in Beyoncé's 'Formation' video, the video of Baker's banana skirt dance similarly shows a disrespectful attitude about respectable norms and white culture. Shown as a before-show short in movie theatres in the United States and Europe, the clip depicts an African jungle scene complete with thick foliage and a large tree branch that hung above the stage. Below the branch, black men with drums pound out a beat while a white explorer sleeps beside a tent at the edge of the stage. Baker enters in the banana skirt crouched down from on high on the branch and goes over to inspect the explorer. Seeing him asleep, she begins her dance. The dance and its corresponding skirt shocked audiences because of their lack of coverage – the black woman showed all for those who paid to see (Figure 3).

However, the skirt and dance also muddle what appear at first glance as racist and misogynistic overtones because the signifiers are left undefined. It is unclear what the bananas in Baker's skirt represent or even who she is dancing for because the white explorer sleeps through her dance. For Cheng (2013), it is impossible to define the fetishistic qualities of the dance or the costume because the signifiers seem to fly in many directions at once, preventing any sort of totalised image of colonial desire from ever taking hold. For example, Cheng argues that the banana skirt by itself delivered racialised femininity for white audiences 'armed with a ring of embarrassingly fruitful phalluses' that made it impossible to tell if the audience was supposed to desire the bananas, or the lack thereof underneath (46). And, for Cheng, because of the skirt's phallic nature, one

Figure 3. Josephine Baker in costume for her famous 'banana dance'. Image: Walery/Getty Images.

may read the skit as potentially homoerotic, with the white man dreaming of the African phallus, or alternatively, of the fact that the primitive eroticism of black femininity stems from its potentially masculine nature (46).

Using Cheng's interpretation of Baker's banana skirt routine, it becomes clear why Beyoncé might focus on the dancer as an inspiration for her own disrespectable politics. Baker appears in control of her body in the clip, and because it is difficult to decipher the ways in which her audiences were supposed to read the skit and skirt, one can imagine that she had some space through which to play with her identity on stage. It is through this play that we might see Baker's version of disrespectability politics. For example, much like Beyoncé's own dancing on top of the police cruiser in 'Formation', the phallic nature of the bananas on the skirt could demonstrate Baker's potential power over the sleeping explorer. Although we can assume that he is in the jungle to fulfill a white fantasy about black feminine sexuality, she will not give him the pleasure of submission. It is she who wears the phallus, she who openly thrusts in the direction of the white man, and she who decides who can gain pleasure from her movements. Furthermore, Baker's dancing (and the phallic skirt) seem to show her interest in exploring her own sexuality despite the restraints placed upon her by the white coloniser. She doesn't even look at him while she shakes the skirt, let alone lay with him as he sleeps. She seems to turn inward, refusing to acknowledge anything but the pleasure she receives from the dance.

Baker's intimate interactions with Paris' couture industry further speaks to how Beyoncé may have seen her as an inspiration for her own disrespectable politics. Looking at Baker's relationship with Poiret in particular allows us to imagine her actions as a retooling of primitivism, one that gave her room to imagine her identity beyond the constraints of white supremacy. For example, when Caroline Reagan first introduced Baker to Poiret, various accounts detail their meeting in his salon.[12] Some biographies, such as Bennetta Jules-Rosette's, indicate that Poiret manipulated the power dynamics between them to control her. She narrates that on their first meeting, Poiret stripped Baker naked in front of the rest of his white models (Jules-Rosette 2007, 142).

However, Jean-Claude Baker and Chris Chase tell a different version of Baker's first meeting with Poiret in *Josephine Baker: The Hungry Heart*. Written from the perspective of her unofficially adopted son Jean-Claude Baker, the book oscillates between loving admiration for Baker and a damning sense of neglect. Even so, this ambivalence produces one of the best researched biographies of Baker because it is clear from the first page that Jean-Claude desperately wants to know the truth about her. In order to find out this truth, Jean-Claude sought out interviews with those who knew Baker best, including Caroline Reagan, Paul Colins, even members of the band who travelled with her to Paris for the first time.

The evidence that Jean-Claude provides about Poiret's first meeting with Baker offers a uniquely intimate take on the situation. It is important to consider that he directly quotes Caroline Reagan when explaining what happened when Baker first met Poiret. This direct quotation provides a level of authenticity and detail that other accounts lack. Even beyond the direct quote, Jean-Claude explains that in multiple instances, Reagan's relationship to Baker and Baker's dancing has been erased in other accounts in preference for stories about the men in her life. For example, he argues that Reagan had much more control over Le Revue Nègre's French translation than many presume and that it was her decision to take Baker to Poiret, not Paul Colin's. Reagan's recollections indicate that we should take seriously his argument that not only did Reagan first bring Baker to Poiret but that she also did not sit quietly for the aging king of fashion.

Jean-Claude's articulation of Baker's first meeting with Poiret focuses on the dancer's stubborn insistence on controlling her style. Quoting Reagan, he explains that on meeting Poiret, Baker refused all of the designs that he recommended. Instead, she 'asked for a piece of paper and a pencil; she drew, while laughing. She wanted fringe from the shoulders to the hem, light pink at the top, shading to dark at the bottom' (Baker and Chase 2001, 120). She named her design 'American Beauty' (120). Given that by the mid 1920s Poiret's designs were falling out of style, it makes sense that he would allow Baker to take control of the design process. Perhaps he hoped to appease her enough to wear his fashions because he desperately needed the free advertising. Or, alternatively, given his history of helping burgeoning designers, he allowed her to try her hand at dress creation.[13] Either way, it is clear that Baker got the upper hand in the meeting: she refused to submit to his ideas and, because she knew what she wanted to look like, forcefully asked for it.

Baker's choice to draw and name her own design for Poiret in Jean-Claude Baker's account speaks to the style of disrespectability politics that she created through her clothes. She does not let Poiret push her around but uses their meeting to get the exact dress that she wants. Clearly, given the other accounts of this meeting, we can presume that Poiret hoped that Baker would get naked and let him dress her. Her age, gender, and race placed her in a less powerful position than the designer, who, despite his failing celebrity, still commanded a sizeable group of fans. Yet, she snapped the code of respectable behaviour that Poiret expected of her by laughing instead of bowing down to his recommendations.

Moreover, that Baker drew her desired gown with fringe from head to toe draws attention to her use of primitivism to break normative depictions of black feminine sexuality. The fringe and colour recall her popular Danse Sauvage, where the pink, feathered loincloth that she wore emphasised her body's freedom of movement and exoticism. However, her insistence on designing and naming the dress 'American Beauty' also shows how it represented her history, her migration from US chorus girl into European celebrity, instead of the primitivist relationship to Africa through which her audience viewed her. In naming the dress, Baker seems to argue that she is not a primitive African but a modern, successful American capable of designing styles even better than Poiret. She calls attention to her actual heritage, much like Beyoncé's proud claiming of her own in 'Formation'. Calling out those such as Andre Levinson, whose reviews compared her to African sculpture, Baker proudly claims her own history and names it beautiful. Perhaps her actions may not appear as forward or as radical as Beyoncé's in 'Formation', but her willingness to create her own fashions in front of Poiret still demonstrate the type of snapping that Cooper (2017a, 2017b, 2017c) describes when she writes about disrespectability politics. Like Beyoncé's declaration of her 'Texas-bamma' heritage, with 'American Beauty' Baker disrespectfully proclaims her African American background and celebrates how beautiful it is.

Baker in the now: a call for a disrespectable future

Beyoncé's callback to Baker in her performance and interview provides us with a new lens through which to interpret the dancer today. It asks us to explore how, through fashion and performance, Baker reimagined herself and resisted the normative, white supremacist representations of black women. On stage, Baker's costumes brought into play the relationship between her African American body, white European colonialism, and the fashion industry's reliance on primitivism for the production of its fashions. This left her audiences begging for more of her dancing and fashions, which, in turn, gave her the means to disrespectfully decline their requests for her to fulfil the primitivist type through which they read her.

Beyoncé's reference to Baker, and subsequently, her more radically black feminist performance in 'Formation' demonstrates how Baker's fashions and dancing inspire black feminist experimentation in the contemporary moment. Like Baker, Beyoncé must navigate a similar binary political landscape, one where black women are over-sexualised, yet expected to act submissively. Baker's energy, her freedom of movement and seeming ability to choose her own presentation in the public sphere, acted as a catalyst to propel Beyoncé into the radical black feminism that she performed in 'Formation' and *Lemonade*. Beyoncé asks us to take a second look at Baker and contemplate what she might add to current discussions about black feminism. It seems, going by Beyoncé's example, that looking back to Baker might help us question notions of respectability that still keep black women in submissive subject positions today. Folding time on itself, Baker and Beyoncé's dancing and costumes disrespectfully say 'Enough!' to white racism and sexism. Unable to act politely in the face of white, primitivist violence, they do what they must to demonstrate the value of their desires, bodies, and very selves. Perhaps, as Beyoncé's song lyrics imply, Baker's influence over her might encourage other black feminists to 'get in formation' and make their own ratchet sartorial and performance choices in pursuit of a more radically disrespectful future.

Notes

1. In *Josephine Baker in Art and Life: The Icon and the Image,* Jules-Rosette argues that even though Baker eventually achieved a modicum of control over her image, her initial performances in Paris relied on and perpetuated the types of racial stereotyping the French had begun to associate with French femininity. She played up the 'sexual savage' stereotype to gain popularity in the French theatre scene (129). hooks (2014), in *Black Looks: Race and Representation,* explains that this type of stereotype harkens back to Sarah Baartman, the African 'hottentot venus' put on display in France as an oddity because of her large buttocks (123).
2. Even within the academic black feminist community, Beyoncé's articulation of her style of feminism has set off some rather controversial debates. bell hooks for example, described her as a 'terrorist' and an 'anti-feminist' at a talk at the New School (quoted in Trier-Bieniek 2016, 1). hooks's declaration of Beyoncé's negative role in the fight for black feminist equality, in turn, caused other black feminists such as Hobson (2016) to defend Beyoncé, arguing that academic black feminists must evolve to embrace the more publicly minded articulations of the movement that might not be couched in academic language or packaged in respectable attire or actions (21). In either case, this debate signals to Beyoncé's importance to the future of black feminism. Her voice and persona matters to the movement, even if, in the case of bell hooks, it might be considered detrimental.
3. For more information on Destiny's Child and black feminism, see Weidhase (2015).
4. Beyoncé uses this line to most probably respond to the media's relentless criticism of her daughter's natural hair. As Eggert (2016) argues, the internet had teased the girl for her matted, unruly hair for years, even creating a change.org petition to encourage Beyoncé and Jay Z to comb it.

5. Rose (1989) explains that Baker's recollection of the St. Louis race riots of 1917 propelled her to Europe – not only did she fear racial violence but choosing to leave gave her a feeling of control over her surroundings (15).
6. Jordan (1995) describes this time lag as a 'turning away from modernity' in order to shield oneself from the horrors it created (282). For Jordan, early twentieth century primitivism described Africa and its peoples as less evolved than the West because the West needed a space to hide in that did not get devastated by modern capitalism or the brutal warfare that defined World War I.
7. In a 2016 exhibition entitled 'Flapper Style: 1920s Fashion', The Kent State Fashion Museum argued that change social norms, encapsulated by a growing population of women who engaged in sports activities and more hands-on jobs 'required simplified and streamlined fashions, whether dancing the night away or spending the day on the links. Generally, the fashion of the decade was a tubular silhouette enhanced with pleats, panels, and fringe'.
8. For more information on the design aspects of the French colonial expositions, see Finamore (2015).
9. In the early parts of the twentieth century, American fashion retailers still preferred to sell French designs because consumers considered them the height of fashionable attire. For more information about the relationship between French and American fashion, see Evans (2013).
10. For more information about Poiret's orientalist fashions, see Pham (2013).
11. Kraut (2007) argues that, although Baker often worked with some of the best choreographers available to her, she would 'forget her lines' and come up with improvised, emotionally charged moves right on the spot.
12. Biographies, such as Jules-Rosette's, debate whether or not Reagan introduced Baker to Poiret at all (2007, 142). There is some evidence that Paul Colins first took her to see the designer but much of that evidence is made up from quotes from Colins, who may have wanted to claim responsibility for their relationship.
13. For more information about Poiret's work with up and coming designers, see Koda and Bolton (2007).

Disclosure statement

No potential conflict of interest was reported by the author.

References

Archer-Straw, Petrine. 2000. *Negrophilia: Avant-Garde Paris and Black Culture in the 1920s*. London: Thames and Hudson.

Baker, Jean-Claude, and Chris Chase. 2001. *Josephine Baker: The Hungry Heart*. New York: First Cooper Square Press.

Brooks, Daphne. 2007. "The End of the Line: Josephine Baker and the Politics of Black Women's Corporeal Comedy." *Scholar and Feminist Online* 6 (1/2). http://sfonline.barnard.edu/baker/brooks_01.htm.

Carlos, Marjon. 2016. "Meet the Stylist Behind That Beyoncé Throwback Gucci 'Formation' Video Look." *Vogue*, February 9. https://www.vogue.com/article/super-bowl-beyonce-gucci-alessandro-michele-formation-music-video-stylist.

Cheng, Anne Anlin. 2013. *Second Skin: Josephine Baker & the Modern Surface*. New York: Oxford University Press.

Cooper, Brittney C. 2017a. *Beyond Respectability: The Intellectual Thought of Race Women*. Champaign: University of Illinois Press.

Cooper, Brittney C. 2017b. "Dis Respectability Politics: On Jay-Z's Bitch, Beyoncé's 'Fly Ass, and Black Girl Blue." In *The Crunk Feminist Collection*, edited by Brittney C. Cooper, Susanna M. Morris, and Robyn M. Boylorn, 181–187. New York: The Feminist Press.

Cooper, Brittney C. 2017c. "(Un)clutching My Mother's Pearls, or Ratchetness and the Residue of Respectability." In *The Crunk Feminist Collection*, edited by Brittney C. Cooper, Susanna M. Morris, and Robyn M. Boylorn, 217–221. New York: The Feminist Press.

Eggert, Jessica. 2016. "Blue Ivy's Hair: Beyoncé Swiftly Shut Down Her Daughter's Critics in New Song 'Formation'." *Mic*, February 8. https://mic.com/articles/134635/blue-ivy-s-hair-beyonc-swiftly-shut-down-her-daughter-s-critics-in-new-song-formation.

Evans, Caroline. 2013. *The Mechanical Smile: Modernism and the First Fashion Shows in France and America, 1900–1929*. New Haven: Yale University Press.

Finamore, Michelle Tolini. 2015. "Fashioning the Colonial at the Paris Expositions, 1925 and 1931." *Fashion Theory* 7 (3–4): 345–360. doi:10.2752/136270403778051943.

Ford, Tanisha C. 2015. *Liberated Threads: Black Women, Style, and the Global Politics of Soul*. Chapel Hill: University of North Carolina Press.

Francis, Terri. 2007. "What Does Beyoncé See in Josephine Baker?: A Brief Film History of Sampling La Diva, La Bakaire." *Scholar and Feminist Online* 6 (1/2). http://sfonline.barnard.edu/baker/francis_01.htm.

Gates Jr, Henry Louis. 1998. "Josephine Baker and Paul Colin: African American Dance Seen Through Parisian Eyes." *Critical Inquiry* 24 (4): 903–934.

Griffiths, Kadeen. 2017. "This is what Beyoncé's Lemonade Meant to Me as a Black Woman & this is why it Needed to Win Album of the Year." *Bustle*, February 14. https://www.bustle.com/p/this-is-what-Beyoncés-lemonade-meant-to-me-as-a-black-woman-this-is-why-it-needed-to-win-album-of-the-year-37653.

Hannel, Susan L. 2005. "The Influence of Jazz on American Fashion." In *Twentieth Century American Fashion*, edited by Patricia Cunningham and Linda Welters, 57–79. New York: Bloomsbury Publishing.

Hartman, Saidiya. 2008. "Venus in Two Acts." *Small Axe: A Caribbean Journal of Criticism* 12 (2): 1–14.

Higginbotham, Evelyn Brooks. 1995. "African-American Women's History and the Metalanguage of Race." In *We Specialize in the Wholly Impossible: A Reader in Black Women's History*, edited by Darlene Clark Hine, Wilma King, and Linda Reed, 3–25. New York: New York University Press.

Hobson, Janell. 2016. "Feminists Debate Beyoncé." In *The Beyoncé Effect: Essays on Sexuality, Race, and Feminism*, edited by Adrienne Trier-Bieniek, 11–27. North Carolina: McFarland and Company.

Hobson, Janell. 2017. "Celebrity Feminism: More than a Gateway." *Signs: Journal of Women in Culture and Society* 42 (4): 999–1007.

hooks, bell. 2014. *Black Looks: Race and Representation*. New York: Routledge Press.

Jordan, Glenn. 1995. "Flight from Modernity: Time, the Other, and the Discourse of Primitivism." *Time and Society* 4 (3): 281–303.

Jules-Rosette, Bennetta. 2007. *Josephine Baker in Art and Life*. Chicago: University of Illinois Press.

Knowles-Carter, Beyoncé. 2016. *Lemonade*. New York: Parkwood Entertainment.

Koda, Harold, and Andrew Bolton. 2007. *Poiret*. New York: Metropolitan Museum of Art.

Kraut, Anthea. 2007. "Whose Choreography?: Josephine Baker and the Question of (Dance) Authorship." *Scholar and Feminist Online* 6 (1/2). http://sfonline.barnard.edu/baker/kraut_01.htm.

Lemke, Sieglinde. 1998. *Primitivist Modernism: Black Culture and the Origins of Transatlantic Modernism*. New York: Oxford University Press.

Pham, Minh Ha T. 2013. "Paul Poiret's Magical Techno-Oriental Fashions (1911): Race, Clothing, and Virtuality in the Machine Age." *Configurations* 21 (1): 1–26. doi:10.1353/con.2013.0003.

Rose, Phyllis. 1989. *Jazz Cleopatra: Josephine Baker in Her Time*. New York: Vintage.
Rovine, Victoria L. 2009. "Colonialism's Clothing: Africa, France, and the Deployment of Fashion." *Design Issues* 25 (3): 44–61.
Shah, Hemant. 2009. "Legitimizing Neglect: Race and Rationality in Conservative News Commentary About Hurricane Katrina." *Howard Journal of Communications* 20 (1): 1–17. doi:10.1080/10646170802664821.
Sharpley-Whiting, T. Denean. 1999. *Black Venus: Sexualized Savages, Primal Fears, and Primitive Narratives in French*. Durham: Duke University Press.
"Take Back New Orleans." 2005. *New York Daily News*, September 2.
Torgovnick, Marianna. 1990. *Gone Primitive: Savage Intellects, Modern Lives*. Chicago: University of Chicago Press.
Trier-Bieniek, Adrienne. 2016. "Introduction." In *The Beyoncé Effect: Essays on Sexuality, Race, and Feminism*, edited by Adrienne Trier-Bieniek. North Carolina: McFarland and Company.
Weidhase, Natalie. 2015. "'Beyoncé Feminism' and the Contestation of the Black Feminist Body." *Celebrity Studies* 6 (1): 128–131. doi:10.1080/19392397.2015.1005389.

Just Use What You Have: Ethical Fashion Discourse and the Feminisation of Responsibility

Kathleen Horton

ABSTRACT
The rise of fast fashion has meant that young women (even those on relatively low incomes) are able to 'regularly consume and discard fashionable clothing' [Buckley, Cheryl, and Hazel Clark. 2012. "Conceptualizing Fashion in Everyday Lives." *Design Issues* 28 (4): 18–28. doi:10.1162/DESI_a_00172., 21]. While this development may be aligned with the democratisation of fashion—the fact that the supply chains that deliver fast fashion are not consistent with the principles of global democracy is now also relatively common knowledge in the democratised West. This, along with growing awareness of the ecological harms associated with the fashion industry has contributed to what Elke Gaugele [2014. *Aesthetic Politics in Fashion*. Vienna: Sternberg Press] has termed the 'ethical turn' in fashion. However, despite the fact that young women are often not deemed capable of translating their (ethical) attitudes into (ethical) behaviours [McNeill, Lisa, and Rebecca Moore. 2015. "Sustainable Fashion Consumption and the Fast Fashion Conundrum: Fashionable Consumers and Attitudes to Sustainability in Clothing Choice." *International Journal of Consumer Studies* 39 (3): 212–222], nor able to be 'trusted to consistently make good decisions' [Brooks, Andrew. 2015. *Clothing Poverty: The Hidden World of Fast Fashion and Second-Hand Clothes*. London: Zed Books, 241], they are also increasingly being called to recognise their individual role in the politics of global fashion supply chains. Drawing on examples from scholarly and popular discourses as well as online peer to peer communications, this article explores the historical moment of fast fashion as an instance of both the feminisation of consumption and the feminisation of responsibility.

Introduction: in the era of fast fashion

The term 'fast fashion' emerged in the early 2000s in relation to commercially aggressive global retailers such as the Spanish Zara and the Swedish Hennes and Mauritz (H&M), who provide a quick turnover of 'on trend' product to a predominantly youthful female market. Fast fashion— understood as a market segment—is framed nearly exclusively as meeting the desires of young women to be 'in fashion'. And, as fast fashion is consistent with a marked trend that has seen the lowering of the relative cost of clothing over the last fifteen years, it plays to an ever increasing and broadening global audience, thus linking it to the 'democratisation' of fashion (Lipovetsky 1994, 63). As Buckley and Clark (2012, 21) note, it is only with the emergence of brands such as 'Primark' and 'Forever 21' in the last 20 years that young women (even those on relatively 'low incomes') are able to 'regularly and routinely consume and discard fashionable clothing'. Fashion historians frame the rise of ready-to-wear in the early to mid twentieth century through the political language of access and authenticity. In this narrative, ready-to-wear emerges as a powerful and dynamic form of 'fashion for all' (Rouse, as quoted in Sullivan 2016, 34) in relation to more exclusive forms of fashionable dress such as haute couture but also as seen against the history of fashion as a class based system, whereby upper class taste and distinction set the aesthetic standards and drive fashion change (Bourdieu 1984; Simmel 1957; Veblen 1899). Although the advent of fast fashion in the twenty-first century does not represent a complete rift with past forms of fashionable clothing provision, the expectation of low-cost, high-speed product has inflected nearly all sectors of the market, including high end luxury and non-branded basics. Consequently, the term fast fashion has gained cachet as paradigmatic of fashion in the twenty-first century.

However, the social and economic benefits that a much broader demographic of young women may currently enjoy as a result of participating in fast fashion are potentially undercut by knowledge of the many critiques of fast fashion on both social and environmental grounds. These critiques have emanated from academic, industry and popular media forums—including for example, the field of sustainable fashion spearheaded by Kate Fletcher in the United Kingdom, the publication of highly influential texts such as Lucy Siegle's *To Die For: Is Fashion Wearing Out the World?* and consciousness raising documentaries such as Andrew Morgan's *The True Cost* (2015), which is readily available on Netflix. In addition, the critique of fast fashion is a recurrent feature of hyperbolic fashion journalism—where the mode of second person address ('How your fast fashion habit is ruining more than the earth', *Vogue Australia*, 2018)—leaves the reader under no illusion as to who is to blame, while celebrities such as Emma Watson and Livia Firth add a layer of intermediary glamour to the refusal of fast fashion. All of these sources are undoubtedly contributing to a cultural scenario in which it is 'common knowledge that the booming surplus of cheap clothing is causing problems worldwide' (Dougher 2015). In fact, according to Phạm (2017) the 'high cost of cheap fashion' has become a 'cliché in the popular discourse about ethics and fashion'. Consequently, one might argue that the historical moment of fast fashion constitutes an ethically precarious terrain for consumers of the global north, who must reconcile the celebratory, affirmative and democratic aspects of fashion consumption with the call to recognise their own role in what Louise Crewe (2017) terms the 'harm chains' that make up the global commodity market.

The idea that the broader field of twenty-first century fashion has engendered an 'ethical turn' across both questions of production and consumption is noted by both Gaugele (2014) and Tseëlon (2014). Gaugele uses the term to refer to the various ways that the fashion industry (post-2008 global financial crisis) has tried to recast itself along more moral lines via 'the commodification of trust and honesty' (as typified by the label, Honest By), along with the 'integration of 'social critique as ethical capital' (207). Tseëlon links the 'ethical turn' to the impact of globalisation on the fashion industry, including the intensification of the 'human cost' associated with global supply chains and the 'flattening' of the relationship between corporations and their customers (14–18). This analysis is consistent with that of Barnett et al. (2011, 2–4) who argue that consumption has been remoralised over the last 30 years in light of the 'systematic inequalities' brought about by globalisation. A high profile example of the ethical turn in fashion is Fashion Revolution.org, a fashion activism platform founded as a response to the Rana Plaza factory collapse of 2013, in which over 1100 garment workers lost their lives. Fashion Revolution's yearly hashtag campaign, #whomademyclothes? invites consumers to demand greater transparency in a bid to address the injustices of fashion supply chains. The ethical turn in fashion is also often implicitly linked to the assumption that capitalism and consumption are 'incompatible with environmentalism' (Miller 2001, 227). As Crane notes, 'sustainable fashion … requires ethical consumers' (2016, 249).

The role of the global north consumer in the fast fashion matrix is a critical and complex issue that is often framed through the questions of choice and agency—or the lack thereof. For example, the fashion industry predictably characterises the consumer's 'insatiable demand for newness' (Barnes and Lea-Greenwood 2006, 269) as the driver of fast fashion. However, critics of fast fashion as a system of clothing provision argue that consumers are positioned by the system to become embroiled in a competitive form of 'superfluous' consumption that serves the interests of 'capitalist production' (Brooks 2015, 82). Ethical fashion product is promoted as a conscious alternative to the consumption of fast fashion (McNeill and Moore 2015). However, in the context of a market flooded by cheap clothes, individual consumers are deemed neither capable of translating their (ethical) attitudes into (ethical) behaviours (McNeill and Moore 2015), nor able to be 'trusted to consistently make good decisions' (Brooks 2015, 241). That is to say, the agency of even the most well-meaning and mindful consumer is often perceived as somehow corrupted by fast fashion.

In this article, I explore the 'ethical turn' in the era of fast fashion explicitly in relation to questions of gender. The central objective of my exploration is to interrogate the ways in which young women are uncritically positioned as the main protagonists in the frenetic consumer culture of twenty-first century fashion, across both scholarly and popular discourses, while simultaneously being held (and self-identifying) as more responsible. In fact, the article argues that the era of fast fashion represents a particularly intense version, not only of the feminisation of consumption, but also what Sylvia Chant identified as the 'feminisation of responsibility and/or obligation' (2006, 2014). Taking my cue from Southwell's analysis of sustainability in the context of gender (2015), this article looks at the ways in which young women are assumed to both bear a greater 'liability' in relation to the ills associated with fashion consumption in the contemporary era along with experiencing a sense of 'duty' in relation to this liability (Chant 2014, 299–301). The article has two sections. In the first I present an overview of some of the key discursive positions in relation to women, fast fashion and ethical consumption and in the second I briefly consider how ethical fashion discourse is emerging in the context of peer-to-peer video blogs as young women try to grapple with the morality of being the economic subjects of advanced capitalism. Consequently, this article stands to counter some of the more pervasive and predictable representations of the market segment known as 'young women' in relation to fashion consumption.

Young women, fast fashion and ethical consumption

Since at least the early nineteenth century, fashion consumption has been conceptualised, marketed and indeed experienced as a highly feminised field, which has in turn led to sustained critique along gendered grounds. Craik points out that 'the history of "femininity" in western culture was entwined with consumerism', an association intensified in the mid nineteenth century with the rise of the department store, when women's connection with 'domesticity through household management' was replaced with associations of 'leisure and pleasure' as defined through consumer goods (1994, 70). The Marxist political critique of women, fashion and consumerism developed in tandem, with the characterisation of fashion as a particularly 'cruel, inhuman' form of capitalism (Sullivan 2016, 36). In the context of the 'misery' that arose in the 'production of all kinds of commodities', the case of fashion was made all the worse by the fact that it resulted in 'marvels beyond necessity ... (Marx)', 'which serve the personal adornment of the ladies of the bourgeoisie (Engels)' (Sullivan 2016, 37). At the turn of the twentieth century, Veblen extended this class-based argument to align with nineteenth century critiques of the 'irrationality' of the fashion system along with its material forms, resulting in a longstanding ideological stance that positions women as the 'unwitting "victims" of fashion' (Entwistle 2015a, 28).

More nuanced understandings of fashion consumption beyond the realm of 'oppression' were developed in the 1980s via influential feminist texts such as Wilson's *Adorned in Dreams* (1987), that actively 'recuperated ... the pleasure(s)' both bodily and social, of fashion consumption in relation to questions of gender (Wilson 2003, ix). In addition, broader developments in cultural studies (such as Hebdige's 1979 study of Punk) and *The Sociology of Everyday Life* (de Certeau 1984) highlighted the agency of consumers—as expressed through their oppositional or creative use of everyday commodities. In emphasising the use phase, these perspectives also highlight a crucial distinction between fashion understood primarily as a form of 'consumer culture' and fashion consumption as a much broader set of sociocultural practices that occur well beyond the 'act of purchase' (Warde 2010, xxiv). For example, Woodward's *Why Women Wear What They Wear* (2007) repositions the taken for granted 'site' of fashion consumption from the department store/shopping mall to the bedroom. She highlights the ways in which acts of dressing are daily *practices* for all women everywhere regardless of how much they may or may not follow 'fashion', and she also shows how 'getting dressed' often involves 'negotiations' as opposed to liberating 'choices' (2007, 2). In recent years popular texts such as *Women in Clothes* (Heti, Julavits, and Shapton 2014) are contributing to the broader discourse of fashion consumption (beyond that established via fashion magazines) as an everyday practice that is both socially binding and complexly nuanced.

While both scholarly and popular debates concerning women, fashion and consumption can therefore be seen as having moved beyond the highly moralistic, the era of fast fashion has arguably *re*moralised the issue of fashion consumption. However, given the fact that fashion is not the only industry that operates on the logic of high speed/low cost novelty, Entwistle warns that the renewed moral indignation directed towards fashion consumption might be connected to the 'lingering suspicion' that fashion is 'more trivial' than the 'obligatory smartphone' (2015b, 27). Entwistle points out that many contemporary critiques of fast fashion consumption seem to line up with Veblen's late nineteenth century characterisation of fashion as an 'inherently irrational and wasteful system' (28). A case in point might be Brooks' *Clothing Poverty: The Hidden World of Fast Fashion and Second Hand Clothes* (2015). In the text, Brooks brings important considerations from the field of cultural geography to understanding the network of global connections linking the production, circulation and consumption of fashion in 'late-capitalism' (241). However, his discussion of consumption in the global north relies on a persistent and implicitly gendered understanding of fashion as a symbolic system of emulation and competition. For example, part of the moral indignation that he expresses in relation to fast fashion is the 'charade' of it being associated with 'youth, independence and even female emancipation' (81). Rather, he argues that fashion 'restricts social mobility', through placing 'consumers in a never-ending contest of purchases' that serve the interests of 'capitalist production' (82).

Young women are routinely singled out as key targets/protagonists/victims, in the era of fast fashion—and two recent examples from the Australian context prove instructive. According to the market research platform, IBISWorld (2017) despite 'variable consumer sentiment' fast fashion has been a growth industry since 'industry giants' Zara and Topshop opened in Australia in 2011. It is also reported that the sector has kept 'consumer demand high' through competitive pricing and the (paradoxically named) 'scarcity effect'. Consequently, the market is predicted to expand at a rate far exceeding the GDP over the next ten years as international players fulfil their 'store roll out strategies'. One might also learn from the same report that 'people aged between 15 and 34 are the primary target market of fast fashion retailers' currently making up 66% of the market. The report also explains that 'fast fashion generally holds greater appeal to women' (and presumably 'girls') who also apparently 'generally wear items of clothing less times than men'. While the report surmises that Australia is in the throes of a 'love affair with fast fashion', it does strike a slightly more sombre tone when it notes that due to the fact that most fast fashion is produced in countries with 'light environmental regulations' the industry may face pressure to pursue more 'sustainable operations' as 'social and environmental issues' come to light over the next five years (Magner 2017).

In a nod to one of the ways that some of these issues might indeed come to the attention of everyday consumers, a recent Australian television documentary series, *War on Waste* (2017) featured a 'fast fashion' storyline. Based around the statistic that six tonnes of clothes are thrown out every ten minutes, the show clearly framed fast fashion consumption in Australia as an ecological and moral waste issue. *War on Waste* has a clear social agenda, to not only raise the consciousness of middle Australia to the ills of overconsumption but to deliver acts of intervention via the largesse and profile of public television. After presenting on the topics of household waste, the role of supermarkets and disposable coffee cups as 'gender and age neutral', the episode that dealt with fashion consumption identified a very specific demographic. In an editorial choice that felt predictable if not a little unkind, the middle-aged male host (who made numerous references to his lack of interest in fashion) met with four 'fashion-obsessed friends' (young women) to witness their shopping 'habits' first hand—at the site of a large urban shopping mall. Throughout this section, the young women were presented as the hapless economic subjects of late capitalism, although they were in effect making the sorts of everyday deliberations about clothing consumption that any subject of 'middle Australia' might—such as: *how much does it cost? do I like it? does it seem like good value for money?* Their 'intervention' was staged first as a visit to a secondhand fashion transfer station—to which the subjects expressed varying levels of surprise, tinged with echoes of partial responsibility, before being put on a 'fashion diet' for a month (despair), during which time they were also educated on how to sustain their enchantment with the material items in their wardrobes (feigned delight). The ensuing logic was that should they become better skilled at wearing clothing—at seeing its fluid aesthetic potential—they could effectively get their fast fashion shopping fix just by visiting their own wardrobe.

While it is hardly surprising that a business report should allegorise the consumer of fast fashion as a young woman giddy with love, the adoption of a piece to camera by the host of *War on Waste* —commenting on his lack of faith in the young women's capacity to make good on their newfound knowledge—reeks of the psychological observation (noted by Daniel Miller) that the tendency to be overly attached to material things always [applies to] 'someone other than ourselves' (Miller 2001, 229). The *War on Waste* segment also demonstrates that young women's frequent characterisation as the 'unwitting' participants in what has become the poster child for the worst machinations of 'late capitalism' does not stop them from being simultaneously identified as more responsible for its ills.

Like fast fashion, ethical fashion can be understood as a market segment but the term is also used more broadly. Littler (2007) notes that 'ethical consumption is a relatively modern term' linked to 'a broad discursive field' that includes 'such diverse practices as buying fair-trade, products-not-tested-on-animals, non-sweatshop brands, organic goods and avoiding "exploitative" products or "unnecessary purchases"' (6). While ethical consumption always implies a moral stance, Littler argues that the term ethics enjoys a discursive freedom over the term morality, being 'more porous, more open to use in multiple ways' (10). Popular understandings of ethical fashion consumption are similarly broad, and often follow a dialectical logic of affirmations and negations enacted by the consumer in order to 'sanction' (Littler 2007, 7) certain types of goods. Many ethical fashion stances adopt discourse borrowed directly from the context of food consumption—such as replacing (animal) leather with vegan leather, and (fast) fashion with slow fashion. Other models of ethical fashion consumption fold aesthetic categories (such as minimalism) into social movements (such as voluntary simplicity) (Shaw and Newholm 2002) in order to refuse the excesses of twenty-first century consumerism.

While ethical fashion can therefore be understood as both occupying a position of moral critique in relation to the broader context of twenty-first century fashion as well as offering an alternative, it is barely a position it is able to maintain without undergoing rigorous criticism itself. For example, Tseëlon (2014) interrogates which issues are prioritised over others, arguing that concepts of sustainability and fair trade take precedence over questions of animal cruelty and the ethics of fashion imagery. Citing market research that indicates that the aspirational market for 'ethical fashion' is on the rise, she surmises that it is a 'high profile niche market whose brand image is bigger than its usage' (7). Tseëlon also provides a useful critique of the 'commodification' of ethical fashion in philosophical terms, noting that while 'there is a tendency in the ethical fashion conversation to apply ... ethics to concrete tangible products or outcomes', the ethical requires 'agency' (13). Agency might be necessary but it is barely sufficient. Andrew Brooks casts 'ethical fashion' as a case of 'responsible' capitalism, whereby consumer choice acts as an impoverished proxy for real political action (2015, 214). And while this critique of ethical consumerism doesn't apply *only* to fashion, fashion is allocated a special place in this regard by virtue of its capacity to signal our identity. Brooks writes, 'Wearing clothes such as fair-trade cotton T-shirts, second-hand dresses from charity shops or organic woolen sweaters is a way to demonstrate solidarity with good causes', that do damage through absorbing some of the opposition to, and critiques of, capitalism' (214). Consequently, Brooks argues we are left a *'tepid revolution in shopping* without a revolution in society' (218).

In tackling the question of gender in relation to the discourse of ethical fashion, it is difficult not to feel as though you are being taken on a frustrating conceptual journey, where gender is everywhere, yet nowhere. First, market research confirms (undoubtedly in a highly circuitous way) that women remain the 'main consumers of fashion and clothing' (Southwell 2015, 107) along with exhibiting the characteristics of being more 'passionate' ... 'positive' and 'more likely to impulse buy than men' (Southwell 2015, 101). This provides the 'feminisation of fashion' thesis with an enduring empirical justification. However, as Southwell points out, both market and scholarly research into sustainability nearly always defaults to a 'gender neutral consumer' (102) who ostensibly assumes responsibility for the various environmental issues on humanistic grounds. At the same time data from the OECD clearly indicates that 'in the home, women exhibit stronger environmental attitudes and behaviour than men' (101), and are more likely to act on them. This gender bias towards both concern and action in relation to the environment is reinscribed in corporate contexts—where 'having women in positions of power' has been found to have a 'positive effect on the environmental and social impact' of the company (Southwell 2015, 101).

Given that there is a gender bias towards women both within the context of fashion and the context of sustainability, it is not surprising to learn that ethical fashion consumption is highly feminised. Following an analysis of articles on the *Guardian* UK website over a five year period (2008–2013), Southwell concluded that 'the vast majority of those publicly expressing concern for sustainable fashion were women' (107). Crane (2016) also cites research into 'two American green forums' that hosted discussions 'related to green consumerism and green fashion', noting that 'participants were mainly women and were younger and more educated than the average American' (257). Moreover, the gender bias towards consumption should also be taken into consideration. In his study of consumer movements in Switzerland in latter part of the twentieth century, Balsiger (2016) notes the 'leading role that women [have] played in consumer movements and in political consumerism' (37). While the 'realm of consumption typically constitutes a social arena, which is assigned to female gender roles' ostensibly because of 'men's disinterest', it is also a site of political power for women (37). Balsiger also notes that while the 'tension' that the reinforcement of gender roles was noted by the campaign makers, they mostly saw consumption campaigns as an emancipatory path for women' (37-38). In fact, to the extent to which the campaigns constituted a 'politicisation of everyday lives', women found themselves in a more 'privileged position' as they had more autonomy to effect change through everyday concrete acts such as 'recycling to buying fair trade' (38).

The tension that Balsiger notes at the heart of these consumer campaigns –(between the restriction of normative gender roles versus the everyday as a site of political action) is also lurking beneath the surface twenty-first century ethical fashion discourse —particularly around questions of consumption although it is rarely acknowledged. It seems pertinent to note, for example, that the flurry of 'how to manuals' for the would-be ethical fashion shopper, including Siegle's *To Die For,* (2011), Cline's *Overdressed: The Shockingly High Cost of Cheap Fashion* (2012); and Press' *Wardrobe Crisis: How we Went from Sunday Best to Fast Fashion* (2016), are all written by women and adopt a confessional mode and implicitly address a female readership—without once making it explicit. Redress's *Dress with Sense: The Practical Guide to a Conscious Closet* (Dean, Tarnberg, and Lane 2017) which is geared to a teenage/young audience, is illustrated throughout with images depicting exclusively feminised fashion scenarios (such as young women shopping, regarding themselves in the mirror and measuring their waist while wearing underwear), while simultaneously showcasing industry leaders of both genders.

The ethical fashion vlogosphere

In this final part of the article I briefly turn my attention to burgeoning ethical fashion discourse as it plays out via peer-to-peer digital platforms. Research into fashion blogs is an emerging area and work has begun to 'show their value as sites of interrogation not only for contemporary practices of dress and discourses on fashion and appearance but also as platforms of investigation of digital media culture' (Mora and Rocamora 2015, 150). In this case I adopted an 'unobtrusive' approach to data collection, which entailed 'trawling' (Hookway and Snee 2017) user-generated vlogs (video blogs), hosted on the video sharing platform, YouTube.[1] While I take vlogging to be part of the broader context of user-generated digital fashion content known as the fashion blogosphere, I also suggest that there are some generic specificities related to YouTube communications that mark them out as a potentially rich and appropriate context of ethical fashion discourse. Therefore, while this analysis *explicitly* draws from and is framed through the existing research into the fashion blogosphere (which predominantly focuses on the genre of personal style blogging) I also hope to extend the frame—albeit minimally.

Like fast fashion, fashion blogs are a defining feature of twenty-first century fashion, emerging in the early 2000s, gaining notoriety around 2009 and continuing to grow since then (Findlay 2015). They are championed for the same reason that they were originally reviled—namely that they are seen to enable 'the devolution of fashion authority from traditional power brokers such as magazine editors and designers to a more diverse assemblage of participants' (Crewe 2017, 107). As Pham notes, 'peer-to-peer communications' and 'amateur opinion,' 'hallmarks of the blogosphere, are an antithesis to the 'fashion industry's top-down, hierarchical, and highly guarded organisation of taste and value' (2015, 55). Consequently, fashion blogs share the mantle with fast fashion as key aspects of the further democratisation of fashion in the twenty-first century—summed up in the pithy phrase, 'the average person is taking ownership of' fashion (Givhan, quoted in Phạm 2013). The second decade of the century has seen the proliferation of online platforms (such as Instagram and YouTube) that in their own way have had an equally disruptive influence on the fashion industry. And internet culture more broadly is understood as a 'hybrid commercial space' where 'user-generated content' and competing values of access monetisation and community work in tandem across multiple platforms simultaneously (Arthurs, Drakopoulou, and Gandini 2018).

Research into the fashion blogosphere has explored questions of gender and identity as they are mediated through online platforms from a variety of methodological and conceptual angles. In her empirical study into amateur 'teen' blogging, Tara Chittenden (2010) noted she was somewhat surprised that her final group of respondents were all female, even given that 'activities such as 'dressing up' and 'diary keeping' are 'gendered'. Agnès Rocamora (2011) has applied psychoanalytic theory to examine aspects of feminine identity through tracing conceptual links between digital screens and mirrors. She concludes that blogs are a potentially liberating space as they produce 'a fashion open to appropriation and interpretation, including that of women's visions of themselves and by themselves'(422). Rosie Findlay (2015) has traced the history of fashion blogging unpacking a cultural transition from 'independence' (pre 2009) to 'aspiration' (post 2009) and increasing focus on 'fashionability and prestige' (172). With the professionalisation of web 2.0, research into the fashion blogosphere has also sought to bring to light and analyse the various immaterial labours, including the aesthetic and the affective, that are central to work of fashion blogging and how these in turn are related to neoliberal notions of the branded and entrepreneurial self (Phạm 2013, 2015).

While, as Findlay (2015) points out, the earliest iterations of fashion blogging were intellectual and discursive in nature, vlogging 'is a practice with antecedents in "camgirl culture" when webcams first made "authentic", video streaming possible' (Arthurs, Drakopoulou, and Gandini 2018, 9). While vlogging has subsequently become a highly male dominated sphere, the form of vlogging which is most successful 'for women vloggers' in terms of internet measures (popularity and monetisation) is beauty vlogs (Arthurs, Drakopoulou, and Gandini 2018). While there are various genres of vlogging, there are key aesthetic features, deriving in part from the context of digital intimacy, that are relatively consistent. First, vlogs are nearly always shot in domestic spaces and in the case of beauty and fashion vlogging, the vlogger frequently positions herself in front of a 'well-dressed' bed. Second, vlogs 'generally feature a single person facing the camera head on' and are framed with a 'close-up shot' of the face (The Vlog Aesthetic). Third, vloggers generally deliver a conversational, unscripted monologue direct to camera—on a topic of their own choosing for around five to ten minutes—with minimal editing. Hosted via YouTube, vloggers frequently explicitly invite comments or 'likes' in line with the internet's culture of vernacular opinion.

The intersection of fashion culture and vlogging is primarily associated with haul videos. A mixture of 'cataloguing, confessionals and tutorials', haul videos feature the vlogger displaying their 'haul' (a range of beauty and fashion product all bought simultaneously) to a soundtrack of benign approval, seemingly normalising the idea that shopping is indeed something akin to an expedition. Haul videos began to make an impact in 2009, in concert both with fast fashion gaining greater market share and the Global Financial Crisis. And, as a form of reality marketing they are an established part of the fast fashion business model. According to Phạm (2015) haul vloggers can be contrasted with personal style bloggers, as they represent 'a wider tension in mainstream Western fashion culture, which wants to hold fashion together as fantasy and fashion as reality culture' (169). Haul videos also arguably speak to a working class culture. While fast fashion/low market retailers were quick to appropriate them for marketing, high-end fashion keeps its distance (Bean 2015) moreover, some haulers themselves feel like they are addressing a demographic of adolescent girls and young women who 'don't have very much money' (Melyssa, quoted in Cline 2012, 15).

What the f**k is ethical fashion?

If ethical fashion is a niche market, one might also assume (correctly) that ethical fashion blogging and vlogging must also be niche. And while blogging is theoretically democratic, the fashion blogosphere has its own hierarchy of celebrity influencers and the "long tail" of the *un*known—and the *un*influential—who may or may not have commercial aspirations and who blog regardless. And it is so in the *ethical* fashion blogosphere. What is more, the discourse of peer-to-peer ethical fashion discourse plays out in both shambolic and predictable manners. Deriving largely from popular forms of journalism, (the influence of *The True Cost* is notable) and refracted through lived experience, it seems to epitomise the 'new kinds of information' endemic to internet culture 'where fact … content, opinion and conversation can't easily be separated (Manovich 2009). The monologues delivered by both the well subscribed and the minimally subscribed adopt tones that are at once confessional, helpful and informational. There are moments of transformation and awakening, and there are numerous tales of redemption and addiction. And the finer points of twenty-first century moral ambiguity are addressed via blog posts such as 'Why its Ok to buy fast fashion second hand'—and subsequently debated in the comments. And, notwithstanding comments in the vein of 'there is no ethical fashion in capitalism', the ethical fashion vlogosphere is overwhelmingly positive.

While ethical fashion registers as a rational (and informed) intervention into the space of everyday/taken for granted fashion consumption, it is an intervention that is frequently precipitated by an emotional rupture either with a specific brand or with the field of fast fashion more generally. Consequently, a recognisable vlog type is one that details a vlogger's changing relationship with fast fashion over a period of time. Frequently these posts confirm a tale of perceived 'democratisation' by beginning with a confession of how excited the vlogger was to finally have the opportunity to enjoy the access to fashionable product that had been formerly outside of their range due to economic constraints. Next the vlogger will often identify a disappointment with the material quality of the clothing, which has very little to do with a moral reckoning and more to do with the right to customer satisfaction. However, this is quickly reframed as an ecological issue associated with clothing that can only be worn a few times before it ends up in landfill. Reflection on the ethics associated with the modes of production is usually what cements the disenchantment. This, in turn, precipitates a renewed sense of responsibility—which is ethically discharged by boycotting the identified brands. Consequently, one comes across posts with titles such as 'Why I quit shopping at Zara'; 'Why I no longer shop at H&M'; and 'Why I quit Forever 21' and 'The Fast Fashion Trap'.

In a post entitled 'Quitting Fast Fashion//One Year Later', published 16 July 2017, the vlogger outlines some of the difficulties both practical and emotional in being one of the very few consumers who do manage to make good on their intention to shop ethically. There are wins and losses over the year—having solved the problem of sourcing 'ethical socks and underwear,' she confesses to buying 'a pair of denim shorts from TopShop or something' (because she needed them to fulfil a functional wardrobe requirement) and succumbing to 'Primark Christmas Sweaters' (Hyde 2017). Not only do such posts shed light on what might be called the ongoing emotional attention ethical consumption might entail—they also clearly highlight how elusive 'cognitive consistency' (Festinger, quoted in Southwell 2015, 107) might be in light of the lived experience of both the utilitarian and social requirements of dress. What is also particularly instructive in the case of the moral slipup with the Christmas Sweaters is the fact that the vlogger notes that her attachment to sweaters is something she shares with her 'family', which in turn registers one of the ways in which unethical things might play crucial roles maintaining everyday social (and we might assume ethical) relations.

Given that 'choosing' to shop ethically is neither easy nor self-evident, one of the most common forms of ethical fashion vlogs is the one that offers pragmatic instruction such as 'No More Fast Fashion//My Tips'. The tips cover alternative sites of provision—with 'thrifting' or 'charity shopping' featuring frequently as the number one ethical option. Suggestions of thrifting are often closely linked to questions of 'personal style'. Vloggers might propose on the one hand that it is easier to shop at thrift stores if you have a sense of your 'own sense of style', while others encourage their audience to *find* their personal style through thrifting. In either case style is presented (as it routinely is in fashion discourse) not only as way to express a sense of individual identity, but also as a strategy to escape fashion—and presumably its moral baggage. In the comments, positive feedback is frequently combined with reflections on the questions of style and broader references to fashion:

> You know I dig it when you bring up ethics but seriously, one thing I appreciate most (especially when speaking to a larger audience) is honesty – small steps are definitely more important than nothing. Also – you NEED the People Tree corduroy collection in your life. DREAMY.

Other suggestions feature more programmatic (or quantitative) approaches—including downsizing, working with a capsule wardrobe, or becoming a minimalist.

Despite that so much ethical fashion discourse in the vlogosphere replays the predictable arguments based on dichotomous logic wherein fast fashion is the enemy, more nuanced conversations take place, often via the comments. It is for this reason that one might propose (following Woodward 2007) that ethical fashion is not so much a market (niche or otherwise), but a set of negotiations—moral perhaps, economic maybe, —but *material* and emotional also. For example, the challenge of either thrifting or buying 'ethical' brands to fit bodies that don't conform to industry standard sizes is also frequently commented on:

> I do think being plus size is one of the hardest aspects of switching to slow fashion. No ethical brands produce plus size clothing, and if they do its only the most basic staples (i.e. not office wear). Thrifting is also more difficult when you are plus size, as those sizes are the highest in demand. I can't wait till these niches are better filled.[2]

At other times the comments register an innocent guilt: 'Aww, now you're making me feel bad about shopping at ZARA. And I loooove ZARA.' And the more ridiculous aspects of finding ethical sustainable everything is also registered through humour, 'I haven't bought brand new clothing in many years. Except for underwear lol.'

While 'how-to' ethical consumption manuals are often understood as a form of 'moralism' (Littler 2007), in the context of peer-to-peer ethical discourse I find it difficult to interpret these vlogs in this way. This is partly due to the overwhelmingly positive and supportive tone in which the advice is given (everyone is just so *nice*) or—to frame this response in more scholarly terms—it is potentially due to the 'affective labour' (Negri and Hardt 1999) that the vloggers are performing. Moreover, the fact that vlogs are indeed generic forms of communication, delivered via everyday technology and ubiquitous digital platforms, does little to detract from (and may even intensify) the authenticity of so many ethical fashion communications. One particular post, 'How to Shop Ethically on a Budget' by Cosmic Raja (2017) with modest views strikes me in this regard. The face of the twenty-something vlogger appears tightly framed. Her makeup and clothing register graphically in line with the communication demands of mobile technologies, and she notes (as many vloggers do) that she has been 'getting a lot of questions' about how to shop ethically. She talks her viewers through the usual options: 'thrifting'; 'upcycling'; 'sharing clothes with your friends' and 'renting' (casually naming a couple of businesses along the way), but it is her final tip that I find most affecting. She suggests that with the prospect of an event coming up that you should refrain from indulging in a fast fashion fix—and 'just use what you have'. At first, I am struck by the banality of this advice—the ground zero of ethical consumerism—but I am quickly unsettled from this moral reading as she goes on to adopt a much more reflective tone, taking her time and momentarily losing eye contact with her audience and offering the sort of advice that she wishes she could follow. It's ok to 'wear that skirt that you've already worn before' because 'people are mostly paying attention to what they're wearing and what's going on in their own heads and ... they're not going to notice and ... even if they did 'who cares right?'

Conclusion

In this article I have sought to interrogate what I see as a fraught political terrain for young women in the era of fast fashion. One of the difficulties in framing this exploration is the fact that the categories of women, fashion and consumption are so intricately linked in cultural and commercial discourses that it can feel like trying to unravel a particularly tangled historical knot. However, as I contend, the ethical tension that arises for young women in the context of fast fashion is well worth exploring as a specifically twenty-first century phenomenon even if it can also be seen to rehearse many of the pervasive historical ideological positionings of women, fashion and consumption. What the contemporary era points to most emphatically is both an enthusiasm to cast young women as the desiring subjects of twenty-first century consumerism, while implicitly reminding them of their gendered responsibilities to take care. That young women are singled out for special mention in relation to fast fashion can be linked not only to the house of mirrors that is market research (which reminds us that they are guilty not only *buying* more fashion but also owing to *liking* it more)—but also to a conceptual slippage that happens when the market segment known as fast fashion is taken to stand in for twenty-first century fashion in general. That is to say, while we are all—in the global north and most parts of the global south—wearing 'fast fashion' these days, it is the shopping habits of young women that are pathologised.

While the discourse of ethical fashion obviously points to a 'crisis' in fashion (we should not need ethical fashion) and while it may originate in critique and blame, there is some evidence that not all young people are mindlessly consuming fast fashion, nor do all experience the call to ethical action as a responsibility too hard to bear. In fact, the ethical fashion sphere is arguably a space where young women are well positioned to play a leadership role. It is hard to say—and well beyond the scope of this article—how ethical fashion practices as they are currently playing out might be validated in a causal logic; that is to say, how they might actually address the overconsumption of fashion and the 'unethical' values that permeate the global commodity chains of fashion. Moreover, as the vlog communications make clear, questions of what might make consuming fashion an ethical choice do not transcend questions of economic and geographic privilege, let alone the sorts of social privileges accommodated by a perfect size 10 body. At the same time, questions of how one might conceive of individual consumer responsibility are imperative to addressing not only the issue of the overconsumption of fashion in the twenty-first century, but the consumption of so many other material things to which we may or may not be overattached.

Notes

1. The vlogs that I draw on were observed between February and June 2018, however I also looked at archives dating back to 2015. The majority of the vlogs that I observed emanated from the UK and North America, however I also observed German, Greek and Australian vloggers. All the videos that I refer to in this article were published by young female vloggers, although the ethical vlogosphere does feature some young men as well.
2. Comment posted by Mae Menk on the YouTube video 'A Beginner's Guide to Ethical/Sustainable Fashion'. https://youtu.be/-VRJ9B03NLI.

Disclosure statement

No potential conflict of interest was reported by the author.

References

Arthurs, Jane, Sophia Drakopoulou, and Alessandro Gandini. 2018. "Researching YouTube." *Convergence* 24 (1): 3–15. doi:10.1177/1354856517737222.
Balsiger, Philip. 2016. *The Fight for Ethical Fashion: The Origins and Interactions of the Clean Clothes Campaign*. Abingdon: Routledge.
Barnes, Liz, and Gaynor Lea-Greenwood. 2006. "Fast Fashioning the Supply Chain: Shaping the Research Agenda." *Journal of Fashion Marketing and Management* 10: 259–271. doi:10.1108/13612020610679259.
Barnett, Clive, Paul Cloke, Nick Clarke, and Alice Malpass. 2011. *Globalizing Responsibility: The Political Rationalities of Ethical Consumption*. Malden: Wiley Blackwell.
Bean, Nadia. 2015. "Can Haul Videos Ever Replace Fashion Shoots?" *I-D*, March 19, https://i-d.vice.com/en_uk/article/gygjjw/can-haul-videos-ever-replace-fashion-shoots.
Bourdieu, Pierre. 1984. *Distinction: A Social Critique of the Judgement of Taste*. London: Routledge.
Boylan, J. 2017. *War on Waste [Television Documentary]*. Sydney: Australian Broadcasting Corporation.

Brooks, Andrew. 2015. *Clothing Poverty: The Hidden World of Fast Fashion and Second-Hand Clothes*. London: Zed Books.

Buckley, Cheryl, and Hazel Clark. 2012. "Conceptualizing Fashion in Everyday Lives." *Design Issues* 28 (4): 18–28. doi:10.1162/DESI_a_00172.

Chant, Sylvia. 2006. "Re-thinking the 'Feminization of Poverty' in Relation to Aggregate Gender Indices." *Journal of Human Development* 7 (2): 201–220.

Chant, Sylvia. 2014. "Exploring the 'Feminisation of Poverty' in Relation to Women's Work and Home-Based Enterprise in Slums of the Global South." *International Journal of Gender and Entrepreneurship* 6 (3): 296–316.

Chittenden, Tara. 2010. "Digital Dressing up: Modelling Female Teen Identity in the Discursive Spaces of the Fashion Blogosphere." *Journal of Youth Studies* 13 (4): 505–520. doi:10.1080/13676260903520902.

Cline, Elizabeth. J. 2012. *Over-Dressed: The Shockingly High Cost of Cheap Fashion*. New York: Penguin.

Cosmic Raja. 2017. "How to Shop Ethically on a Budget." Uploaded January 13. YouTube video, 8:35 min. https://www.youtube.com/watch?v=9dSsLOYoQCQ.

Craik, Jennifer. 1994. *The Face of Fashion: Cultural Studies in Fashion*. London: Routledge.

Crane, Diana. 2016. "The Puzzle of the Ethical Fashion Consumer: Implications for the Future of the Fashion System." *International Journal of Fashion Studies* 3 (2): 249–265.

Crewe, Louise. 2017. *The Geographies of Fashion: Consumption, Space and Value*. London: Bloomsbury Academic.

Dean, Christina, Sofia Tarnberg, and Hannah Lane. 2017. *Dress [with] Sense: The Practical Guide to a Concious Closet*. London: Thames and Hudson.

de Certeau, Michel. 1984. *The Practice of Everyday Life*. Berkeley: University of California Press.

Dougher, Kelly. 2015. "How to Shop Ethically: 10 tips for Reducing Your Fashion Footprint, Now!" *Fashion Magazine*, November 16. http://fashionmagazine.com/fashion/how-to-shop-ethically/.

Entwistle, Joanne. 2015a. *The Fashioned Body: Fashion, Dress and Modern Social Theory*. Cambridge: Polity.

Entwistle, Joanne. 2015b. "Sustainability and Fashion." In *Routledge Handbook of Sustainability and Fashion*, edited by Kate Fletcher and Mathilda Tham, 25–32. Abingdon: Routledge.

Findlay, Rosie. 2015. *Personal Style Blogs: Appearances That Fascinate*. London: Intellect.

Gaugele, Elke. 2014. *Aesthetic Politics in Fashion*. Vienna: Sternberg Press.

Hebdige, Dick. 1979. *Subculture: The Meaning of Style*. London: Routledge.

Heti, Sheila, Heidi Julavits, and Leanne Shapton. 2014. *Women in Clothes*. New York: Penguin.

Hookway, Nicholas, and Helene Snee. 2017. "The Blogosphere." In *The SAGE Handbook of Online Research Methods*, edited by Nigel Fielding, Raymond Lee, and Grant Blank, 380–397. London: SAGE Publications.

Hyde, Kayle. 2017. "QUITTING FAST FASHION // One Year Later". Uploaded on July 16. YouTube video, 7:05 min. https://www.youtube.com/watch?v=WW4qK6DlIg8.

Lipovetsky, Gilles. 1994. *The Empire of Fashion: Dressing Modern Democracy*. New French Thought. Princeton: Princeton University Press.

Littler, Jo. 2007. *Radical Consumption: Shopping for Change in Contemporary Culture*. Berkshire: McGraw-Hill Education.

Magner, Lauren. 2017. IBISWorld Industry Report OD4172: Fast Fashion in Australia.

Manovich, Lev. 2009. "The Practice of Everyday (Media) Life: From Mass Consumption to Mass Cultural Production?" *Critical Inquiry* 35 (2): 319–331.

McNeill, Lisa, and Rebecca Moore. 2015. "Sustainable Fashion Consumption and the Fast Fashion Conundrum: Fashionable Consumers and Attitudes to Sustainability in Clothing Choice." *International Journal of Consumer Studies* 39 (3): 212–222.

Miller, Daniel. 2001. "The Poverty of Morality." *Journal of Consumer Culture* 1 (2): 225–243. doi:10.1177/146954050100100210.

Mora, Emanuela, and Agnès Rocamora. 2015. "Letter from the Editors: Analyzing Fashion Blogs—Further Avenues for Research." *Fashion Theory* 19 (2): 149–156. doi:10.2752/175174115X14168357992274.

Morgan, Andrew. 2015. The True Cost. United States: Untold Creative.

Negri, Antonio, and Michael Hardt. 1999. "Value and Affect." *Boundary 2* 26 (2): 77–88.
Phạm, Minh-Hà T. 2013. "Susie Bubble Is a Sign of The Times." *Feminist Media Studies* 13 (2). Routledge: 245–267. doi:10.1080/14680777.2012.678076.
Phạm, Minh-Hà T. 2015. *Asians Wear Clothes on the Internet: Race, Gender, and the Work of Personal Style Blogging*. Durham: Duke University Press.
Phạm, Minh-Hà T. 2017. "The High Cost of High Fashion." *Jacobin*, June 13, 2017. https://www.jacobinmag.com/2017/06/fast-fashion-labor-prada-gucci-abuse-designer.
Press, Claire. 2016. *Wardrobe Crisis: How we Went from Sunday Best to Fast Fashion*. Melbourne: Black Inc.
Rocamora, Agnès. 2011. "Personal Fashion Blogs: Screens and Mirrors in Digital Self-Portraits." *Fashion Theory* 15 (4): 407–424. doi:10.2752/175174111X13115179149794.
Shaw, Deirdre, and Terry Newholm. 2002. "Voluntary Simplicity and the Ethics of Consumption." *Psychology & Marketing* 19 (2): 167–185.
Siegle, Lucy. 2011. *To Die For: Is Fashion Wearing Out the World*. Great Britain: Fourth Estate.
Siegle, Lucy. 2018. "How Your Fast Fashion Habit is Harming More than the Earth." *Vogue Australia*, March 21. https://www.vogue.com.au/fashion/trends/how-your-fast-fashion-habit-is-harming-more-than-the-earth/news-story/b67985de72be083a05570255ee8bdc2c.
Simmel, Georg. 1957. "Fashion." *The American Journal of Sociology* 62 (6): 541–558.
Southwell, Mirjam. 2015. "Fashion and Sustainability in the Context of Gender." In *Routledge Handbook of Sustainability and Fashion*, edited by Kate Fletcher, and Mathilda Tham, 100–110. Abingdon: Routledge.
Sullivan, Anthony. 2016. "Karl Marx: Fashion and Capitalism." In *Thinking Through Fashion: A Guide to key Theorists*, edited by Agnes Rocamora, and Anneke Smelik, 28–45. London: I.B. Tauris.
"The Vlog Aesthetic." Accessed March 31, 2018. http://www-personal.umich.edu/~annaob/vlogaesthetic.html.
Tseëlon, Efrat. 2014. "Introduction: a Critique of the Ethical Fashion Paradigm." In *Fashion and Ethics*, edited by Tseëlon Efrat, 3–68. Bristol: Intellect.
Veblen, Thorstein. 1899. "Conspicuous Consumption." Chap. 4 In *The Theory of the Leisure Class*. Accessed December 14, 2018. https://www.gutenberg.org/files/833/833-h/833-h.htm.
Warde, Alan. 2010. "Editor's Introduction." *Consumption V1*. London: Sage.
Wilson, Elizabeth. 2003. *Adorned in Dreams: Fashion and Modernity*. London: I.B. Tauris.
Wilson, Elizabeth. 1987. *Adorned in Dreams: Fashion and Modernity*. Berkeley: University of California.
Woodward, Sophie. 2007. *Why Women Wear What They Wear*. Oxford: Berg.

Performative Rhetorics in Invisibility: Phoebe Philo's Undone Authorship

Erin O'Connor

ABSTRACT
This inquiry analyses the rhetoric of intentionally unfinished fashion contained in the collections from Céline as designed by Phoebe Philo and explicates the implications of this approach to fashion as a feminist text. Shoshana Felman's seductive promise of speech, modified with insights from Paul de Man's theory of autobiography as both giving face and defacement, is applied to Philo's 'new minimalism' in order to highlight its appeal to modern female audiences. Using insights from the philosophy of Jacques Derrida, I examine ways in which wearers may seek to create a signature citationality via clothing that produces its own 'unwriting' therefore allowing the wearer to believe she inscribes her own iteration while maintaining control. Wearers are offered the chance to identify with a designer who is enlightened beyond fast and flashy fashion while hinting at the notion of the clothing having the substantialising effect that language has (instead of representational). Through this examination, clothing is shown to be a decision, and clothing is also shown to be a fiction. These decisions and fictions are open to failure; yet Felman offers that this failure acts as an opening remaining inadvertent or unacknowledged. Philo's designs invite an exploration of clothing as performative rhetoric.

In Hans Christian Andersen's fable of the 'Emperor's New Clothes' a needy, materialistic emperor is deceived through the weaving of language to publicly spend great amounts of wealth to have visiting weavers make clothing for him. This promised clothing was so magnificent that it would become invisible to anyone not fit for office or unusually stupid. Thus, the king ends up naked and exposed in front of his subjects all of whom secretly worried they would be called stupid or unfit for believing their own eyes. Language, in this fable, is not only used to persuade him that where there is nothing there is something; the key is that he relies on what others say about his appearance as more real than what he can feel with his sensing body. Thus, the tale is one of conspicuous consumption: eager public consumption of expensive 'goods' by the king, and fearful consumption of a lie by his followers. Desire for approval is often an exercise in giving the complete power of valuation over to language's substantialising effects, even at the expense of bodily experiences. As an extreme version of performative rhetoric, this fable points to the absurdity of what language can create. But what should we make of inconspicuous consumption and language? Here, I examine the work of a clothing designer who has built her house, and our current aesthetic of women's work wear, on the unique idea that women might feel powerful and persuasive when they feel less visible. I argue that it is a uniquely feminist approach to shift clothing design away from either the side of language and its 'statement making' or the side of 'the body' but instead to mediation between the two as a form of performative rhetoric that simultaneously produces what it enunciates.

Phoebe Philo came to the fashion house of Céline as head designer in 2010 and left in 2018, ushering in an aesthetic many have called a 'new' minimalism. Most of the descriptions used for Philo's pieces circle around the terms invisibility and strength. Like the story of the emperor with no clothes in reverse, the women who wear the brand feel that the visible clothing gives them an invisibility that is equated with a version of power, specifically connected to gender roles. In focusing on Philo's work in the form of what she produces along with her broader cultural impact, I offer a chance for answering the question: how does clothing function within performative rhetoric?

This contributes to a method for feminist approaches to studying clothing as a dimension of communication and influence. Can we ever be what we say? Can we say what we want with our physical presence? Can we control visibility without taking ourselves out of the picture? Put another way, does invisibility give us space to write ourselves? To explore this I will look at three dimensions of performative rhetoric and their resonance with this designer's work. First, I examine Derrida's citationality and the scene of the inscription of the mark and how this applies to communication through clothing. There is a tension at stake for the wearers and discussions of Philo's work, between luxury manifesting in not having to show yourself and yet feeling luxurious in recognisably designer clothing. This at least hints at the notion of clothes having the substantialising effect that language has (instead of a representational effect only).

Second, I ask if something can be undone on purpose and examine the control sought after in high end fashion's design and use and in how we dress ourselves generally. With Shoshana Felman's concept of a 'misfire' that reveals hope beyond language, I ask if we can plan for or even acknowledge our misfires while simultaneously examining how women's fashion has reacted to the more forgiving and fluid clothing styles usheredin by Philo's work. Clothing is functioning both as beyond language and as a type of language, and I look at how, when the body speaks in spite of us, clothing often mediates.

This question of control leads me to the third part of this discussion, in which I complicate authorship in the 'writing' (in this case, the designing) process. Philo's work as a text also offers a unique perspective from which to examine authorship. The discussion from many writers depicting Philo's work (and designer goods) relies on a strong sense of authorship – of being 'in the know' on who to watch and buy – and those who wear the clothing get to be this sort of woman of whom the designer speaks. Yet, the way women are interacting with Céline's clothing lines, the immediate copies available at Zara, and even the way Philo discusses her work, as well as the clothing itself expands and collapses the category of designer/author in new ways. Authorship of a given design and what can or cannot be owned (a pattern like the famous Diane von Furstenberg wrap-dress? a colour like Tiffany Blue?) remains a battleground for copyright lawyers, but for everyday people, contending with what is for sale, the lines between knock-off, mimics, and trends hide in plain sight. The material artifacts appear before us without explanation but often as citations, and we take them up every day to do the explaining for us, to be complimented on our choices of good taste, to enter the social parts of our lives and so on. I close with considering how Paul de Man's undecidability contributes to a feminist approach to understanding our dressed bodies and influence in communication.

While the text I have chosen to explore are Phoebe Philo's rich designs, the beauty and complexity of this text also lies in the multilayered media surrounding those designs. Her designs are presented in runway shows that are photographed and streamed online; they are written about and reviewed in fashion magazines as collections; they are featured in editorials in magazines like *Vogue*; they show up on Instagram feeds and blogs. In addition to the multiple texts spinning out from the designs, there are texts spinning around Phoebe Philo as a public figure as well. From magazine features with in-depth interviews to special events featuring 'A Conversation with … ' to her taking a bow after a show and answering a few questions backstage, Philo herself is documented and represented as much as her work. These texts are how most people like me get 'access' to the designs and we must function within the hyper-mediated aspect of this access. Examining the rhetorical aspects of this work allows me to look at how these designs are taken up and circulated via many dimensions in a discursive sphere. Rather than requiring direct access to the designs or one-on-one information from the designer in order to examine the work, the salience of these texts is in the way meaning emerges in the tangle of mediums, experiences and connectivity.

Performative rhetoric, clothing, and fashion as communication

Three terms will be important to understand at the outset: performative rhetoric, clothing, and fashion, at least with regard to Philo's creations and understanding of the term. Performative rhetoric is most often associated with speech-act theory, as outlined in J. L. Austin's lectures, *How To Do Things With Words (1962)*. Austin offers a provisional distinction between 'constative' language (that is descriptive of 'what is') and 'performative' language (that creates, inaugurates, and produces). Austin collapses the distinction between 'saying' and 'doing', opening questions of language and being. While many researchers have followed this opening in differing directions, here I will be focusing on rhetoric's substantialising effects.

Most (in)famously, Judith Butler (1990) explores performative rhetoric in *Gender Trouble: Feminism and the Subversion of Identity* by arguing that gender is performed through 'words, acts, gestures, and desires' that are 'performative in the sense that the essence or identity that they otherwise purport to express are fabrications manufactured and sustained through corporeal signs and other discursive means' (136). Using this as a framework, performative rhetoric can be defined as utterances that do not only describe but through language and embodiment constitute the things they say.

In this direction, I follow Jaques Derrida (1972) who begins 'Signature, Event, Context' with a call to expand the word 'communication' to 'a semantic domain that precisely does not limit itself to semantics, semiotics, and even less to linguistics' (1) – this is a call to performative language. Rather than simple exchange of meaning, the term takes communication and meaning as rupture, force, and displacement that is proliferated as it is utilised. He offers two proposals to expand our language discovery. The first locates absence in the very origin of language and writing; any chance at specificity in writing depends upon absence of all the other meanings (7). The second proposal extends this absence first found in writing to all of language, undoing the hierarchy of speech over writing.

As a critique of Austin's narrowly defined performative language, Derrida locates the limitless potential Austin so carefully tried to contain as applying only to special language and expands it to every mark or inscription of difference – locates it in ordinary language. For Derrida, the most basic form of communication generates the 'mark', meaning any inscription of difference, and so, of meaning. The mark can exist and function beyond the moment of inscription and can carry force and meaning beyond the original author's/speaker's intention. Instead of basing language on an idea of a pure form with impure effects (as does Austin), all of language becomes iterations within webs of possibilities; 'It is simply that those effects do not exclude what is generally opposed to them, term by term; on the contrary, they presuppose it, in an asymmetrical way, as the general space of their possibility' (19). This is Derrida's emancipatory hope – that everything cannot be fully programmed and the context can never be fully determined; performative rhetoric holds space for this hope. The social and political messages urged on audiences, readers, consumers, viewers and so on, are not deterministic but productive and disruptive of both creator and consumer, in this case, designer and wearer.

The second term needing some scaffolding is clothing. For years feminist scholars looked at clothing and fashion as sites of oppression and confinement. These studies tended to centre media representing clothing (advertising, films) as guiding texts. More recently, feminist studies of clothing have included more complex standpoints on the entanglement of expressive and oppressive aspects in clothing. Negrin (2008) centres her work in fashion on the paradox of a postmodern 'body'. Valerie Steele has championed fashion and embodiment as cultural texts and served as founding editor in chief starting in 1997 to academic journal *Fashion Theory: The Journal of Dress, Body, and Culture*. Susie Orbach's (2009) *Bodies* and, foundationally, Elizabeth Grosz's (1994) *Volatile Bodies: Toward a Corporeal Feminism* both touch on clothing and bodies as co-constitutive. Kim Sawchuck (1987) offers a Derridian direction for feminist fashion scholars stating, 'these inscriptions of the social take place *at* the level of the body, not *upon* it' (55), and I follow her lead as scholars move the focus away from fashion as representation of a centralised power towards how specific clothing (texts) are taken up and constitutive in particular contexts.

Central to my exploration is that texts throughout popular culture have rhetorical impact on audiences (Brummett 1991). Implicit in this foundation is that the choice of text will greatly effect what rhetorical dimensions can be explored. Clothing items, specifically Philo's designs, as well as the writing about those items, form the text under consideration for my exploration as an echo and answer to Parkins' (2008) call that, 'Still missing is a strong feminist theoretical literature that considers the cultural significance of fashion as a textual and material system' (501). To understand clothing in the context of Philo's work, I look to how it is described and detailed in writing and images. Examining interviews with Philo, articles about her, and her collections (at least images of them via advertisements, magazine shoots, and fashion websites) gives me the opportunity to think about both clothing as a performative rhetoric on the wearer and the viewer/non-wearer. Specifically, clothing as I will use the term simply means the material goods we put on ourselves, while fashion is the larger network of meaning those materials are located within. Wanting clothing to 'say' something is a common enough idea – even Philo discusses her draw to designing by saying, 'I really think it comes up and out of me, an idea of wanting to use clothes to say something' (Crisell 2014). Perhaps we also want our clothing to do something and for us to be able to do something in them – and do things for those who we encounter.

Philo's own disclosures of her creative process rely on a sense of limitations and parameters that create space for spontaneity and creativity. She uses the term 'a real life' to describe a meaning created in the doing of life, and her clothing offers freedom of movement, materials and fabrics that structure a kind of predictability and protection within that daily flow. 'I find it reassuring to use fabrics that perform in a very honest, straightforward way ... I don't like clothes imposing themselves on women. They are to be used in a real life' (Blanks 2013). In talking about wearing Philo's designs, women inevitably seem to talk about their various forms and roles: being a mother, the actions of their daily lives, and a description of appreciation rarely found in designer interviews. Her sense of work coming from only her 'gut' and its relation to time (as a limitation) is fascinating to performative rhetoric in that both (self and time) serve as a sort of naturalising force in her narrative. What clothing is in this narrative remains part of what I will explore with these texts as my guide.

Part of the context for Philo's work is that she is considered a *fashion* designer, meaning, her work is for a fashion house producing haute couture and ready-to-wear garments. This brings me to the third term structuring this exploration: fashion as it relates to language and communication. Elizabeth Wilson's (1985) foundational text *Adorned in Dreams: Fashion and Modernity* describes fashion as a form of dress 'in which the key feature is rapid and continual changing of styles' as well as that which 'sets the terms of *all* sartorial behaviour' in Western societies (3). This bold enclosure of all clothing and dress into fashion's network is an important redirection in considering fashion as a text and language in that Wilson positions it all in a *system of meaning*; the material fact of clothing does not exist outside of a system of meaning to the point where even being unfashionable can be seen as a reaction to or against that system. This sense of systematisation is picked up by Barnard (2002) in *Fashion as Communication* when he states that fashion and clothing are 'cultural phenomena insofar as they [are] signifying practices' and 'some of the ways in which a social order [are] experienced and communicated' (59). He is careful to outline the many functions of fashion, summarising, '[t]he unifying function of fashion and clothing serves to communicate membership of a cultural group both to those who are members of it and to those who are not' (60). Roland Barthes' (1967) detailed analysis of the 'rhetoric of fashion' in *The Fashion System* sets up a linguistic semiology in which, like his theory of language, the objects named have arbitrary differences yet their significance is known only from those differences. Barthes argues all sign systems are closed in this way. Barthes, in a very structuralist mode, attempts to separate the connotative (for him this is the rhetorical system) from the denotative language (vestimentary code) in fashion.

Yet in Austin's teachings, language is not only connotative or denotative, but also performative. Austin is clear that at times to say a sentence 'is not to *describe* my doing ... or to state that I am doing it: it is to do it' (1962, 6). Wearing clothing, as part of a fashion system, is not communication meant to only describe or to state, but in the *wearing* to make it so.

As Parkins offers, 'one of fashion's greatest strengths for feminism is its ability to problematise the unnecessary antagonism between poststructuralist and materialist approaches, which threatens to impoverish feminist theory' (2008, 502). Parkins' work brings fashion to feminism through Karen Barad's epistemological theory of agential realism. For Barad, knowing and becoming are already intertwined, which gestures to performativity as an opening in continuing the discussion of feminist explorations of fashion. Barad's (2003) embrace of 'performative metaphysics' shows forces and practices are always material-discursive: at once productive of matter and of meaning. With Barad, we lose the ontological gap between subjects and objects, which representation is designed to mediate. Looking at fashion through the designs of one person and how these are taken up by wearers and observers (of the clothing and of the phenomenon of a designer's influence), allows us to look at clothing as constituting the very thing the wearer would like to say while also moving beyond clothing as representing a mind behind the design or body wearing it.

Citationality and the scene of inscription

Clothing, especially highly fashionable clothing, is most often discussed as a form of signification, both by researchers and consumers. While the exact meanings of specific materials, items and goods are debatable, they are generally understood to mean something. At stake here is what Barry Brummett (2008) outlines in *A Rhetoric of Style*, wherein, '[r]easons, motives, and so forth are activated aesthetically in a culture that is aesthetically dominated, as is ours' (127). Starting with the pragmatic experience of longing to know (via clothing), 'what it will mean to wear a certain pair of jeans or shoes in public', clothing as a form of signification becomes a way 'to predict how people will react' (30).

Of course, it is not so predictable, though. One way to understand why signification is so hard to pin down is to consider Jacques Derrida's (1972) assertion that every sign can be cited, 'put between quotation marks', and 'in so doing it can break with every given context, engendering an infinity of new contexts in a manner which is absolutely illimitable' (12). The confluence of space, citationality and detachment in the mark culminates in his chosen example of 'the instance of the juridic signature' (19). A signature paradoxically functions as 'the pure reproducibility of a pure event' (20) in which authenticity functions in reproducibility; the signature must be cited and reproduced in citation as an indicator of authenticity. Put another way, we can only prove authenticity of identity with signs that are repeatable. They can only be repeatable if they work in new contexts, which, in turn, generate new meanings and versions of authenticity.

Every sign, then, is a citation. In order to make sense, the very possibility of communication requires the mark's ability to be detached from its 'original' desire, usage and intention, rendering every sign and iteration a 'citation' of a previously ongoing mark's usage. We know a mark and a sign by what it is not; we know presence because of our sense of absence.

How might this function in appearance and dress as it does in writing and speaking? Put another way: is clothing a form of communication because it is part of this network of both iterability, difference and citationality? When asked to comment on the clothing she wears from Philo, actress Isabelle Huppert remarks, 'How can I look my best? ... You are not visible with Phoebe's clothes. It's not too obvious. It's a way of not being seen'

(Vargas 2014). This approach to clothing certainly sounds like a citation of absence, dressing yourself to hide yourself, feeling your presence because of your sense of absence. It's a strange coupling; 'look[ing] my best' becomes equated with 'not being seen'. It seems that with clothing, absence and presence, concerning the wearer and the designer, creates and limits possibilities for meaning and identity formation. Philo herself leads this charge, offering, 'I have an innate fear of fame. I don't know where it comes from, but I have never thought that being famous looked like a good place to be. I love being incognito. I very much value my freedom' (Marriott 2014). At work regarding Philo's designs is both citationality (that the wearer wants to have others know she can afford a real Céline piece) and perhaps the 'pure reproducibility of a pure event' (Derrida 1972, 20) as the wearer's iteration of identity, especially class identity, creates a signature look that relies on absence of other designs and the taste of the wearer and observer. Still, that invisibility is a coded and weighted invisibility that allows another customer to claim, 'Yet as subtle as the Céline code is ... there are giveaways that are recognizable to those in the know, such as a longer sleeve or a topcoat without a closure' (Vargas 2014). There is a sort-of cited-invisibility, or even cited undone-ness, at play.

For many in the fashion world, up through Philo's first collection in 2011, the 'pure event' where one's fashion sensibility was most on display as an event was attending fashion week and getting photographed by street fashion photographers. Fashion critic Suzy Menkes (2013) lamented this takeover by the 'showoffs' in a piece titled, 'The Circus of Fashion' in which she remembers, 'I can't help feeling how different things were when cool kids loved to dress up for one another – or maybe just for themselves'. She decries the fashion blogger's constant posture of 'look at me wearing the dress!' as missing the point of great fashion being great whether you would want to wear it on the street or not. For Menkes, and many other cultural authorities, reducing all of fashion to bow at the throne of conspicuous consumption created less room for that sense of social order fashion brings. This lament for order (hierarchy) was both widely criticised for being elitist and widely pointed to as the beginning of the end of maximalist streetwear.

Thorstein Veblen put forth the idea of 'conspicuous consumption' in 1899 as a form of class distinction wherein the usual rules of economics are reversed – the higher the price, the more in demand the item becomes. The price of a Veblen good is not reliant on the cost of production but rather the class distinction it creates. However, in the case of Céline, clothing and accessories are specifically inconspicuous fashion wherein invisibility is linked to greater power. 'The clothes are quiet and not meant to make a statement. And so you look invisible. Able to be viewed for more than your surface appearance. This is power dressing.' (Vargas 2014). The class distinction is to become invisible yet somehow retain the power of class distinction.

In light of the 'fashion circus' mentality that fashion only works when it is creating an event in which you are getting looked at (through photographers snapping your image or 'likes' and followers on social media), the eventfulness of Philo's designs seems to transfer that power to the wearer having some control over being looked at. 'The idea that quiet fashion now conveys power is ironic' comments Vargas, 'given that for years that spot has been defined by bright colors, broad shoulders, wide lapels, cinched waistlines – caricatures of exaggerated severity' (2014). It is an attunement to the ways we give our power away in the era of social media and a quiet reclaiming. This is what is meant by 'new minimalism' in a cultural sense but there is also a fashion sense accompanying this as well.

Minimalism is a movement across genres, including art, music and architecture that has resonance across history for fashion. Architect Ludwig Mies van der Rohe famously summed up this aesthetic, stating, '[l]ess is more' (see Johnson 1947, 49). His designs were characterised by each element serving multiple purposes with the appearance of simplicity smoothing over many details and functionalities. In fashion specifically, minimalism can be seen as early as Coco Chanel's early twentieth century adoption of utilitarian dock worker fabrics for women's everyday clothing but it is most often associated in the United States with the 1950s and 60s emphasis on the materiality of the clothing designs, rather than any explicit symbolism or emotional content. This aesthetic resurfaced in the 90s after the maximalist trend with its shoulder pads and sequins of the 1980s but this time without any fear of the figure of the body shaping the clothing as well. Philo's version of minimalism is not alone – at the time of her first, very structured collection in 2011 she was riding a wave

Figure 1. Designer Phoebe Philo typifies a minimalist aesthetic. Paris Fashion Week Womenswear Spring/Summer 2017, 2 October 2016 in Paris. Photo: Pascal Le Segretain/Getty Images.

of a return to the 90s aesthetic. Yet, Philo most typifies the aesthetic throughout her whole workflow (see Figure 1). 'Reduction and revision have been founding principles of Céline since Philo became creative director of the label five years ago', states Lisa Armstrong (2014) for *The Telegraph*. 'This is a designer who pores over each piece, subtracting until she's reached that distinctive Céline equilibrium between the austere and the luxurious. It's design as a meditative pursuit rather than a process of embellishment – a kind of haute-minimalism'. The question is, how does this this sort of utility of structure and subtraction remain *luxurious* and desirable, or even recognisable?

One explanation is that there are more levels of signaling wealth than Veblen's original theory suggests. In their study, 'Signaling Status with Luxury Goods: The Role of Brand Prominence', Han, Nunes, and Drèze (2010) discuss two new distinctions for wealthy customers of luxury brands. The first group, the 'parvenus', wants to be visually associated with images of wealth and feel a 'need for status' (16–17). 'Parvenus possess significant wealth but not the connoisseurship necessary to interpret subtle signals' (17) making them more likely to buy items with prominent or 'loud' branding. The second group, the 'patricians', are more interested in 'inconspicuously branded products that serve as a horizontal signal' to each other (other wealthy people) rather than to the masses.

Is Philo's definition of invisibility entirely reliant upon the sense of visibility of other brands, then, in fashion? As with the patricians and the parvenus, the giveaways signal the designer-connection and make it visible for some. But the signal is not merely that the buyer has taste or wealth but that she is a certain kind of woman. The ultimate luxurious experience is not having to show (off) yourself to the masses. Han, Nunes and Dreze found that Gucci and Louis Vuitton, in fact, charge more for quieter handbags (with little to no branding) than their loudly branded bags (19). What's more, they found that counterfeiters are more likely to copy those louder goods (although that is not always the case with mainstream fast fashion, like Zara or Forever21). Following their findings, Céline designs are simply an increasingly nuanced way for patricians to signal to each other.

Yet, *Vogue* magazine's Sarah Mower declares, 'No designer has been more copied than Philo herself – all over fashion, from student collections to young designers to the mass market' (2017). Philo is responsible for what has become current women's workwear style, beyond knock-off versions of her specific items. 'Look around this winter, on subways and buses' Mower offers, 'wherever there's a woman in a camel coat, gray pants and white boots – that's Phoebe Philo who did that'. And she is certainly counterfeited as well. 'The main criticism against Céline is that the clothes are too expensive. For that, we now have Zara' (Vargas 2014). On cheap brands copying her designs, Philo herself only says, 'Most of the time I find it really flattering and exciting' (Sykes 2014). Even without loud branding, the clothing designs ripple through the market at every level leading to the possibility that it is not the brand name that is generating the desire for owning and wearing these clothes but the designs themselves. As the highest compliment to Philo, Mower states, 'she belongs to that rarest order of designers who are able to change the way people dress to such a point that it's so normalized, no one sees it anymore' (2017). If the signals were meant only for other patricians, it would seem that the gig is up; invisibility is on sale racks everywhere.

As chief designer at Chloe from 2001 to 2006, Philo's work spans much longer than her recently ended tenure at Céline and the significance of her work has been characterised in *Vogue* as no less than a 'lightning conductor of the female energy of the times, twice over'

(Mower 2016). 'It felt like a clean slate', she says of leaving Chloe to start at Céline. 'But it also felt interesting because Céline was founded by a woman, and what it had stood for historically was clothes for women by women.' (Rawsthorn 2010) Connotations can be set free from material goods, just as Derrida sets writing free from a secure signified. This creates new conditions in language but if this generative power extends to objects like clothing, what does it look like? If every mark must be readable outside of the scene of its inscription, every mark is set free from intention (1972, 10). In order for clothing to remain readable, iterable, or wearable it must be able to function outside of any designer's, and perhaps any wearer's, intention or guidance, while remaining haunted by what is to come. Philo offers, 'I felt it was time for a more back-to-reality approach to fashion, clothes that are beautiful, strong, and have ideas, but with real life driving them' (Berrington 2008). Grounding clothing in 'real life', or as alive, functions as citation for her, yet also holds the context open, boundless, and untraceable.

Wearers want to attribute Philo's clothes to having a blank identity but then having all identities; 'Céline gives women style that is glamorous and feminine without being too girly. The bloke part is in there' is how another customer, Pauline Daly, describes the clothing (Vargas 2014). One example of this is the line of 'mannish' shirts feature in Autumn/Winter 2016 with ironed-in creases and just a little too long collars and cuffs. The effect of the shirts is that of menswear for women but with the feminine wearer's own twist. Unlike women's suits mimicking masculine cuts in a 'feminised' version, this has the effect of a woman who shops in the men's section and outright takes what she wants (see Figure 2). I find it telling that the clothing's potential for blank identity relies on not being 'too girly' or, perhaps, the absence of proscribed and written femininity. Yet, it is as if the presence of masculine style allows for rewriting – the surface appearance enables more than surface when it is skewed masculine. How might absence be different from invisibility? The Céline citationality is widespread across economic classes yet the originals do not wear thin in their allure for those who can afford them. Perhaps we could say those wearing her styles (if not her 'authentic' designs) are seeking to create a signature citationality via clothing that produces its own 'unwriting', thereby allowing the wearer to believe she inscribes her own iteration. Perhaps those wealthy buyers believe all the downstream consumers are trying to be like them.

I argue, instead, that for most designers, the moment of inscription belongs to the fashion house; the scene of inscription is orchestrated and shared for purchase, to be cited by ready-to-wear, luxury pieces that will be copied and circulated as copies of an original, authentic piece, to the masses who cannot afford participation otherwise. But for Philo's designs, the moment of inscription belongs to the wearer; the clothes are not meant to be seen as authentic signature pieces with copies, but activated only when worn by women; the authenticity functions in reproducibility, not of the original precious runway piece but of the design itself.

Undone on purpose

In *The Scandal of the Speaking Body*, Shoshana Felman (2002) introduces the promise as the ultimate performative utterance. She shows that our body cannot help but speak and the body that speaks is always already wrapped up in productive failure. It fails in that the body as our unconscious 'cannot know what it is doing' (67) yet is still what

Figure 2. Celine Spring/Summer 2011 ready-to-wear collection show on 3 October 2010 in Paris. Photo: Pierre Verdy/AFP/Getty Images.

the act of language relies on upon. Our uncontrollable bodies (situated at the unconscious) tell by insisting and persisting that we cannot keep our promises, and we don't even realise it. Felman states it is a scandal, that telling, which arises

> … of the incongruous but indissoluble relation between language and the body; the scandal of the seduction of the human body insofar as it speaks the scandal of the promise of love

insofar as this promise is par excellence the promise that cannot be kept; the scandal of the promising animal insofar as what he promises is precisely the untenable. (5)

The promise is ultimately performative because it will produce and generate force and meaning beyond what we intend, beyond what we promise. Felman separates self-referentiality with time: the subject of the ego is the speaking subject who promises and the subject of enunciation is self-produced by (the speaking body's) disclosure whose words carry meaning in excess of what is intended. The body disrupts the positioning and posing of the speaker; it makes our utterances possible and undoes and exceeds them from the start. There is no dichotomy between mind and body because of the body's pervasiveness in language, then.

Perhaps, what I promise as the subject of ego with my appearance and clothing is that I am who I show myself to be. I can intend that only wealthy people can recognise who I show myself to be or I can intend that no one look at me, even. Yet I can never keep that promise, even in front of the mirror; as the subject of enunciation, my dressed body is both conscious and unconscious, directive and excessive. Thinking of dressing as not just language but specifically as Felman's promise, develops the performative dimension's pleasure of mastery coupled with its lack of control. Philo discusses her work as 'building collections where I'm able to be spontaneous and yes, there's some disruption, corruption, distortion and organized chaos ... a bit of a fight going on ... a feeling of it being built up, then a slight ripping apart' (Blanks 2013). And yet, can the excess, the failure of the language in the moment of the saying/wearing be so planned? Do her designs simply acknowledge this or is she (and by extension, her customers) trying to account for and limit the fissure? Which leads me to ask, what sort of promises are made with clothing?

While most styles – certainly those designed by Philo – rely on our ability to play with floating signifiers that we do not take overly seriously (i.e. wearing a cowboy hat does not a cowboy make), that we read 'statements' made with clothing as disclosures of identity indicates we still hold out that clothing is telling the viewers something about the wearer and the designer. Philo mentions she finds it 'strange' that after shows she is peppered with questions about what she intended the pieces to be about; as if further description could be action – more action than the very existence and sight would indicate. This could be taken as the items' failures to speak fully, to master the signification. But Felman's sense is that the failure is an opening. She states, '[t]he act of failing thus opens up the space of referentiality – or of impossible reality – not because something is missing, but because something else is done, or because something else is said: the term 'misfire' does not refer to an absence, but to the enactment of a difference' (57).

On the side of invisibility, that enactment of difference may be that we want to try to get out of this promise made through clothing. There is a long, detailed history of women being told what their appearance is promising to those around them. There are examples throughout popular culture where women are judged to be bad mothers, childish, asking for it, unprofessional, incompetent, too confident, bitchy – all by what their clothing is 'saying'. Women cannot keep the promise of whatever we are saying with our clothing, and what's more, we don't want to be beholden to whatever someone else reads into it. Felman sees a new materiality in Austin's ideas, one in which language produces the referent to which it refers, and there is discomfort with this.

As women tangle with how their clothing may speak of their lives, another aspect of invisibility and clothing is that many women experience dangerous and dehumanising invisibility. For many women, this has to do with a seeming aging-out of visibility; the older we get, the less we are acknowledged as existing in shared space. In an episode of Netflix's series, *Grace and Frankie* (Gordon 2015), the two women, both in their seventies, desperately try to get the attention of several store clerks with no success to the point where they simply walk out of the store with their items unpaid. The red-bandana hat and bright caftan worn by Frankie and the sharp professional clothing on Grace make no difference at all. Grace eventually yells, 'I exist!' before being ushered out of the store by Frankie who summarises in the car, holding her stolen goods 'can't see me, you can't stop me'. On a more serious note, there is the terrifying statistic that more than 60,000 black women are missing in North America. Not just treated as invisible but as gone and forgotten. According to the Black and Missing Foundation black women make up roughly 8 percent of the population in the United States but nearly 37 percent of missing women (Jones 2017). The Black Lives Matter movement has been grappling with how quickly and automatically the movement's activism has excluded Black women, leading activist-poet Claudia Rankine to state 'The invisibility of black women is astounding' (Cocozza 2015). This reinforces the fact that the power being negotiated by Philo and her fans is, as all power, not only gendered and economic but aged, abled and raced.

How much can clothing produce and shape the body while the body and language also push back? Paul de Man (1984) quotes Wordsworth talking about the 'right kind of language as being 'not what the garb is to the body but what the body is to the soul' (79). Wordsworth is agitated over language (rhetoric) 'clothing thought' and insists that good language is 'incarnate thought', or naked thought (79). Felman's answer to this call for pure, unadorned thought is to point to the creative force arising in language's (consciousness) and body's (unconsciousness) 'undecidability and their constant interference' (67).

Does clothing, then, side with language or the body, here? Philo offers, '[t]here is nothing else in life that we keep as close to us, literally wearing it on our bodies as we do clothes' (Blanks 2013). Clothing both adorns the body and extends, or contours, the body, placing clothing in a situation similar to the mouth for Felman: as mediation between the language and the body (37). Every promise is a promise of consciousness (34) but the mouth blurs any chance of a binary. For de Man, what naked flesh and clothing share, 'in opposition to the thoughts they both represent' is 'their visibility, their accessibility to the senses' (79). In this very undecidability, the production of meaning and embodiment is made possible (57–58). Fashion reviewer Cathy Horyn (2016) sees that Philo 'recognizes that ambivalence' between the need to dress and the desire to represent a 'self', and claims the designer 'actually builds on it', perfectly exemplifying how ambivalence opens productivity. While many other designers often build ambivalence through androgyny, Philo builds this through purposefully unfinished details, folds of materials that get adjusted by the wearer and playing with surprise such as unexpected volume or attention to materials only the wearer will see. A great example of this is the 2017 collection's black and white print button-up silk shirt. As a tricky material, the silk is presented already wrinkled and worn in a fit that often annoys women; the button-up is pulling apart at the buttons revealing diamonds of flesh behind the material. Any customer could purchase this shirt in a size larger for a more expected fit but the presentation pays attention to how wearer's bodies often work against the ways clothes are designed. Philo's shirt is blurring the distinction between intentional (self-directed) openings or revelations and unintentional openings and disclosures.

Felman's subject of enunciation, thus, is produced by discourse and is NOT the agent of what she says, or in this case, wears. Her words carry meaning in excess of what she means to say. History is made up of trivialities – minor decisions, ambiguities in terms of acts (83) that are not in opposition to the generalisable but remain unclassifiable and get left out of histories. Misfires are where we encounter the experience that language is not everything, and in its failing we get the affirmation of something beyond language – a generative fissure establishing the possibility of everything.

As Leonard Cohen observes with his lyrics, 'there is a crack in everything; that's how the light gets in', there is a sense in Felman of this act of failure as opening always being inadvertent or unacknowledged. Can the fissure be produced intentionally? Can the undone be 'done' or cited on purpose, or is that missing the point? In Philo's design work, there is often a leaving-off or leaving-out certain elements – an unfinished hem open to fray, or a skirt's silhouette just slightly off-kilter. For example, in Autumn of 2016 she sent slacks with 'printed cuffs of chiffon flopping over the shoes – like an errant bit of trash that gets stuck on your toe' (Horyn 2016). This gestures towards the presence of fissure but does not purport to master it or foreclose further misfires.

Fiction and decision in authorship

Sophie Hicks, a customer of Philo's, states that '[i]f you want to feel right in your clothes and you don't want to show off [your wealth], then you wear Céline. There are no connotations to do with class or background' (Vargas 2014). This is complete fiction considering she's claiming this while wearing a $4400 outfit that is recognisably designer, even if only to 'insiders'. Clothing is a decision: we must dress. Yet clothing can be completely made up: I may not be who I present myself to be. Even when I think I'm dressing without intended connotations, I'm telling a story and my actions are grounded in materiality and economy. For Paul de Man (1984), all texts are based on fictional structure, which is a system of substitutions in which any attempt to write renders the author the *reader*. Simultaneously, all texts are based on autobiography where there is self-representation of its very own self (70). For clothing as a text, when we assemble what we will wear, we are both author *and* reader, wearer and viewer, representation and original.

This is the performative dimension of clothing that works like language; Judith Butler (1993) writes, 'performativity is construed as that power of discourse to produce effects through iteration,' to 'produce what it declares' (20, 107). This resonates with de Man's conception of language as the bestowing of visibility and the giving of figuration, or the giving of face, yet it is founded in a fictional structure that, like Derrida, centres this productivity on absence. 'To the extent that language is figure (or metaphor, or prosopopeia) it is indeed not the thing itself but the representation.... Language as a trope is always privative' (de Man, 80). Language is always giving absence. Performative language is no longer about how we use language, but aspects of what language does to us and in spite of us.

Philo remarked to *Vogue*, 'I came about it through wearing it … It's always that' (Mower 2017). Using clothing as a sort of autobiography is not a terribly new idea, neither for the wearer nor for the designer. Whether it is telling the story of the wearer, or that of the designer, we tend to believe what we see. A person's dress is experienced in the present moment by the wearer and the observer. Yet with this performative shift in language and writing, we can explore not how we use clothing but what clothing does to us and in spite of us. Philo's clothing gives visibility even as it gives privacy; creates spaces for the wearers and their various roles in life while erasing the connotations that often accompany those roles (mother, wealthy, feminine, etc.).

With clothing, as with language, it does not have to be either/or. de Man wants us to remain in the 'whirligig' of language's undecidability between the text and the author and which is producing whom. By troubling the waters of autobiography-as-genre he demonstrates that the entire concept resists cohesion, saying of autobiographies that, '[e]ach specific instance seems to be an exception to the norm' concluding that 'generic discussions … remain distressingly sterile when autobiography is at stake' (68). Muddying the distinction between autobiography and fiction he questions, 'Are we so certain that autobiography depends on its reference[?]' (69). Staying within the undecidable, autobiography becomes generative and 'the interest of autobiography, then, is not that it reveals reliable self-knowledge – it does not – but that it demonstrates in a striking way the impossibility of closure and totalization' (71). With the clothing as the text, we are both the written-I and the writing-I, giving face to a self while defiguring a self.

So what does undecidability look like, feel like, with the clothed body? I suggest that this impossibility of closure and totalisation is exactly what we can experience in clothing and this is a uniquely feminist approach to clothing. 'It would be overdoing it to read this interim collection as a statement or to read any profound prescribed meaning into any one thing', writes Sarah Mower. 'The meaning is what the woman herself gives the piece, the context she puts it in, the extent to which it becomes part of her life: That's Céline-style feminism for you' (2016). The ability to rewrite a self into the text (the clothing) while also letting the text become part of that self/life sounds like Iris Young's version of a feminine language which, 'moves and twists, starts over again from different perspectives, does not go straight to the point' (1985, 179). And it sounds like Barad's sense that language produces rather than represents a reality, and matter is a process and affective materialisation. This language is not only generative, but replaces the 'sterility and oppressiveness' of a phallogocentric organisation of meaning and language, while the materiality of these designs is in flux.

This openness of undecidability has implications for language itself; an autobiographical text is not the same as a book/essay/etc. Rather, it is what is produced in the act of reading. A text can be anything because every cognition, experience, or sense-perception requires a reading and already is mediated by language. The reading creates the subject, and autobiography is 'a figure of reading or of understanding that occurs, to some degree, in all texts' (de Man, 70). Thus, writing ourselves as subjects is always already an encounter with language. de Man distinguishes (and then blurs) the writing-I and the written-I in that the author of the autobiography must present to her self-description a face; she must deface herself to bring herself into being in the text. 'Our topic deals with the giving and taking away of face, with face and deface, figure, figuration and defiguration' (76).

The emphasis on the face is the condition of existence of a person. For de Man, instead of a category, autobiography is a moment that occurs 'as an alignment between two subjects involved in the process of reading in which they determine each other by mutual reflexive substitution' (70).

Even writing about Philo's designs proves difficult and Cathy Horyn, the *New York Times*' fashion reviewer, writes, 'by elusive I mean the peculiar effect of her designs, especially at Céline, was difficult to pin down. In writing about her collections, I never felt that I nailed one to my satisfaction' (2017). Horyn, however, offers:

It left me free to imagine. Because Philo's clothes were not just simply for women; they were also about women – their distractions, their routines, the way they stuff a bag under an arm or concoct an outfit out of a dress and trousers, their sideways longing for red-lipped glamour, their disdain for basics, their love of uniforms, their wisdom and maturity. It was all there, every season, expressed in the clothes (2017).

Perhaps her designs somehow accomplish both the feeling of right decision and enough space to write the wearer into the clothing. In tipping the hat (so to speak), her minimalist style has designer 'tells;' it seems that in dress selection there is a desire to display a reading that productively defaces, or substitutes the face of another as 'yours'. Like Cixous's (1976) twofold project in *The Laugh of the Medusa* wherein she seeks 'to break up, to destroy; and to see the unforeseeable, to project' (875) 'to bring about something new' (876), the defiguration and projection in Philo's work is destructive and open. There is a reordering: if I buy/wear the clothing, it produces my body, generating an authenticity or depth of personhood. But just like the autobiography, each instance of writing the self through clothing resists cohesion, remains un-generic and undecidable. Just as, 'Things look accidental but are actually entirely purposeful' in Philo's work (Vargas 2014), clothing also includes things that look purposeful but are also open to actually being entirely accidental.

Further study and conclusion

In a post-#metoo era of Instagram fame and takedowns, perhaps the ultimate power is to become invisible. Philo, who announced in December 2017 that she is leaving Céline and leaving fashion all together, certainly knows what it is to crave invisibility. Horyn (2017) mourns, '[g]oing forward, we will see less intuitive design, less design that is respectful of the wide range of feminine emotions, experiences and ages'. Wearers of Philo's designs have gotten the chance to create a signature citationality via clothing that produces its own 'unwriting', thereby allowing the wearer to believe she inscribes her own iteration, her own story. Her fans have been offered the chance to identify with a designer who is enlightened beyond fast and flashy fashion, who hints that clothing has the substantialising effect that language has (instead of representational). These decisions and fictions within Philo's clothing as a form of performative rhetoric are open to failure; yet Felman offers that this failure acts as an opening beyond language's limitations, a place of Derrida's emancipatory hope and of de Man's giving of figuration. While we cannot foresee the unforeseeable, exploring the performative rhetoric of Philo's work opens the door just bit more to the creativity available in writing our own stories, bodies, and languages.

Disclosure statement

No potential conflict of interest was reported by the author.

References

Armstrong, Lisa. 2014. "Céline Autumn/Winter 2014 at Paris Fashion Week." The Telegraph, March 2. http://fashion.telegraph.co.uk/Article/TMG10671216/870/Céline-autumnwinter-2014-at-Paris-Fashion-Week.html
Austin, J. L. 1962. *How to Do Things With Words*. Cambridge: Harvard University Press.
Barad, Karen. 2003. "Posthumanist Performativity: Toward an Understanding of How Matter Comes to Matter." *Signs: Journal of Women in Culture and Society* 28 (3): 801–831.
Barnard, Malcolm. 2002. *Fashion as Communication*. New York: Routledge.
Barthes, Roland. 1967. *The Fashion System*. Los Angeles: University of California Press.
Berrington, Katie. 2008. "Phoebe Philo." *British Vogue*, April 22. http://www.vogue.co.uk/article/phoebe-philo-biography
Blanks, Tim. 2013. "Phoebe Philo: A Real Life." *Purple Fashion Magazine*, May 19. http://purple.fr/magazine/ss-2013-issue-19/phoebe-philo/
Brummett, Barry. 1991. *Rhetorical Dimensions of Popular Culture*. Tuscaloosa: University of Alabama Press.
Brummett, Barry. 2008. *A Rhetoric of Style*. Carbondale: Southern Illinois University Press.
Butler, Judith. 1990. *Gender Trouble: Feminism and the Subversion of Identity*. New York: Routledge.
Butler, Judith. 1993. *Bodies That Matter: On the Discursive Limits of 'Sex.'*. New York: Routledge.
Cixous, Helene. 1976. "The Laugh of the Medusa." *Signs: Journal of Women in Culture and Society* 1 (4): 875–893.
Cocozza, Paula. 2015. "Poet Claudia Rankine: 'The invisibility of black women is astounding'." The Guardian, June 29. https://www.theguardian.com/lifeandstyle/2015/jun/29/poet-claudia-rankine-invisibility-black-women-everyday-racism-citizen
Crisell, Hattie. 2014. "Phoebe Philo on Creative Freedom at Céline, Her 'Innate Fear of Fame,' and More." The Cut, March 30. https://www.thecut.com/2014/03/phoebe-philo-on-freedom-at-cline-fear-of-fame.html
de Man, Paul. 1984. *Autobiography as Defacement: Rhetoric of Romanticism*. New York: Columbia University Press.
Derrida, J. 1972. *Limited Inc*. Evanston: Northwestern University Press.
Felman, Shoshana. 2002. *The Scandal of the Speaking Body: Don Juan with J.L. Austin, or Seduction in Two Languages*. Stanford: Stanford University Press.
Gordon, Bryan, dir. 2015. "The Dinner." In *Grace and Frankie*. Netflix.
Grosz, Elizabeth. 1994. *Volotile Bodies: Towards a Corporeal Feminisim*. Bloomington: Indiana University Press.
Han, Young Jee, Joseph Nunes, and Xavier Drèze. 2010. "Signaling Status with Luxury Goods: The Role of Brand Prominence." *Journal of Marketing* 74 (4): 15–30.
Horyn, Cathy. 2016. "The Mystery of Phoebe Philo: The Designer has a Private Language, but Her Clothes Speak to Today's Woman." New York Magazine, October 3. https://www.thecut.com/2016/10/the-mystery-of-phoebe-philo.html
Horyn, Cathy. 2017. "Phoebe Philo and the Death of Leisure Time: Philo is a Designer for a Slower Era." New York Magazine, December 22. https://www.thecut.com/2017/12/phoebe-philo-leaving-Céline-cathy-horyn.html
Johnson, Philip. 1947. *Mies Van der Rohe*. New York: Museum of Modern Art.

Jones, Roxane. 2017. "Missing Black and Latina Children Are a Crisis for All of Us." CNN, April 2. https://edition.cnn.com/2017/04/02/opinions/missing-girls-in-dc-jones-opinion/index.html

Marriott, Hannah. 2014. "Phoebe Philo: 'I find mediocrity hard'." The Guardian, March 31. https://www.theguardian.com/fashion/fashion-blog/2014/mar/31/phoebe-philo-Céline-interview-vogue-festival-alexandra-shulman

Menkes, Suzy. 2013. "The Circus of Fashion." The New York Times, February 10. https://www.nytimes.com/2013/02/10/t-magazine/the-circus-of-fashion.html

Mower, Sarah. 2016. "Céline." *Vogue*, May 9. https://www.vogue.com/fashion-shows/pre-fall-2016/Céline

Mower, Sarah. 2017. "Phoebe Philo in Her Own (Few) Words." *Vogue*, December 22. https://www.vogue.com/article/phoebe-philo-Céline-quotes

Negrin, Llewellyn. 2008. *Appearance and Identity*. New York: Palgrave Macmillan.

Orbach, Susie. 2009. *Bodies*. London: Profile Books.

Parkins, Ilya. 2008. "Building a Feminist Theory of Fashion: Karen Barad's Agential Realism." *Australian Feminist Studies* 23 (58): 501–515. doi:10.1080/08164640802446565.

Rawsthorn, Alice. 2010. "Phoebe Philo's Third Act." *T Magazine*, February 25. https://www.nytimes.com/2010/02/28/t-magazine/28well-philo.html

Sawchuck, Kim. 1987. "A Tale of Inscription/Fashion Statements." *Canadian Journal of Political and Social Theory* 11 (1–2): 51–67.

Sykes, Pandora. 2014. "Phoebe Philo Says It's Ok to Copy Céline. So Here's How." *Grazia*, March 31. https://graziadaily.co.uk/fashion/news/phoebe-philo-say-s-ok-copy-Céline/

Vargas, Whitney. 2014. "Phoebe Philo's Prophetic Fashion." *T Magazine*, February 14. https://www.nytimes.com/2014/02/14/t-magazine/phoebe-philo-Céline-prophetic-fashion.html

Veblen, Thorstein. 1899. *The Theory of the Leisure Class*. London: The MacMillan Company.

Wilson, Elizabeth. 1985. *Adorned in Dreams: Fashion and Modernity*. New Brunswick: Rutger's University Press.

Young, Iris. 1985. "Humanism, Gynocentrism, and Feminist Politics." *Women's Studies International Forum* 8: 173–183.

Index

Abzug, Bella 14
activism 16; Fashion Revolution.org 111; Martha Ansara 11–12
Aden, Halima 51
adornment 32
advertising: in films 24; queer messaging in 50
aesthetics 70; of Beyoncé's 'Formation' video 97; 'grounded' 68, 69; of new minimalism 131, 132
'affective economy' 68
affectivity 55, 56, 57, 58, 65, 69, 70; androgynous fashion 61; blogs 59, 60; 'cruel optimism' 58, 65; emotions 57; negative 57
Africa, primitivism 98, 99, 100
African American women 15, 22; celebrity icons 24; 'consciousness of resistance' 31, 32; dressmaking 30; Moynihan report 31; racial masquerade 27; *see also* black feminism; *Mahogany*
'age studies' 77
ageing 76–77, 78; and invisibility 136; Sherman on 84; in Sherman's photographs 81–82; 'society portraits' 84, 85, 86, 87, 88; *see also* young women
Ahmed, Sara 57, 68
Aldrich, Robert: *Whatever Happened to Baby Jane?* 87
Alex, Joe 101
Allen, Lily 64
Andersen, Hans Christian: 'Emperor's New Clothes' 124
Andrews, Jessica 15
androgynous fashion 55, 56, 61, 63, 69, 70, 70–71n1; audience responses to 64–65; 'cruel optimism' 65; 'grounded aesthetics' 68–69; shaming 61, 62; Tumblr blogs 67, 68
Ansara, Martha 34, 10, 11, 16; *Film for Discussion* 12–13, 14, 17; politics of 17–18
Anthropologie 59
Archer-Straw, Petrine 98
Armstrong, Lisa 132
Arnold, Eve 58, 87

art: and celebrity culture 79; Cindy Sherman 80–82; and fashion 78–79; and women's magazines 83
Artforum 81, 82
Asian motifs 27; *Cleopatra Jones and the Casino of Gold* 35; in *Mahogany* 38
Atlantic City, protest against the 1968 Miss America pageant 10, 11, 16
audiences 60; of androgynous fashion 64–65; direct engagement 61–63; imagined 63; *see also* direct audience engagement; indirect audience engagement
Austin, J.L. 127, 135; *How To Do Things With Words* 126
Australia: fast fashion in 113; feminism in 18n3; women's liberation movement 10
Australian Film Institute 12
authentic feminism 14
authenticity 129
authorship of designs 125–126
autobiographical texts 138–139

Bad Hearts Club 67
Baker, Jean-Claude 104; *Josephine Baker: The Hungry Heart* 103
Baker, Josephine 92, 93, 94, 98, 105; banana skirt 102, 103; dancing 98; disrespectability politics 103; *La Revue Nègre* 100–101, 103; primitivism 100, 101, 104; *see also* black feminism; dance; disrespectability politics; primitivism
Balsiger, Philip 115
Barad, Karen 129, 138
Barnard, Malcolm: *Fashion as Communication* 128
Barthes, Roland: *The Fashion System* 128
'bashing' 63
Basquiat 80
Batchelor, David 32
Beard, Mary 84
beauty 34, 45, 10, 14, 15
beauty contests, protests against 10

Bennett, Bruce 62
Berlant, Lauren 58
Beyoncé 36, 92, 94, 101, 103; *B'Day* 92; black feminist performance 94–95; 'Formation' video 95, 97, 98, 102, 104, 105
Bis, Dorothée 82, 83
black feminism 25–26, 29, 30, 35, 38, 39, 92, 99; Beyoncé 94, 95, 105n2; disrespectability politics 97; *Ebony* 33–34; 'Formation' video 95–96; Josephine Baker 93; ratchet politics 97; in the United States 30–31
black women: images of in Tumblr blogs 67; invisibility of 136
Blanc, Charles 32
Blaxploitation films 34, 35; *Cleopatra Jones* 34
blogs 55, 58–59, 60, 66, 116, 117; *Advanced Style* 84; corporate 59; and ethical fashion 118, 119, 120; independent 58–59; *see also* corporate blogs; Tumblr blogs; vlogs
Bogle, David 39
Borschke, Margie 65
Bowie, David 26
boyd, danah 63
Braidotti, Rosi 56
bright colors: in Blaxploitation films 34, 35; chromophobia 33; as 'lurid' 29, 35; *see also* chromophobia; flamboyance
Brooks, Andrew 114
Brooks, Daphne 101; *Clothing Poverty: The Hidden World of Fast Fashion and Second Hand Clothes* 113
Brownmiller, Susan 17
Brummett, Barry 129
Buckley, Cheryl 110
Bündchen, Gisele 61
burkas 16
BUST magazine 14, 16
Butler, Judith: *GenderTrouble: Feminism and the Subversion of Identity* 126

Camp, M.H. 31
capitalism 34, 24, 35, 70, 98; late 113; Marxist critique of fashion 112; 'responsible' 114–115; *see also* consumerism
celebrity culture 78–79
celebrity icons 24
Chant, Sylvia 111
Charles, Jacques 101
Chase, Chris: *Josephine Baker: The Hungry Heart* 103
chav style 62
Cheng, Anne Anlin 93, 102, 103; 'Ornamentalism' 27
Chittenden, Tara 116–117
Cho, Alexander 66
chromophobia 32, 33
Chung, Alexa 61

cinema, and advertising 24; *see also* filmmaking; films, Blaxploitation
citationality 129, 130
Civil Rights 35, 97
Cixous, Helene: *The Laugh of the Medusa* 139
Clark, Danae 50, 110
Clarke, Maxine Beneba 45
Cleo 14
Cleopatra Jones 34, 35
Cleopatra Jones and the Casino of Gold 35
Cline, Elizabeth: *Overdressed: The Shockingly High Cost of Cheap Fashion* 116
clothing 11–12, 126, 127, 128, 133, 136; of African American slaves 31; bright colors 32; and 'consciousness of resistance' 31–32; and emotions 58; 'ethnic' 49; and invisibility 136; of Josephine Baker 94; new minimalism 124, 125, 130–131, 132; overalls 12; performative dimension 137–138; as signification 129, 130, 132, 135; skirts 12; Student Non-Violent Coordinating Committee (SNCC) 96; trans 51–52; *see also* costume design; *Mahogany*; Philo, Phoebe
Coachella music festival 15
Cobb, Jasmine: *Picturing Freedom* 30
Cohen, Ari Seth 84
Cohen, Leonard 137
Coleman, Rebecca 57
Colins, Paul 103
colonialism 30, 98, 105
color, chromophobia 32, 33
Coming Out Show 34
commercial fashion 13
communication 126, 127
communist women 12
connotations 133
'consciousness of resistance' 31, 32
consciousness raising 129, 34, 13, 17, 18n4; *Film for Discussion* 13–14
conspicuous consumption 124, 130
constantive language 126
consumerism 14, 25, 49, 60–61, 79, 111, 112, 114–115; chav style 62; conspicuous consumption 124, 130; and ethical fashion 119, 120; racial masquerade 27; Reina Lewis on 47; 'selling dreams' 57–58; unobtainability 58; *see also* fast fashion; feminization of consumption
contemporary fashion communication: audiences 60; blogs 58–59, 60; corporate blogs 59; *see also* affectivity; Tumblr blogs
Cooper, Brittney 94, 97, 98, 104
corporate blogs 59; Anthropologie 59; Topshop 59
costume design: flamboyance 25–26; Josephine Baker 104; *Mahogany* 22, 23, 25, 26, 34; orientalism 27; in silent films 24

counter culture styles 10, 14
Craik, Jennifer 112
Crawford, Joan 87
Crewe, Louise 110
'cruel optimism' 58, 65
cultural appropriation 15
Cultural Boneyard, A 66, 67, 69
cultural remix 65, 66, 70; Tumblr blogs 67, 68
cultural studies 77
cultural studies research 34–45
Currid, Elizabeth 79

Dalton, Kate 101
Daly, Pauline 133
dance: and Baker's banana skirt 102, 103; Beyoncé 98; 'Formation' video 95, 97, 98, 102, 105; Josephine Baker 94, 98, 100–101; and primitivism 99, 100, 101, 104
Darwin, Charles 28
Davis, Angela 14; 'The Black Woman's Role in the Community of Slaves' 30–31
de Beauvoir, Simone 76, 81; *The Coming of Age* 77; *The Second Sex* 75
de Certeau, Michel: *The Sociology of Everyday Life* 112
de Man, Paul 124, 126, 136, 137, 138, 139
Derrida, Jacques 124, 125, 126, 127, 129, 133, 139
Didion, Joan 77
digital culture 116; Reina Lewis on 46–47; vlogs 116; *see also* vlogs
digitalization of fashion communication 56
direct audience engagement 56, 61–62, 65, 70; imagined audiences 63; online 'bashing' 63
discrimination, chromophobia 32–33
disrespectability politics 94, 97, 103, 104
Diva 43
Dobson, Pamela 34, 35
Dyer, Richard 25, 67

Ebony 33
Eckert, Charles: 'The Carole Lombard in Macy's Window' 24
ego, the 135
embodiment 44, 127
Emin, Tracey 78
emotions 57, 65, 66; 'affective economy' 68; blogs 59, 60; 'cruel optimism' 58, 65; gendered 58; happiness 57, 58; 'selling dreams' 58; *see also* negative emotions; positive emotions
Entwistle, Joanne 112
ethical fashion 109, 110, 111, 114, 116; Reina Lewis on 50
Experimental Film Fund 12

'Facetune' app 89
fashion 129, 34, 45, 10, 14, 15, 75; affectivity 56, 57; of African American slaves 31–32; and ageing 77, 78; androgynous 55, 56, 63, 65; and art 78–79; Asian motifs 27; authorship of designs 125–126; blogs 66, 116, 117; burkas 16; commercial 13; commercial collaborations 79, 80, 82; counter culture styles 10; cultural appropriation 15; *Ebony* 33; Elaine Welteroth 14–17; ethical 50, 109, 110–111, 114, 116, 118–120; fast 45, 76, 109; and feminism 10; functions of 128; fusion 49; girly culture 69; *Mahogany* 22, 26; Marxist critique of 112; modest 42, 43, 46, 49, 51, 52; Muslim 45, 46, 48–49, 51; and neoliberalism 47; new minimalism 130–131, 132; overalls 12; plus-size 52; and primitivism 99, 100, 101, 105; racial masquerade 27; ready-to-wear 110; 'selling dreams' 57–58; and signification 129, 130, 132; skirts 12; sustainable 50, 51, 110, 111, 113, 115; vlogs 117; *see also* androgynous fashion; consumerism; contemporary fashion communication; dance; ethical fashion; fashion photography; fast fashion; *Mahogany*; primitivism; queer fashion; women's magazines
Fashion Fair, Dior's 'New Look' 76
fashion photography 82–84; 'society portraits' 84, 85, 86–87, 88; *see also* Sherman, Cindy
Fashion Revolution.org 111
Fashion Rocks 92, 101
fast fashion 45, 76, 109, 110, 111, 113, 120; *War on Waste* 113–114
Featherstone, Mike 58
Felman, Shoshona 125, 135, 136, 139; misfires 135, 137; *The Scandal of the Speaking Body* 133–134
female gaze 42, 46; Reina Lewis on 43, 44; religiously inflected 44
feminine mystique 45, 13, 17
femininity 13, 22, 23, 32, 56, 61, 66, 112; and androgynous fashion 61–62; black 31, 33, 93, 94, 99
feminization of consumption 111, 115
feminism 129, 34, 45, 14, 15, 46, 76; in Australia 18n3; authentic 14; black 25, 26; burkas 16; consciousness raising 34; Elaine Welteroth 14–17; and fashion 10; 'intersectional' 16; in *Mahogany* 25; Martha Ansara 11–12, 13–14; neo 76; post- 76; second-wave 16, 17, 18n13, 75, 77, 81; second wave consciousness raising 34; third-wave 18n13; and women's magazines 45; *see also* black feminism; consciousness raising; second-wave feminism; Sherman, Cindy
festivals: Coachella 15; Performa 80
fiction 137
Film Australia 12
Film for Discussion 34, 12–13, 16–17
filmmaking 12; Sydney Women's Film Group 12–13

films, Blaxploitation 34; *see also Mahogany*
Findlay, Rose 117
Firth, Livia 110
Fixmer, Natalie 16
flamboyance: as bad taste 28; of *Mahogany*'s costume design 25–26; and slavery 31
Fleetwood, Nicole: *On Racial Icons: Blackness and the Public Imagination* 24
Fletcher, Kate 110
Fonda, Jane 77
Ford, Tanisha 96
Ford, Tom 76
Foxy Brown 34
Francis, Terri 93
Friedan, Betty 77; *The Feminine Mystique* 45

Gaines, Jane 25; 'Costume and Narrative: How Dress Tells the Woman's Story' 23–24
Gates, Henry Louis 101
Gaugele, Elke 109, 110
gay liberation 41
gaydar 43
gaze theory 43, 45, 46; female gaze 43–44
gender 16, 26, 41, 66, 69; and ethical fashion 111; feminization of consumption 115
Gilbert, Sophie 129
Gilman, Charlotte Perkins 31, 32
girly culture 69
global north, fashion consumption in 113
Goffman, Erving: *The Presentation of the Self in Everyday Life* 63
'good life' 58
Gordy, Berry 23, 25, 29, 30, 34
Gould, Bob 34
graffiti 29
Grazia 61, 63
Greer, Germaine 10, 14, 17, 77
Grey Panthers 78
Grier, Pam 34
Griffiths, Kadeen 95
Groeneveld, Elizabeth 14
Grosz, Elizabeth 56; *Volatile Bodies: Toward a Corporeal Feminism* 127
'grounded aesthetics' 68, 69
Guardian 34, 15

Hanna, Kathleen 14
Hannel, Susan 99
happiness 57, 58
Harper's Bazaar 82, 83
Hartman, Saidiya 97
Hasegawa-Overacker, Paul: *Guest of Cindy Sherman* 79
Hegel, G.W.F. 95
Hemmings, Clare 45
Hicks, Sophie 137
Higginbotham, Evelyn Brooks 96

hijab 15–16, 51
Hill, Anita 32
Hirst, Damien 80
historical narratives 17
Hobson, Janell 94
Holloway, Karla F.C. 32
Hollows, Joanne 14
Hollywood 24
Horne, Peter: *Outlooks: Lesbian and Gay Sexualities and Visual Culture* 42
Horyn, Cathy 136, 139
Hurricane Katrina 95, 96, 97

Idrissi, Mariah 50, 51
images: of Cindy Sherman 80–82, 89; in *A Cultural Boneyard* 67; reblogging 66; 'selling dreams' 57–58; 'society portraits' 84, 85, 86, 87, 88; in *Wink, Pout, Ask Me Out* 67; *see also* fashion photography; Tumblr blogs
imagined audiences 63
inclusion 51
independent blogs 58–59
indirect audience engagement 55, 56, 60, 65, 70; Tumblr blogs 66, 67, 68
Information Communication Technologies (ICT) 45; Reina Lewis on 46–47
inscription 125, 127, 133
Instagram 89, 139
internet 56
'intersectional feminism' 16
intersectionality 44
invisibility 132, 133, 135, 136

Jacobs, Marc 83
Jarvis, Helen 11
Johnson, Beverly 33
Johnson, John H. 33
Jones, Carla 45
Jules-Rosette, Bennetta 101
Jurgenson, Nathan 60–61

Kabuki theatre 26
Kael, Pauline 28, 29
Kawakubo, Rei 83
Kearney, Mary Celeste 69
Keckley, Elisabeth 30
King, Toni C. 33
kitsch 28
Koons, Jeff 78, 79
Kruger, Barbara 79; 'The Drop' 80
Kusama, Yayoi 78

La Revue Nègre 100–101, 103
language 127, 134, 136; connotations 133; constantive 126; misfires 125, 135, 137; performative rhetoric 124, 125, 126, 128, 129, 135, 137–138

INDEX

Larsen, Nella: *Quicksand* 27
late capitalism 113
Legge, Kate 13
lesbian and gay lifestyle magazines 42
Levinson, Andre 98, 104
Lewis, Reina 41; on consumerism 47; on the digital culture 46–47; on ethical fashion 50; on the female gaze 43, 44; on 'lifestyle' 48–49; on modest fashion 42, 45, 46, 47, 48, 51; on Muslim fashion 48; *Muslim Fashion: Contemporary Style Cultures* 44–45; on neoliberalism 47; *Outlooks: Lesbian and Gay Sexualities and Visual Culture* 42; on queer fashion 42, 43, 48; on religious cultures 43–44; on surveillance 46; on sustainable fashion 50
Life magazine 10, 14, 99, 100
lifestyle, Muslim 48–49
Lincoln, Mary Todd 30
lipstick 13
Loos, Adolf 31, 32
Loreck, Hanne 83
Louis Vuitton 79, 132
Lowenstein, Wendy 12
Lumby, Catharine 34
Luna, Donyale 33
'lurid' 29, 35

MacDonald, Barbara: *Look Me in the Eye: Old Women, Ageing and Ageism* 77
MacRobbie, Angela 76
Magarey, Susan 45, 10, 17
Mahogany 22, 24, 31, 37; Asian motifs 38; audience 34; and *Cleopatra Jones* 34; costume design 22, 23, 34; flashback scene 28; 'L' train scene 29; Marshall-Fields scene 36; Miriam Thaggert on 24–25; opening scenes 26; orientalism in 27; plot 35; politics 24; racial masquerade 27; rainbow dress 36, 38; Tracy's return to Chicago 39; use of bright colors 33; *see also* black feminism
makeup 11–12, 12, 13
Manovich, Lev 68, 70
Marie Claire 14
marriage 13
Marwick, Alice 63
Marxist critique of fashion 112
masculinity 56, 62; female 70–71n1; in *Mahogany* 35; of Philo's clothes 133
Mason, Dick 12
McCall's 45
McDormand, Frances 50
McQueen, Alexander 79
Meagher, Michelle 86
Meinhold, Roman 58
MeJane 34, 10, 12, 16
Menkes, Suzy: 'The Circus of Fashion' 130
#MeToo movement 45, 78

middle class, respectability politics 96
Millett, Kate 10
miniskirts 12, 13
minoritized cultures 47
Mirren, Helen 77
misfires 125, 135, 137
Miss America pageant 14; 1968 protest against 10, 11, 16
Mitchell, Joni 77
Miyake, Issey 26
modest fashion 44, 49; Reina Lewis on 42, 43, 45, 46, 47, 48, 51, 52
Monroe, Marilyn 13
Morgan, Andrew: *The True Cost* 110
Morgan, Robin 10
Mort, Frank 48
Mosely, Rachel 14
Mosmann, Petra 34, 10, 14
Motown 23, 29, 34
Mower, Sarah 132, 138
Moynihan report 31
Ms. Magazine 14
Mulvey, Laura 43, 81
Munich, Adrienne 39
Murakami, Takashi 78
Muslim fashion 46, 48–49; hijab 51; lifestyle magazines 42; Reina Lewis on 45, 48
MuslimGirl.com 15–16

narratives 10, 15, 17; costume design 23–24; historical 17; 'selling dreams' 57–58; in Tumblr blogs 68
Neal, Mark Anthony 23, 29
negative emotions 57; 'bashing' 63; 'cruel optimism' 58, 65; shaming 61–62
Negrin, Llewellyn 127
'negrophilia' 98
neofeminism 76
neoliberalism 75, 117; Reina Lewis on 47
new minimalism 124, 125, 130–131, 132
New Orleans, Beyoncé's 'Formation' video 95–96
New Women 99
Newsreel 11
Nyong'o, Lupita 67

online interaction 56
Ora, Rita 61
Orbach, Susie: *Bodies* 127
orientalism 27, 41, 101

Paglia, Camille 14
pamphlets 34, 11
Parkins, Ilya 41, 42, 129
Parkinson, Hannah Jane 129
patriarchal society 70
Performa 80

performative rhetoric 124, 125, 126, 127, 128, 129, 137–138; promises 135; texts 127, 128
Perkins, Anthony 35, 38
Pham, Minh-Ha 110, 116, 117
Philo, Phoebe 124, 125, 126, 130, 133, 136, 138, 139; creative process 128; materials 136–137; new minimalism 130–131, 132
Pickford, Mary 87
'Pictures Generation' group 81
plus-size fashion 52
Poiret, Paul 103, 104
Poison and Butterflies 66, 67, 68
political awareness 15
politics 129, 11; of 'disrespectability' 94, 97, 103, 104; LGBTQ 51–52; in *Mahogany* 24; Martha Ansara 14, 17–18; racial 35; ratchet 97, 98, 105; respectability 96, 97; *Teen Vogue* 15
positive emotions 57
post-feminism 76
poststructuralism 56
prejudice, chromophobia 32–33
Press, Claire: *Wardrobe Crisis: How We Went from Sunday Best to Fast Fashion* 116
primitivism 93–94, 96, 97, 100, 101, 104; and fashion 99
Prince, Richard 78
Probyn, Elspeth 56
promises 135
protests, against beauty pageants 10

queer fashion 44, 66; Reina Lewis on 42, 43, 48; 'tomboy' 51

racial masquerade 27
racism 14, 22, 24, 27, 105; chromophobia 33; Moynihan report 31
Radner, Hilary 76
ratchet politics 97, 98, 105
ready-to-wear 110
Reagan, Caroline Dudley 101, 103, 104
reality TV 63
reblogging 66
recycling 50–51, 115
red dress, the 32
religious cultures: Muslim fashion 45, 46, 48–49; Reina Lewis on 43–44, 48
religiously inflected female gaze 44
respectability politics 94, 96, 97
Ritzer, George 60–61
Robertson, Mavis 12
Rocamora, Agnès 117
Roeper, Richard 29
Rolley, Katrina 43
Ross, Diana 22, 23, 24, 30, 33, 34, 38; *Secrets of a Sparrow* 22
Rossellini, Isabella 77

Ruggerone, Lucia 58
Runnin' Wild 100

Said, Edward 27
Sassy 14
Sawchuck, Kim 127
scientific racism 98
Screen 81
second-wave feminism 45, 10, 15, 16, 17, 18n13, 75, 77, 81
Segal, Lynn: *Out of Time* 77
self-actualization 58
self-expression, images of in Tumblr blogs 67
Selfridges 79
'selling dreams' 57–58
sexism 14, 22; chromophobia 33; red dress 32
sexual oppression 11
sexuality 16, 41, 76; female 43
Shah, Hemant 95
shaming 61, 62
Sharpley-Whiting, T. D. 98–99
Sherman, Cindy 75, 76, 78, 79, 83, 89; on ageing 84; 'Centrefolds' 82; collaboration with Supreme 80; collaborations 82–84; and feminist criticism 80–82; 'History Portraits' 82; 'portraits' 80; 'Project Twirl' 84; 'Retrospective' exhibition 78; 'Sex Pictures' 82; 'society portraits' 84, 85, 86, 87, 88
Siegle, Lucy: *To Die For: Is Fashion Wearing Out the World?* 110, 116
signification 129, 129–130, 132, 135
silent films, costume design 24
sisterhood 34, 15
Skeggs, Bev 63
slavery 30, 97; and black feminism 30–31; 'consciousness of resistance' 31–32
social media 48, 55, 56, 58, 60, 61, 63; blogs 55, 116; indirect audience engagement 65; Instagram 89, 139; Reina Lewis on 46–47; Tumblr blogs 55, 66; user-generated content 65; YouTube 116; *see also* blogs; YouTube
'society portraits' 84, 85, 86, 87, 88
Solomon-Godeau, Abigail 85; 'The Coming of Age: Cindy Sherman, Feminism and Art History' 81
Sontag, Susan 77
Southwell, Mirjam 115
speech-act theory 126
Spencer, Shea 82
Stanton, Elizabeth Cady 14
Steele, Valerie 127
Steinem, Gloria 14, 77
Stenberg, Amandla 15
Student Non-Violent Coordinating Committee (SNCC) 96, 97
styles 56
Summers, Anne 45, 12

Supreme, collaboration with Cindy Sherman 80
surveillance, Reina Lewis on 46
sustainable fashion 110, 111, 113, 115; recycling 50–51; Reina Lewis on 50; *War on Waste* 113–114
Swanson, Gloria 87
Sydney Women's Film Group 12–13, 16–17, 18n14
Sydney Writers' Festival 129

Tarlo, Emma 47
Teen Vogue 129, 34, 14, 15, 16, 17, 18
Teller, Juergen 83
texts 127, 128, 137; autobiographical 138–139
Thaggert, Miriam 24–25, 28
Third World bookshop 34
third-wave feminism 18n13
Thornley, Jeni 12
'tomboy' 51
Topshop 59
Torgovnick, Marianna 93–94
Trump, Donald 15
Tseëlon, Efrat 110–111, 114
Tumblr blogs 55, 70; 'affective economy' 68; *Bad Hearts Club* 67; *A Cultural Boneyard* 66, 67, 69; cultural remix 66; images 67; *Poison and Butterflies* 66, 67, 68; *Wink, Pout, Ask Me Out* 67
Turner, Julia 129, 34
Twigg, Julia: *Fashion and Age: Dress, the Body and Later Life* 77
Tyler, Imogen 62, 63

undecidability 126, 138
United States, black feminism in 30–31
user-generated content 65

van der Rohe, Ludwig Mies 131
Varda, Agnes 11
Vargas, Whitney 130
Veblen, Thorstein 31, 32, 112, 113, 130, 132
Vietnam war 11
visuality 49
vlogs 116, 117, 121; and ethical fashion 118, 119, 120

Vogue 10, 14, 17, 33, 59, 132
Volcano, Del LaGrace 45

War on Waste 113–114
Warhol, Andy 79
Warrington, Ruby 15, 17
Watson, Emma 110
wearable technologies 55
Web 34.0 65
Weinbaum, Alys Eve 27
Welteroth, Elaine 129, 34, 45, 14, 15, 16
White, Graham 31, 69
White, Shane 31
white supremacy 92; primitivism 93–94, 96, 97, 99, 100, 101, 104, 105
white women, racial masquerade 27
Wiegman, Robyn 25, 36
Wilder, Billy 87
Wildfang 51, 52
Williams, Billy Dee 35
Williamson, Judith 81
Wilson, Elizabeth: *Adorned in Dreams: Fashion and Modernity* 76, 112, 128
Wink, Pout, Ask Me Out 67
women's liberation movement 34, 10, 11, 13, 14; in Australia 10; sexual oppression 11
women's magazines 45, 10, 14; and art 83; *BUST* 16; *Diva* 43; *Ebony* 33; *Grazia* 61, 63; *Harper's Bazaar* 82, 83; 'selling dreams' 57–58; *Teen Vogue* 15, 16, 17, 18; *Vogue* 10, 14, 17, 33, 59, 132
Women's March Against Trump 78
Women's Marches 129
Wood, Julia 16, 63
Woodward, Kathleen 77; *Why Women Wear What They Wear* 112
working class glamour 67, 69

Yamamoto, Kansai 26
young women: and ethical fashion 118–120; and fashion consumption 112, 113, 114; vlogs 117
YouTube 15, 46, 50, 116; vlogs 117